VOCATIONAL EDUCATION

DPH Education Series

VOCATIONAL EDUCATION

U K SINGH • K N SUDARSHAN

DISCOVERY PUBLISHING HOUSE
NEW DELHI-110002

First Published - 1996
Reprinted - 2015

ISBN: 978-81-7141-338-6

Vocational Education

Published by:
DISCOVERY PUBLISHING HOUSE PVT. LTD.
4383/4B, Ansari Road, Darya Ganj
New Delhi-110 002 (India)
Phone: +91-11-23279245, 43596064-65
Fax: +91-11-23253475
E-mail: discoverypublishinghouse@gmail.com
sales@discoverypublishinggroup.com
web: www.discoverypublishinggroup.com

Printed at:
Infinity Imaging Systems
Delhi

Preface

The *DPH Education Handbook* has been created to provide access to information about contemporary topics in education. Practitioners and students at all levels in education have a need to know what is happening today, in addition to historical treatments within the literature.

Each chapter within the Handbook is designed to provide the user with needed "state-of-the-art" information as well as further sources of information. One of the significant features of each chapter is the inclusion of specific programmes, projects and activities so that the researcher can locate human resources as well as the literature.

The handbook will be of use to graduate and post graduate students in education and to practicing teachers, administrators, librarians and planners. The chapters and the further sources of information cited in each book should lead the reader to thousands of people and documents for either research or programme planning purposes.

An effort to achieve universal and effective education is based on a recognition of the rights of students to basic education that enables them to thrive in a complex society, as well as a realization the technological and economic growth is facilitated by increasing the numbers of students, even those with poor academic progresses, who are, in fact successful in learning. Thus, recent and current efforts improve education serve both private and social interests.

This series is addressed to administrators, planners and educators working in the field of education and training with a view to stimulating interest and attention in the areas of education and its related fields. It is also addressed to a growing number of teachers and instructors who will be practitioners in education and who will need to be acquainted with the modern aspects of educational practice and development. Many ideas, generalisations and discussions presented in this series should also prove useful to employing organisations committed to provide training facilities within their establishments—leading to effective mutual participation by institutions and organisations.

The editors wishes to thank the contributors, as well as those organizations that gave permission to publish their extracts, chapters etc.

Editors

Contents

Contents

1 Vocational Education : Concepts, Principles and Issues

Vocation and vocational education

Through the ages man has worked for his livelihood, has learned through accumulated experiences how to face and control natural forces and how to live within the limited physical resources for the good of all. All this mass of rich human experience achieved through work has stimulated man to seek means and methods of increasing his efficiency in work. As a result, the method of learning through organised experiences has come into use. Apprenticeship or training under guild organisation originated during ancient times and continued during the middle ages, was among the first forms of organised learning. The vocational institute or school, which is relatively of recent origin, is a modern example of institutionalized learning to work through consciously organised instruction.

Since the beginning of time occupational knowledge and manual skill have, in one form or another, been transmitted from man to man and from generation to generation. This transmitting process, whatever its form of organisation, has developed into the educational process that has now given rise to expansions and developments of what may be termed as vocational education. The diffusion of the occupational knowledge and the transmittal of the manipulative skill, underlying occupations and callings of man, may be interpreted as the forerunner of the various concepts of vocational education. In this broad sense, vocational education becomes that part of the total experience whereby man learns to carry on a gainful occupation proficiently and efficiently. The term "vocational education" as used in this broad sense is meant to cover both unorganised and organised methods of transmitting knowledge, skills and competences.

The age-old methods of learning on the job with no or little assistance and supervision is the unorganised form, while specific vocational education through the institutionalised process is the organised form. In a strictly utilitarian sense, "vocational education or training implies a series of organised and controlled learning experiences used to educate or train any person or persons for a given employment". The instructing process is organised to the extent the instructional objectives are clearly defined and understood and the instructor knows exactly what knowledge and skill it his duty to impart most effectively.

Through the ages, however, there has been but one way for the unskilled worker to learn to do his work, namely, the "pick up" method, in which observation, imitation and individual initiative constitute the sole means of training. It is only in the recent years that any serious attention is given to the training of unskilled worker to do his tasks efficiently. The unprecedented developments in science and technology have tended to expand vocational areas for which organised education or training is required. Vocational education and training has thus become both a consequence and a cause of progress.

Vocational education : concepts and meanings

There are several differing concepts and meanings of vocational education or training. Most of these have arisen from traditional practices and the meaning of terms used and their implications. An examination of these will reveal the basic differences for certain practices and relationships in vocational or occupational education, which are fundamental in nature and in programmes.

One such concept is that vocational education is the education or training of workers. Its origin may be traced to the early apprenticeship training practices. This concept implies that any kind of education or training in which a worker participates is vocational education. It also suggests that humans have dissimilar abilities and the persons having neither the capacity nor the desire to study the traditional curriculum be prevailed upon to opt for vocational trades more adapted to their taste and abilities. Implicit in the concept is the meaning that working class children be trained for factory work simply because that is their destiny. This kind of thinking does not fit in with the principle of equal educational opportunity.

Another concept is that vocational education is the education for manual work. This concept centres on the ideas of ability to work with hands rather than mind—with a curriculum of certain manual activities like leather work, wood work, metal work, drawing work, for example. The knowledge and skills learned from such education or training just underlie mental activities relevant to the curriculum but without relevance to specific occupational competence. This concept has resulted in the present-day practice of placing drop-outs, physically handicapped and socially disadvantaged young people in vocational courses without considering learners' interest and ability. A sizeable proportion of vocational institutions (other than I.T.Is.) in our country many perhaps be described as manual training institutions.

Yet another concept is that vocational education is education in certain specified subjects, which may be of vocational or technical nature, generally confined to secondary stage of education. This concept implies that a specified part of the curriculum is vocational or technical, the remaining part falling under general or liberal education coverage. Here vocational education is not designed to take the place of general education but to supplement it. The essential merit of the idea is that the total education imparted has both cultural and utility values fitting an individual for progressing in his chosen field of activity with in-built opportunity for vertical mobility. Technical high school type of education in our country is the example.

One more concept is that vocational education is that education which is craft-oriented. The major objective of craft-oriented education or training is to aid learners in greatest work efficiency possible in earning their living by providing special instruction in single crafts or trades. The education or training given in this manner lacks academic or cultural aspects of education. Educators, therefore, feel that any craft or trade-centred system of education or training is a divisioning process, segregating vocational education from general education mainstream. The learners that are unable to profit from the traditional academic learning generally opt for this sort of industrial training, as is given in our I.T.Is. Although the institutions are equipped to offer practical preparation for most of the recognised trades, the courses are not in accord with the objectives of a mass system of common or comprehensive schools as in vogue in U.K., U.S.A. and Japan.

Finally, there is the concept that vocational education is education for productive purposes or socially useful productive work. When the object is a product or a service for consumer use, the work involved is termed as productive work or socially useful productive work. Implicit in this modern concept is the meaning that as the individual seeks and finds new and improved ways of working through education or training, he increases his vocational efficiency. Gainful pursuits, regular occupations or vocations are becoming increasingly important in our industrialised society. Vocational education for productive work basically provides learning experience of an avocational nature, training learners to fit the requirements of a hierarchical work force. This concept is in accord with the present-day movement of "education for individual needs", education with the purpose "to prepare persons who would contribute to industrial, agricultural and commercial efficiency". This concept also leads to the theme that "all education, when considered in relation to the great masses of the people of a country, must be measured finally by the single test of usefulness and utility". Education imparted in this manner should aim at the development of proficient workers as well as good-citizens.

These concepts and definitions of vocational education reveal varying interpretations, meanings and purposes. A review of the development of vocational education and the litterature associated with it points to the fact that such variations exist and come about as a result of the history and development of a country and many diverging opinions arising in determining the ways and means of the education system fitting in with the mores and traditions of the societies it constitutes.

Viewed in the historical perspective, the development of vocational education or training has taken place through the following successive stage : (i) individual initiative and resourcefulness; (ii) unconscious absorbtion and imitation; (iii) conscious imitation and organised training in the home; (iv) conscious and organised training through exclusive apprenticeship or guild system practices; (v) pick-up learning under specialisation; and (vi) organised training through such means as vocational or occupational institutions and modernised apprenticeship under training-in-industry process. Within recent years the progress of science and technology has called increasingly for the systematic organised training of skilled personnel to man great numbers of new jobs and many old jobs with profoundly modified process. Operations once performed manually are now largely performed through machines, thus the emphasis in training shifting from the acquisition of manipulative skill to the acquisition of technical knowledge intelligently on the job or the activities associated with it. This fact has led to the central idea of organising education systematically and efficiently through the establishment of vocational institutions and modernised training at work places.

To-day, as always, the instructional process is said to be conscious and organised to the extent the methods in transmitting knowledge and skills are well-organised both pedagogically and administratively. In terms of pedagogical details, the methods of instructions as practised in institutions may be better organised than those followed in training establishments of industry. But the institutional system suffers from the weakness of its inability to secure and use participating experiences as subject-matter for training. On the other hand, the training given by the shop or offices is likely to be less pedagogically oriented—with the emphasis given to the training more adapted to the needs and the occupational psychology of the learner. Viewed from the directness of aim, the recognition of group characteristics and the use of the real experience as an instruction device, training-in-industry is regarded as an effectively successful vocational instruction system.

General principles of vocational education

Principles of vocational education serve a useful purpose in the delineation of policies, processes and procedures underlying vocational education. Principles of vocational education are derived from past experiences and judgments that have proved to be satisfactory and effective. Principles growing out of the deliberations and general agreement among individuals and bodies interested in and concerned with vocational education find incorporation in the basic vocational education laws.

The general principles of vocational education are delineated below. The are established principally on the basis of rich experience and judgment of the late Dr. Charles, a leader in vocational education in the U.S.A. He was the first director of the Federal Board for Vocational Education in U.S.A. Dr. Charles was acknowledged as a great authority on vocational education in his life time. Truly, the principles of vocational education enunciated here have stood the test of time and they are as valid now as ever before.

1. Vocational education will be efficient in proportion as the environment in which the learner is trained is a replica of the environment in which he must subsequently work.

2. Effective vocational education can only be given where the training jobs are carried out in the same way with the same operations, the same tools and the same machines as in the occupation itself.

3. Vocational education will be effective in proportion as it trains the individual directly and specifically in the thinking habits and the manipulative habits required in the occupation itself.

4. Vocational education will be effective in proportion as it enables each individual to capitalise upon his interest, aptitudes and intrinsic intelligence to the highest possible degree.

5. Effective vocational education for any profession, calling, trade, occupation or job can only be given to the selective group of individuals who need it, and can profit by it.

6. Vocational education will be effective in proportion as the specific training experiences for forming right habits of doing and thinking are repeated to the point that these habits become fixed to the degree necessary for gainful employment.

7. Vocational education will be effective in proportion as the instructor has had successful experience in the application of knowledge and skills to the operations and processes he undertakes to teach.

8. For every occupation there is a minimum of productive ability which an individual must possess in order to secure or retain employment in that occupation. If vocational education is not carried to that point with that individual, it is neither personally or socially effective.

9. Vocational education must recognise the conditions as they are and must train individuals to meet the demands of the labour market even though it may be true that more efficient ways of conducting the occupation may be known and that better working conditions are rightly desirable.

10. For every occupation there is a body of content which is peculiar to that occupation and which practically has no functioning value in any other occupation.

11. Vocational education will render efficient social service in proportion as it meets the specific training needs of any group at the time they need it, and in such a way that they can most effectively profit by the instruction.

12. Vocational education will be socially efficient in production as in its personal relations with learners it takes into consideration the particular characteristics of any particular group which it serves.

13. The administration of vocational education will be efficient in proportion as it is elastic and fluid rather than rigid and standardized.

14. While every reasonable effort should be made to reduce per capita cost, there is a minimum below which effective vocational education cannot be given, and if the course does not permit this minimum of per capita cost, vocational education cannot be attempted.

Vocational education—involving the institution, the home, and the industry or business—frequently evolves processes and procedures different from those of general education. This fact makes it necessary to understand the importance of the principles presented above.

Vocational education versus general education

The term general education is used to mean the education that should prepare persons to live more intelligently as citizens and to understand and enjoy life. To that end, general education implies the knowledge, skills and attitudes needed by persons for successful and purposeful living.

The term vocational education is used to mean the education that should prepare persons to work more efficiently. Efficient vocational education implies specific education and training in the usable knowledge, skills and competencies for the occupation in question.

However, different concepts of the relationship of general education and vocational education are there. Mostly they arise from differences in educational philosophy. Some educationists and administrators contend that a general or fundamental content is the best preparation for a vocation. They advocate that courses in such areas as general agriculture, domestic science and general business provide appropriate education or training for both general and vocational needs and be included in the general education subjects. However. vocational educators differ on the point that courses designed this way do not provide education for the specific competencies needed in preparing for a vocation. These educators contend that courses of a specific nature as well as those of a general nature are needed in education of workers. In a democratic system of education, they believe, every citizen should have the opportunity, as part of his training, for both types of education.

In the present-day situation, general education and vocational education are major divisions of the total education process. Each of them is of equal importance, and both of them are necessary in the education of workers. This suggests that general education and vocational education have much to contribute to each other and to the total education process. Both general and vocational educators should, therefore, strive to achieve the proper co-ordination of these two divisions of education within the total education process.

Polyvalent education

The modern trends are to avoid multiple-streams at the school stage of education. Dividing education in water-tight compartments of general education and vocational education, and thus segregating the students at an early age, is rather unsound and unfair educationally. It would be unwise for students nearly at the age of fourteen or so to opt for a vocational education or training course with a seemingly doubtful career development and prospective future. However, if they are offered a common or comprehensive system of school education bivalent in character and content, that is, a combination of general academic subjects and vocational subjects, such an arrangement could not only provide academic learning but also learning experiences for some vocation. A scheme of education of this kind organised under one shelter—increasingly adopted in U.K., U.S.A. and Japan—tends to promote employability of students and also help them develop their understanding and practical sense so useful in all walks of life. In a broad-based polyvalent education system with multi-options strategy, students get acquainted with academic knowledge, information and practice of several trades or subjects which all stand them in good stead in any occupation. With such a comprehensive organisation, vocational diversification at an young age is dispensed with. Rigid bifurcation too early in student life tends to stratify personal development and retard progressive outlook of young people. Uniformly organised secondary education without a vocational or occupational education component or any options within the choice of subjects, is an unintegrated system of education, and is thus out of tune with the current thinking and practice.

However, in circumstances where sufficiently intensive vocational education or training cannot be built in the secondary education system, as is mostly the case in our country, vocational bifurcation or diversification has inevitably to be accepted. Yet, wherever feasible, efforts should not be spared to include vocational bias in the mainstream of general education as it would satisfy an important requirement of complete education, that is, preparing a young person in education essentially with his own effort and choice, directed towards individual growth combined with satisfying the needs of the modern society. Such education becomes realistic and useful.

The Education Commission too visualised the future trend of school education to be towards a fruitful mingling of general education and vocational education—general education containing some elements of vocational and technical education, and vocational education, in turn, having an element of general education. The Commission did not favour a complete separation between general education and vocational education.

Further or extension education

It is not possible to give learners a ready-made complete package of knowledge and skills for life at any one time or period. In the modern context, workers are continually in need of adaptation, readaptation to changing demands and exigency of situation, and are therefore constantly required to face renewal of knowledge and skills. The sweeping changes in products, processes and techniques arising from scientific and technological discoveries and innovations result in far-reaching change in training policies, methods and standards required to meet the new exacting demands. This calls for organised systematic ways to train and retrain workers for a wide variety of occupations, spread over large geographical areas, equipped with higher and newer grades of occupational knowledge and skills. As efficiency in the use of human effort progress, as sub-division of operations and tasks lead more to specialisation of jobs, as the scale of production increases, the occupations tend to become less general and more specific. This leads to demands for knowledge, skills and competences that are immediate, direct and specialised.

In the modern world of industry and business, the incoming generations tend to nurture ambition and aspiration to step up the ladder of job hierarchy. This rightful desire for upward mobility is strengthened when opportunities are offered to the workers, within their organisation or outside it, for the training or further training which fit them for the new job responsibilities.

The fundamental principle of the present-day vocational education is that every learner should be given as much education or training he wants at a particular time. Instead of complete preparation for a life occupation, it may be just enough when an individual is equipped sufficiently with knowledge and skills which may help him in meeting his immediate social or economic needs and responsibilities. Through a well-devised system of further or extension education, persons may get prepared for newer or higher occupational callings and responsibilities under the rapidly changing socio-economic order. Further education can help a person in upgrading his job or in seeking alternative occupation or in getting training related to any other personal growth and development.

Further education in vocational and technical areas covers a field of great diversity and usefulness, as is the case in U.K., where—"it is the fastest growing and in many ways the most successful and inventive areas of English education". When properly organised and developed, further education system can provide immense scope and vertical mobility of young working persons towards their goal of better and higher academic and professional achievements leading to better and richer employment benefits. By adopting modern methods and routes of study, facilities for further education can be provided extensively and economically for the emerging class of skilled persons that will have the ability and academic standing to enter advanced education and training programmes. For example, widening the range of routes available—part-time day/evening, block release, sandwich, directed private study or correspondence route or mixing of routes—should give the widest possible opportunity for students to study for various courses. Similarly, devising specialised courses based on the principle of multiple-entry credit system, may make it possible for motivated students to enter a higher stage of course with the minimum of academic entry requirements.

A system of further education of the envisaged kind shall thus prove to be a major integrative factor, a highly motivating force for successful career development of young persons who have had the basic initial groundings in vocational education.

Occupational preparation

To put the discussion on occupational preparation in proper perspective, it will be useful to highlight the distinguishing aspects of education and training.

It is important to underscore the fact that education by itself, except in certain cases, rarely generates the potential for entry to the first job. The contemporary education based on traditional curriculum weighed with academic or cultural content is hardly the means to fit persons into places in the modern work force. Training, which is regarded as an addition to education, is needed to prepare persons for the different occupational levels. The essential purpose of training should primarily be—to increase the work efficiency, to improve the conditions of the individuals, to provide means whereby the individuals may increase their earnings and improve their job status. Education, in its liberal sense, is a humanising process. Training, in its utilitarian sense, is a career building process. Education is a face-to-face instructional activity mostly carried out within tne precincts of an educational institution. On the other hand, training constitutes a out-of-the class activity mostly carried out in work places. Systematic training implies a concerted process directed towards conformity to the requirements of work places and conditioning the trainees to work culture and work discipline. Training presupposes a certain minimum of education acquired by a trainee. In short, training is a sort of super structure, to be built on the edifice of education preparatory to training. That way, there is innermost co-relation between education and training.

Educators and professional experts believe that a comprehensive process of occupational preparation should include both education and training. They argue, rightfully of course, that such a preparation will enable students to achieve their maximum in the knowledge, skills and behavioural accomplishments necessary for a successful satisfying life. To meet the requirements of good citizenship combined with efficient service in the context of the modern economy and technology, learning experiences must be enlarged and enriched by supplementing in - class activities with out-of-the class experiences.

A good system of preparing young people for a wide range of diverse vocations or occupations thus call for organised and co-ordinated efforts in integrating vocational education and training. The integrated process of education and training could be developed along four inter-related stages: (i) Academic education: (ii) Pre-occupational education and training; (iii) In-plant or on-the-job training;

and (iv) In-service training. These four stages should mean...

Academic education

(a) Theoretical knowledge—in terms of definitions, basic principles and fundamentals, descriptions and applications—about subject-matter related specifically to the work the student should perform in the shop/laboratory/field during a given educational period.

(b) The knowledge of the necessary elements of maths, science and similar educational subjects in the general and applied fields to the extent it is considered essential to the career field the student is preparing to enter.

Pre-occupational and training

(a) The knowledge of materials, tools and techniques, operations of specific pieces of equipment, safe work practices and procedures, work standards, and the application of technical information in the practical solution of problems typical to the career field the student is preparing to enter.

(b) The knowledge providing information about the broader occupation field, current developments in the field, work habits and relations and other related information, if any.

(c) Practical, shop and laboratory skill development training related to trades or occupations, communication skill development training, and other related skill development training, if any.

In-plant or on-the-job training

This kind of job entry training should be aimed at exposing the trainee to the actual working methods and techniques related to occupational tasks. The training process should be directed towards acquisition of manipulative skills, occupational competences and work culture and work discipline groundings.

In-service training

This kind of occupational training be directed towards upgrading knowledge, skills and competences of skilled workers so organised that they may advance up the ladder of job hierarchy while in service as and when the opportunity may arise. This extended system of occupational training should also correspond to career-long further training and retraining in specialised occupational areas.

For the first two stages of occupational preparation, the major responsibility must belong to institutions catering to vocational education and training. For stages three and four, the responsibility for accomplishing the training tasks is best discharged by employing organisations.

Institutions can at best turn out readily trainable but not fully trained skilled personnel. The training at the institution level can be feasible only in the areas of basic skill related to trades or occupations, practical training in some manipulative skills and some degree of conceptual skills commensurate with the theoretical topics of the course concerned. Training specific to particular occupations can best be imparted at the beginning of and during employment, or preferably after a further definite occupational responsibility.

The training system should thus be conceived as an integrated process-which may take place partly in institutions and partly in work places, the two parts matched closely. In the final analysis, the most effective training programmes are those that lead to real jobs; which should mean organisations should train persons to meet their genuine needs. In a wider sense, training must be viewed as 'post-institution' investment leading to increased production and better productivity. Viewed purely from the economic point of view, training is a cost of production of labour.

Levels of industrial work force

There are recognised levels of industrial work force. The technologist, the technician and the skilled worker or craftsman make up the "production team" that produces the goods and services that are the foundation of the nation's industrial economy. There is not always a distinct separation between the three levels. Some overlapping in the job requirements and responsibilities is there. However, this classification of trained technical humanpower spectrum has been generally accepted in our country.

The technologist or engineer holds a degree or equivalent qualification in technology or engineering. His work functions and responsibilities relate to management, execution, research and development activities.

The technician is a person qualified by education usually in a technical institution like polytechnic or by training under operating conditions in well-established training organisation within industry. The technician holds the intermediate position between the technologist on the one hand and the skilled workers on the other. The technicians's work functions and responsibilities relate to activities like construction, fabrication, production, maintenance, testing, operation, installation, drafting and estimating, and so forth.

The craftsman or skilled worker is one who has completed training in a vocational institute or has completed apprenticeship programme in a trade or is engaged in a vocation in which vocational knowledge, skills and competences are acquired. I.T.I. trained personnel and National Apprenticeship Certificate holders belong to this category. I.T.Is. provide vocational education and training—with knowledge and skills in occupational trades, mostly of industrial nature, leading to vocational careers. Training of this kind prepares skilled workers needed for plants, factories and industrial establishments. The training system represents a transition from general secondary education to vocational education leading to employability for current, new and emerging occupations.

The growth and diversity of industry and advances in science and technology have led to ever-increasing demand of skilled craftsmen. With on-the-job training and experience, and with further education and training when availed of, such qualified craftsmen will have ample opportunities for stepping up the ladder of job hierarchy to advanced technical positions as shop-floor supervisors or foremen or middle-level technicians.

Several industrial organisations, both large and medium, provide some kind of training for their employees. The training-in-industry programmes include job training, extension programmes training and supervisory training. Such programmes in which both labour and management participate, can provide much needed training for a sizeable section of the skilled work force.

In the industrial sector job hierarchy, this chain of skilled and trained technical humanpower occupies the central or commanding position at the level of managerial, technological and engineering skills. They are the personnel who plan, organise, control and supervise processes and operations and undergo activities with job functions appropriate to the position they hold in organisations.

Below the level of skilled workers, there exists another class of workers or tradesmen. They are referred to as semi-skilled and un-skilled workers. An un-skilled worker is one who performs work that chiefly requires muscular energy and very little judgment. Semi-skilled workers may be classified somewhere in between skilled and un-skilled workers. Semi-skilled workers have some knowledge, experience or hand skills with abilities to work as craftsmen, artisans or handymen. Carpenters, smiths, fitters, painters, weavers, masons, plumbers, tanners-are some such semi-skilled workers that form the work force at the lower rungs of production, manufacturing, construction, operational or maintenance processes underlying mostly middle-scale and small-scale industrial organisations and government establishments. They are the personnel who have to their credit some degree of experience of skills acquired either through the traditional father-to-son apprenticeship practice or by undergoing vocational or occupational education or training in institutions or places of work.

Semi-skilled workers form a recognisable segment of work force in industrial establishments that help restore balance in the demand-supply relationship underlying skilled workers. Through the process of further education or training in vocational institutions or apprenticeship at the shop-floor level, semi-skilled personnel tend to qualify to attain the accepted standards of skill and ability appropriate to skilled operations. Vocational and technical institutions catering to vocational or occupational training at certificate level of course organisation provide the necessary facilities for training of semi-skilled workers and handymen. Such a training system, when properly planned and organised at the State level, tends to supplement the I.T.I. system of training in a large measure. Though the training given in trade certificate level institutions cannot be rated as terminal in character, the end-product may be recognised as trained in semi-skills, which can be up-graded in content and depth by organising programmes of further or extension education and training in the context of the current industrial developments and needs. To that end, the State level vocational institutions, other than I.T.Is., have an important role to play.

Shifting structure of industrial work place

During the past thirty years the course of industrial development in our country has been marked by a massive increase in the size of production units and the corresponding quality production; by the steady introduction of sophisticated machinery and process; by diversifying the industrial production; and by divisioning and sub-divisioning of labour processes. These developments have given rise to a new order of industrial work place, a phenomenon of changing nature of industrialisation. As a result, modern industrial requirement in terms of work force are now cast in an altogether different mould. A major aim of the efficiency movement in modern industry is to facilitate the greatest productivity with the least expenditure on humanpower and other resources. Industrial and business leaders therefore look to the school or institution to develop a new type of student or trainee with behavioural pattern necessary for the modern age. A well-trained and adaptable worker conscious of obligations and efficiency, a better citizen—is the modern requirement.

As a consequence, jobs are becoming highly specialised and standardised, especially in corporate organisations. Divisioning and sub-divisioning of labour process is the order of the day. The diversity of industry's work force with its various levels of hierarchy require different types of workers—with different personality structure with different levels of intelligence and initiative, and with different levels of skill and competence. New jobs arising in the emerging high-tech economy require skills that many workers simply do not possess.

Requirements for the new emerging jobs are spelled out not in terms of knowledge and skills but in terms of behavioural pattern—habits, values and personality traits conducive to assembly line techniques and turn-key industrial processes. In the modern setting, this specialisation of work force means requirement of less craft or skill and requirement of more culture of work. Order, regularity, punctuality, rationality, adherence to work techniques and schedules, the ability to co-operate with co-workers—are the important attributes of work culture.

At the same time, processes and methods of industries have become increasingly more depended on the principles of modern science and technology. More and more jobs emphasize on the need of sophisticated knowledge and skill on the part of the skilled worker in areas like ideas of materials, ideals of organisation, ideas of costs, and so on. Corporate leaders emphasize the necessity for a new stress on far more maths, science, technology and basic skills. Workers in a rapidly changing labour market will need to be generalists, adaptable enough to change courses and change for new careers with a minimum of disruption.

In to-day's industrial environment, the emphasis is on two categories of work force: a sizeable number of workers which need skill, competence and work culture attributes; and a comparatively large number of workers which need skill only in a narrow range of operations. This should mean evolving programmes of education and training with two broad complementary objectives—programmes designed to fit the students or trainees with functional specialities would contribute to their usefulness and thus to their integration into the emerging work culture; and programmes designed to fit the students or trainees with skill and competence commensurate with the job tasks. This should also mean that the traditional curriculum will have to give way to a new dispensation with a mix of knowledge, skill, competence and work culture. Perhaps it may be appropriate to evolves specific programmes of training and retraining for the emerging urban working class.

Needs and demands

Each society needs a certain number of educated citizens, more or less specially qualified, at the desired levels of educational attainment. Ordinarily, this need stems in the first place from the national economy, but it may also be generated by other sources, including the State itself, which has to plan and implement policies and programmes leading to humanpower development and utilisation.

Before commenting on the supply-demand relationship related to skilled workers, it will be worthwhile to refer to the relationship between needs and demands in generalised terms.

First, the co-relation between needs and demands is not always harmonious. Second, in many cases needs precede and exceed demands. But in many others, demands are greater than needs. Third, in many sectors of employment needs and demands fail to coincide. This is more marked when educational systems and economic fluctuations do not match. Fourth, educational needs and demands are both increasing enormously. Among the multiple causes for this kind of expansion are population growth, economic development, increase in knowledge and skills, social transformations and political motivations.

This general analysis apart, expanding economies need ever-large number of skilled workers. Technological advances and changes transform traditional occupations or create entirely new job categories requiring training and retraining on a large scale. New thrusts of a country presuppose a parallel effort in preparing persons to man the emerging occupations. To this may be added the emergence of new demands from hitherto stagnant, traditional rural economies. This leads to pressure for education from parents and young people, especially from the disadvantaged and under-privileged classes hitherto more or less excluded from organised education. The facts to-day amply demonstrate that the requirements of development and the opportunity of new employment possibilities act as a strong stimulus to the expansion of occupational education and training.

It is quite rational to understand that the growth in the demand of vocational education and training should be fundamentally determined by the needs of economic development. The law of supply and demand of the labour market, conditioning the preparation of qualified skilled workers in accord with skilled humanpower forecasts and economic development plans, should hold good all times. Yet the fact remains that the present-day socio-economic forces and compulsions tend constantly to require the education system to operate in advance of real employment outlets. Above all, parents generally do not agree their children being deprived of the education relevant to the modern thrusts of the economy, even when there is only a limited or minimum capacity for absorbing them in gainful employment. "The combination of such needs and interests accounts for the unprecedented pressure of the demand for education at all levels and in all forms"— as rightly analysed in "Learning to Be", UNESCO. This and other concerns stemming from various socio-economic and political considerations, sometimes tend to motivate governments in our country for pushing educational development.

Humanpower data available provide little guidance on the extent of vocationalisation of education at the secondary school stage level. Humanpower needs are generally expressed in terms of matriculates or numbers of students successfully competing courses of general education. Student population in terms of products of vocational or technical schools or centres, craft-training institutes—are not represented in the work force studies and forecasts. Thus there is inadequacy of the available data about vocational or occupational education. Also very little is known about the size of the potential market for trained skilled personnel or the costs and benefits to the individuals and the society of this important part of the country's total education provision. The lack of data and studies adds to the already difficult task of planning effective courses of vocational education for the future.

When the propose and plan of expanding the existing programmes, we should also think of the manner in which the already trained humanpower is put to use. The available statistical data point to the fact that a fair proportion of our skilled personnel is being under-utilised, and in some cases, it is unutilised.

The need to pay due attention to the proper relationship between supply and demand in terms of skilled work force has to be understood in the context of stringency of our financial and physical resources. If the country or state is to achieve its targets of economic growth, it must have adequate supply of skilled hands of reach category of jobs to be performed. On the other hands, if there is a surfeit of trained persons in any job category, it implies waste of scarce resources and organisational efforts. It also adds to the difficult problem of unemployment and the resulting frustration to the educated youth. It has to be reasonably assured that educated and trained skilled persons will not remain unemployed or wastefully under-employed.

Status and value of vocational education

Indian education is essentially centred on one basic purpose—to prepare the student for subsequent education. Far too meagre attention is given to the role of the school or college in preparing students for active citizenship and for employability skills. There is a general notion that preparation for a life career is a second-class activity for second class citizens. This attitude is shared by businessmen, political leaders, labour leaders, educators, administrators, parents and students. Unfortunately, this attitude infests the Central and State governments too—which invest far more on general education than they do for support of vocational and professional education. There is no Central act on vocational education, nor there is any Central funding arrangement operating all over the country. What are the consequences of this national attitude? Well, they are:

— At the secondary stage, the enrollment in vocational education is very low. It was just 2.2 per cent of the total school enrolment in 1966, as per the Education Commission's observation. There is no evidence to show any improvement thereafter.

— Good students shy away from vocational education. Students who opt for vocational education are mostly the drop-outs and cast-offs of the academic stream.

— Teachers and instructors engaged in vocational education enjoy relatively low status or presitge within the teaching profession. Good teachers and instructors are thus seldom attracted to join the vocational stream.

— Facilities for instruction are inadequate both in terms of quality and quantity.

— Courses or programmes offered are far out of context with the realities and needs.

— Achievements in academic subjects far outweigh achievements in vocational subjects. The two parts are usually taught with no relevance to each other. Generally vocational subjects are labeled as "of lower quality", partly because of lower quality of students and partly because of a perverted definition of "vocational subject".

Even the Kothari Education Commission was compelled to make unpleasant comments on the status and value of vocational education. The Commission observed that despite repeated exhortation it is unfortunately still felt that vocational education at the school level is an inferior form of education, fit only for those who fail in general education—the last choice of parents and students.

This attitude must change. At all levels of thinking—national, regional or state—the fact must be recognised that in an increasingly technological era, occupational education and skill development are the keys to a long-range solution, both for the individual and society. Helping young people become employable is an essential national objective.

A concerted effort is therefore needed by government agencies, industrial and business organisations, social and political bodies and all groups and individuals deeply concerned with and interested in vocational education—through enlightened wage policies, improved means and methods of educational organisation, organised vocational guidance and counseling services, the creation of public opinion—to promote the status and value of vocational education.

Unemployment is more often the result of a lack of proper education and skill acquisition rather than of a shortage of job opportunities. We must, in one way or another, see that our education system prepares boys and girls to use their minds as well as muscles for talks that to-day's and—tomorrow's—labour market requires. Vocational education provides the diversity and practicability that our education system lacks so much. An efficient work force is the country's best resource—and vocational education is the best guarantee to workers that they will always be qualified for a job.

Edualisation of educational opportunity

The modern trend is towards universalisation or democratisation of education and imparting it to every citizen irrespective of his ability, attitude and social environment. This is made possible through providing wide options to the students in the selection of subjects including languages, sciences, industrial, agricultural and commercial skills, fine arts, crafts, etc. Admission regulations are made flexible and academic deficiencies, if any, are allowed to be made good en route. Remedial measures and facilities are offered liberally. Conduct of examinations is carried out on widely differing patterns for different categories of students. Further education is provided extensively. These principles of equality and social justice practised in some development countries like U.K., U.S.A., Japan and Germany, are based on the emphasis that opportunities for education should be made available to every person whatever his status in the society or his academic or calibre or ability.

A very important point of view with reference to democracy in education is that modern society requires equality of opportunity for obtaining vocational or occupational education on as extensive a basis as possible. Granted that individuals differ in needs, interests and abilities and that no one type or kind of educational programme is suitable to the needs and capabilities of all persons; yet it would seem more in the spirit of democracy to provide opportunities for many types and kinds of workers to opt for a variety of courses and activities rather than to limit these opportunities to the few who are preparing to enter the vocations or professions.

Our education system has unwittingly created social barriers which militate against the principle of equalisation. In our country, the education of an average student in respect of vocational or technical careers stands neglected. It is this kind of young persons—who would make the rank and file of work force in several fields of employment—that hardly receive the relevant occupational education or training to help them discharge their functions with some degree of efficiency. This imbalance can be overcome by enlarging and modernising the system of vocational education, by dispersing the institutional facilities as widely as feasible, by offering a variety of programmes of education and training to meet the needs and interests and individuals, and by providing other built-in features in the course organisation so as to provide facilities that may be availed of as freely and on as wide as basis as possible.

Constraints, priorities and optimisation

The effort required to pay adequate attention to the proper relationship between needs and demands has to be understood in the context of constraints of our financial and physical resources. Education and training of the number of skilled workers required at different levels of occupations may entail expenditure of an order which the national or state economy may not afford. In planning and formulating vocational education and training programmes, it is imperative to take into account the resources available and the capacity of the administration to provide the necessary finances and other facilities needed. There are to face other constraints that limit expansion and modernisation in the field of vocational-technical education. Availability of—competent qualified teachers and instructors; shop and laboratory equipment of the right type and quality; the facility of training and retraining of teachers and instructors; teaching aids and equipment; instructional materials like text books, reference books, books of programmed instruction, instructional manuals and work books; proper organisation for testing student performance; vocational guidance and counselling service; financial and other aids to students—are the major constraints. There are often overcome by lowering the standards and norms. Diluting standards and norms leads to ineffectiveness of the education and training programmes.

There are internal constraints of this kind in every educational system which limit generating of additional facilities needed for expanding or modernising education. This is all the more so in the case of vocational-technical system of education which is cost-intensive compared to any general education system at the school stage. In such a situation two alternatives come to mind as a matter of solution. When the total cost of proposals goes beyond the finances available, priorities will have to be determined and enforced by the administration. Alternately, it may become necessary to place a much greater emphasis in our plans for expansion and modernisation on the basis of intensive utilisation of the available facilities. It is generally agreed that the existing institutional facilities in terms of space, plant and equipment, under-utilised teaching and instructional staff must be put to their optimum use. Optimisation of facilities can also be thought of in terms of lengthening working days, making full use of the long vacations, organising two-shift working, organising part-time route/ corresponding courses, and generally by creating an environment of hard sustained work.

Question to be answered

We have discussed in generalised terms some important issues, purposes and principles that affect the planning and operation of the vocational education system in our country. There are yet many other question as :

— What shall be the philosophy and objectives governing vocational education?

— For what fields or occupational areas vocational education be designed and organised?

— For whom vocational education is intended?

— What shall be the awards? What shall be the levels and values of the awards?

— What shall be the routes of vocational education?

— What shall be the nature, contents and depth of the curricula for vocational courses?

— How and to what extent shall vocational education be oriented to actual practices or career situations?

— What kind of learning experiences shall be included in vocational education?

— How and to what extent actual occupational knowledge and skill be emphasised in the curricula?

— How and to what extent vocational education be

integrated with general education?

— What shall be the key persons or agencies for designing and formulating the curricula?

— What shall be the standards and norms and how shall they be established and maintained?

— What instructional methods and techniques shall be developed and used?

— How shall the student performance be tested?

— How shall working co-operation between institutions and employing organisations be established and maintained?

— Who shall administer and operate vocational education programmes?

— What shall be the type of organisation? What shall be the character of institutions?

— What shall be the essential facilities and services for establishing and maintaining programmes of instruction?

— Who shall pay for vocational education? What shall be the system for funding and financial aids?

Acceptable answers to questions such as those raised above involve a detailed study and analysis of many concepts, principles, facts and practices in vocational education. The key persons and agencies primarily concerned with the processes and procedures of designing vocational education courses are expected to address themselves to the issues and questions raised here, and to decide whether to accept the presented premises and analysis, to work for reforms, to bring about the significant changes and modernisation in the field of vocational education. Studies like this should not accepted as the final answer about the present. They should, ideally, only raise issues and questions about it.

It is hoped that the exposition, perceptions and arguments presented in this book may serve as a means of evaluating the purposes and scope of the existing programmes of vocational education, and may also serve as a guide in arriving at decisions concerning expansion and modernisation of vocational education.

2 Teaching and Learning Methods

The promotion of technical and vocational aspects of the curriculum needs to be accompanied by changes in the means by which young people learn. The development of new approaches to learning is the basis of curriculum change in Enfield. The focus is not an occupational family or a range of particular skills, but the young people, their possible futures, and their ability to cope with the unknown and the frequently-changing. The emphasis is therefore on learning methods and activities as much as on content.

More must be done to enable young people to live with competence and confidence in the world which will exist at the end of the twentieth century. The more specific and perhaps more easily realisable way of achieving this is through teaching the new technology. But at the same time we have to be aware of the accelerating rate of change—a rate which will ensure that most of the specifics of what we teach will be out-of-date and of little use in ten or twenty years' time. One only has to look at the accelerating rate of development in computing in the last twenty years to appreciate this.

At the same time as ensuring familiarity with the new technology, we have to focus on the students themselves, who will live their adult lives in this unknown future. If we simply *train* them in specific techniques, they will be at a loss when new demands are made upon them. If, however, we encourage their development into mature, flexible individuals, they stand a batter chance of coping. Experience in developing pastoral techniques in Enfield has taught us the importance of helping young people to develop a positive self-image. If they view themselves as individuals of value, they will develop the resources within themselves which will enable them to arrive at a correct estimate of, for example, the blandishments of advertising, the bullying of their peers or the demands of an unfamiliar situation. We cannot predict the nature of the world and of work in 2000 and education should reflect that uncertainty.

In Enfield, we have set ourselves the task of preparing the young in terms of the curriculum as well as in a pastoral sense. The 'way in', we believe, is through 'skills' and skill ownership', both of which are much misunderstood terms. The Schools Council publication. *The Practical Curriculum*, describes 'skill-ownership' as 'more than knowing, although "knowing" is a requisite of skill-ownership and, therefore, skill transfer. It also means that the owner of a skill is conscious and aware of his/her possession of the *ability to organise and effectively carry out such actions as will produce desired results*' (in a variety of contexts)

It may seem unnecessarily cumbersome to refer to the process of gaining skill-ownership' rather than 'learning'. The distinction is made, however, to emphasise a central fact which is not easily accepted by teachers. This is that skills, in the sense used here cannot taught. The student cannot occupy a passive role in relation to the teacher. The student must become actively aware of his/her present stage of development or understanding, will a change to take place and be prepared both to embark on a programme to effect such a change, and also to measure whether and to what extent the desired modification has taken place. It is the teacher's task to design learning situations and methods to encourage and facilitate this, and to initiate discussion with the student to promote this: and the student's task to fulfil the learning objectives which he/she and the teacher have agreed upon together.

TVEI is one of a number of curricular initiatives currently being implemented in Enfield, all of which are based on the premise of the student taking more responsibility for his/her learning. The structure of Enfield TVEI is that a minimum of 20% of the student's time is spent in the Core Programme and 10% in one of five Technical/Vocational options. The principle of helping a student to develop into an autonomous adult underlies both elements. The TVEI scheme in Enfield is based on five key learning objectives. Students are encouraged to be able to:

(a) adapt;

(b) anticipate responses;

(c) gather information;

(d) construct, conduct and evaluate a strategy;

(e) communicate effectively.

All students take 'mainstream' options in the remainder of their time, and have access to work experience.

What follows is a series of accounts written by three teachers, in different schools, of the way they have viewed the implementation of the Core Programme of Enfield TVEI. There is a little overlap, but it is hoped that the reader will find here three distinct personalities, who are working towards the concept of 'skill-ownership' in different ways. They have operated the new scheme for only a year, and are conscious both of the fact that they are working towards a new educational concept, rather than having captured it in its entirety, and also the problem that one's theory can outrun one's practice. However, they describe what they are doing, 'warts and all', in the belief that this is of value. It is in the nature of this approach that there never will be a 'finished product' in the sense of a prescribed syllabus.

Teacher A

The five learning objectives presented a broad canvas on which to formulate a course of greatest benefit to the school. In fashioning these objectives into a learning package I have been concerned, at all times, to maintain their inherent flexibility.

My previous experience included deep involvement in establishing a course based on an integrated curriculum. I was keen to accept the post of TVEI co-ordinator, as I had become firmly persuaded of the merits of moving forward from the traditional subject-based curriculum. The prospect of developing the concept across the ability range was the challenge I welcomed to prove its worth to all students and teachers.

The nature of the course and its origins necessitated a close working relationship with the local authority. Regular in-service training days were held at the teachers' centre with the coordinators from other schools in the borough. These were most beneficial in fusing a team. From an early stage an *esprit de corps* was nurtured which extended to informal meetings in coordinators' homes. At these gatherings ideas were discussed, experiences exchanged and intentions formulated to drive forward the concept.

A key planning issue was staffing. I was convinced that the requirement that students should recognise links between subject areas must be mirrored by a team approach from staff. For this reason I opposed the idea of one tutor being based on the TVEI room for the entire week, as I considered that students needed to work with different types of teachers. Furthermore, my enthusiasm would be better served by a team of teachers from various departments, who shared by attitude. Therefore, three other members of staff were timetabled to work with me on the project.

Creating the right environment for the course was another crucial component of the planning strategy. I wished to create a space which encouraged concentration and task application yet was conducive to talking in a relaxed manner. The staff dining room served this purpose and its new use was agreed. Indeed the first task of the students was to decorate the room; an exercise which, in addition to aesthetic considerations, included the costing of the operation and subsequent purchase of materials. Thus the students' own environment was the fruit of their first experience of planning, decision-making and collectively 'making this happen'.

The resolution of the planning issues in respect of staffing and environment proved a timetabling challenge. TVEI required a tutor to be available at all times regardless of the number of students to be supervised. This was difficult to schedule yet such was the momentum behind the course that all obstacles were overcome.

The question of resources represented the final piece of the planning jig-saw. The need was for packs of material which would guide students in their research, encourage them to question information and look beyond the school for answers. Few such packs existed, although amongst them we found Community Services Volunteers (CSV) to be well presented and reasonably priced. Other sources included CRAC, the Inland Revenue and the Health Education Council. Our own work-sheets began to be written at this time-emphasising the need for initiative and enquiry.

With the planning process complete, the next stage was to develop the classroom methods that would transform ideas into action. Our initial emphasis was twofold: first, deciding the best method of introducing the programme, and second, preparing the necessary learning resources. There was some debate between the view that complete freedom of choice should be offered immediately and the contrary view which held that a more controlled approach was prudent. These perspectives were reconciled in the form of negotiation, which provided for freedom of choice within a controlled and monitored framework.

Each student would select the topics which most appealed to him/her from the scheme's Core Programme. He/she would then prepare a flow-chart maping out a possible scheme of learning, and discuss this with a tutor. This would form a permanent record of the agreement between student and teacher, a contract for learning.

Negotiation began at an early stage when I talked informally to possible candidates for the scheme, at the end of their third year. I explored their feelings towards the scheme and assessed their motivation. When the course was under way in the subsequent year, these early conversations proved a valuable way of re-focussing vision that had become blurred by short-term difficulties. It was possible to remind students of their original goals and ambitions and set them back on target.

Formal negotiations began in September with the beginning of the course. The freedom to select subjects for study was offered with the provision that students fully appreciated the need to plan and discuss progress. Negotiations in our term meant: reviewing possible learning experiences; discussing their value; assessing the best approach; agreeing a course of action; and establishing a procedure for registering progress to the achievement of goals.

Before negotiating process was complete, ideas were also exchanged on complete and innovative methods of recording information gathered. Media such as wall displays, written reports, posters and the like were all considered. For example, the findings of a project on wheelchair users and facilities for the disabled were summarised on a warning poster aimed at the non-handicapped, illustrating the dangers for those confined to a wheelchair.

Not all students were able to perform readily as self-starters. Some found the decision process difficult and were reluctant to guide their own progress. To maintain the momentum of the process, it becomes necessary for the teacher to assume responsibility for decision-making until such time as the student feels sufficiently confident to deal with the challenge.

Such problems, given a little initiative, can readily be translated into opportunities. Thus a student who is unable to deal with an individual programme may function perfectly adequately as part of group or in a pair. An example of this occurred with a comparative study of shopping in the market and supermarket. A student expressed the desire to question shoppers about their preferences, but was reluctant to undertake this alone despite having prepared a questionnaire that was more than equal to the take. A gregarious member of the group volunteered to ask the question whilst the originator of the questionnaire recorded the answers.

The example above indicates that the actual piece of work may be of far less importance than the social and team-work skills which are developed. Such skills are an important foundation on which to build a successful life outside school. Our commitment to a residential component on the course reflects their importance.

Throughout the first year of the scheme we have endeavoured to use as many outside agencies as possible. People other than teachers, from organisations other than schools, help to add a freshness and stability to the learning experience. Students have been encouraged to suggest and invite possible speakers and have responded to this opportunity with enthusiasm. Each of the local political parties has submitted a representative to be questioned, and these session initiated much debate. Visits outside school have also been encouraged, to collect information and sample different environments. Local industry, social services and the council offices have all received parties of students or individuals.

Since 'skills across the curriculum' is one of the organising themes, we have made use of other departments in the school. Technical departments have been a particularly useful source in this respect.

In keeping with the need to weld learning to the world to work and technology we have made extensive use of micro-computers. These are great motivators and are particularly suited to the development of problem-solving skills. In addition to an increasing supply of educational software, many large companies make their own training packages available to schools.

The year has not been without its problems. Many students found it difficult to re-adjust to the conventional subject-based curriculum during the rest of the week. This is in part a measure of how they were able to demolish the barriers between subjects and how they became active participants in learning.

Whilst we have had to adapt the scheme when putting it into the classroom. I am satisfied that its underlying educational philosophy remain intact. The majority of students respond well to the stimulus of making their own decisions and benefit from the widened and enriched curriculum. I am convinced that as a result young people will be able to advance into the world of employment and technology as confident and responsible citizens.

Teacher B

The most important feature of TVEI for my school was that it offered the possibility of change in a system of schooling inhibited in its outlook, way of innovation and conscious that direction was determined by remote external agencies. Such restrictions give rise to conflicts. Education is swamped by schooling. Schooling more accurately reflects the expectations of a society which measures success in terms of percentage pass rates traditional examinations, which sees discipline as collective rather than individual quality and considers imagination, creativity, inventiveness and independence of mind almost subversive. At the same time education is attempting to nurture the individual student by developing his/her potential to the fullest possible extent, broadening perspectives and maximising opportunity. It looks to success and cannot, as does the traditional system, emphasise failure.

The teacher, whilst wishing to promote the concept of a liberal education, cannot ignore the demand of examination boards, employers and parents and must not neglect the preparation of the student for employment or further education beyond sixteen. It is, however, these very demands which have sown seeds of dissatisfaction. Students are increasingly restricted in their choice of subjects beyond fourteen years of age, they are required to specialise well before they are able to appreciate the consequences of their selections, they must drop subjects which they enjoy and in which they display talent, and have a little chance to develop new skills or to explore interesting by-ways. We have promoted a system which makes little real demand on the intellectual or practical abilities of the student and one which sees the teachers often working such harder than their charges.

The planning process of any pilot scheme must be seen as a coherent programme in which course content, methods of implementation, techniques of assessment and consumer response are constantly reviewed. All participants must be given a platform to express opinions and should expect to be involved in all aspects of the course.

It was to our considerable advantage that an outline for the Core Programme and already been prepared by college lecturers, teachers and youth workers in the employ of the local authority. The early planning meetings could therefore concentrate on implementation rather than the development of content. The most pleasing aspect of these meetings was that no common approach emerged but that individual schools were free to progress in ways most suited to their students, staff and particular methods of organisation, with the students as a particularly influential element. Whilst meetings of teachers continued throughout the first year, detailed planning became an integral part of individual student programmes.

All students' timetables are constructed as described in the introduction to this chapter. The way in which individual programmes are put together leads to an emphasis on individual work within TVEI. As a consequence, traditional classroom approaches are not employed, nor are such rooms utilized. A comfortable, well-equipped room is the centre for much of the work, but students are encouraged to make use of other facilities both in and out of school. This has already established contact with other schools, notably those involved in special education, colleges of further education and Middlesex Polytechnic. An appreciation that resources are widely available is most important.

The role of the teacher has altered substantially. It is the student, with any necessary guidance from staff and at times other students, who must organise, develop and prepare schemes of work. The students are also responsible for the collection of resources, seeking specialist assistance and, where new skills are needed, for arranging suitable courses. Such talents do not emerge overnight. In the early stages teacher involvement is considerable, and students are led to solutions. It is clear that, given time, the skills required will develop. Group work is not uncommon but arises from mutual interest rather than from any formal teaching requirement. There are areas of skill development, for example interview techniques, that do need greater co-operation. In all of the base programme units, a framework is provided to establish pathways that each student might follow, objectives are set the progress monitored through discussion. Students are expected to employ a range of methods or recording and presenting completed work. In concentrating on 'skills based learning' and emphasising the role of the students in this process, the hope is that they will begin to develop the five essential attributes noted above.

Formal assessment of progress entails detailed profiling of the whole curriculum. This creates the greatest difficulties and highlights the need for staff as well as student education. A weekly progress record, maintained by each student, is supplemented by agreed statements drawn up three to six times per year, indicating progress made in all aspects of the curriculum. It is envisaged that on completion of the course a summative profile will be drawn up for inclusion in a certification package, a document which will, it is hoped, provide a most valuable 'sales aid' to any student.

Skills or resource based learning methods place particularly heavy demands on learning materials. There is quite clearly a need to ensure that certain materials are immediately to hand, but attempt to stock the base room with every conceivable resource would not only be impossible, but would undermine major element of the course. A large comprehensive school is in itself a most substantial resource, for a vast wealth of information is available at little cost and effort. Beyond the immediate environment of the school are any number of agencies many of which are very willing to provide resources free of charge. Student quickly learn to make use of such munificence.

Teacher C

The aims behind the scheme and approach adopted at my school are:

1. There should be a change of emphasis away from content learning towards skill-based learning, that is, a change from the product of learning to the development of the cognitive processes involved in learning.

   The learning of processes or skills is achieved through their practice. The approach in the classroom needs to be one of experience-based learning, whereby the student is provided with opportunities to develop competence in those skills. The experience may be provided through real life activities or simulated and role play activities.

2. The vocational awareness and interests of the students should take a more central role in their education. For too long vocational awareness has been confined to the periphery of education. Such a change in emphasis may not only provide students with enhanced prevocational preparation but may also make schooling more relevant to students and increase their motivation.

3. Students should take a more active and responsible role in their own learning. This is achieved through the process of negotiation. This term negotiation implies a contract whereby both parties have something to offer the other in return for what the legal profession would call

'considerations'. A negotiated curriculum involves the school offering the students greater choice in deciding what they will study and how they will tackle those studies. Students, in return, provide the 'considerations' of increased motivation, self-reliance and independence. The role of the teacher is altered. He/she becomes a tutor/ counsellor who manages the learning experiences of the students and provides guidance, so that the students may complete their studies in an effective manner. In the process of negotiation, a student may wish to study a subject not conventionally on offer in the school's option system. Such subjects may be studied through self-supported study.

To achieve these aims, we recognised 'the need to create a fully resourced base room which contained audio-visual resources, computer hardware and appropriate software (some specially written) to facilitate effective computer-assisted learning. There was also a need for a careers information bank, a large collection of books, information packs, charts and other resources, and a collection of self-supported study materials. These are specially prepared, so that the students may progress through their studies in a manner akin to a correspondence course. The difference on this course is that the tutor is available to advise. Such a resource base room is used by the students as a self service educational workshop.

Students arriving at the base room negotiate with the tutor the learning tasks to be completed during the lesson, or over a series of lessons. As different students, and groups of students, may be undertaking different tasks during the same lesson, it is of paramount importance to record the decision of the negotiation. The tasks decided between tutor and student are therefore entered on the student's planning sheet. For the students to take a more active and responsible role in their learning, it is important for them to be aware of the purpose of the tasks which they are completing. This is achieved through the use of checklists noting the objectives of the tasks achieved by the student.

An account of part of a typical lesson will illustrate what happens. Eighteen students are due in the base room. Two of the students are attending a children's nursery as part of their vocational awareness. One student visits a school for the mentally handicapped and spends some time working with a speech therapist. The student has an interest in speech therapy as a career. Two girls visit the School Psychological Service. They interview an educational psychologist on the importance of the 1981 Act in treating children with special needs. Three students are completing as survey on industry. The activity is based on a pack produced by the Basic Skills Unit called *Your Local Industry*, which involves the students investigating the nature, size and type of industries in the community. Five students have been studying the topic of money budgeting. They are conducting a survey on teenage income and spending habits. Extensive use of computers in the processing and presentation of the data is required. One student is busy writing a computer program to calculate income tax repayments. Two students are engaged in self-supported study on a subject of their choosing. Three girl students are making light pens for use on the computer. The remaining two students are producing a post on safety in the home.

The reader may feel that the description above sounds interesting but may also wonder how the students react to such a radical departure from traditional classroom teaching. The general impression is encouraging. The course and the lessons are undoubtedly popular with many students. A small number of students, however, do find that they prefer the dependency of traditional teaching and do not wish to avail themselves of the opportunities provided. The course appears self motivating to the vast majority. Homework, as such, is not set on a specified day to complete a specified task. Students who have gained the sense of responsibility for their own studies complete their work at home, though such work is not termed by them as homework, nor does it have the traditional connotations of coercion and drudgery. Students are so keen to continue working that changes of lesson are ignored.

The final question which needs answering must be 'Can this approach, adopted for TVEI groups, be transferred to other parts of the school curriculum?' The answer must be an overwhelming 'yes'. Any approach that engenders such enthusiasm in students and makes education an enjoyable worthwhile and relevant experience is worthy of expansion into other parts of the school curriculum.

One must, however, make one important point. Class sizes can seriously affect the success of this approach. There has been mention of a lesson with eighteen students. It would be impossible for this approach to operate with a class of thirty.

3 Vocational Education and New Technology

The rhetoric of skills is much in evidence. We here of 'skills for the future', 'relevant skills', 'the skill demands of new technology' and the 'skill needed to survive in the modern world'. The aim of this chapter is to examine the notions behind the rhetoric, and to consider whether an education based on skills has either intrinsic worth or economic utility.

The chapter contains what might be considered an unlikely mixture. Examples of the use of the terms skill, vocational and pre-vocational education are followed by a critical discussion of these terms, particularly the notions of specific and generic skills. This use of language is then related to the needs of employers and the language in which those needs are phrased. In particular, the demand which will be made of Britain's education and training systems from the field of information technology are examined by considering both British initiatives and the Japanese approach. Is the rhetoric of skills of value in meeting the educational demands of new technology?

The growth of the language of skills and pre-vocational education

Surely it was James Callaghan who started it all. Callaghan's so-called Ruskin College Speech of 1976 contained an attack on informal, modern teaching methods, a 'concern for standards', and a criticism of the poor relationship between schools and industry. In short, he questioned the very function of schooling by suggesting that schools were not providing the *necessary skills*. Two statements from the Ruskin College speech serve to illustrate this point:

I am concerned ...to find complaints from industry that new recruits from the schools sometimes do not have the basic tools to do the job later.

There is not virtue in producing socially well adjusted members of society who are unemployed because they do not have the skills.

Thus began 'educational newspeak'. Educational objectives were being defined in terms of *skills*—not a new strategy but one which served Callaghan well and, more importantly, provided a framework for the language of Government White Papers in the 1980s. The language of skills, skill-deficits, skill-shortages, skill centres, skill training and skills in new technology is now firmly embedded in educational parlance.

Two points of major importance emerged from Callaghan's speech which have had a potent (though often tacit) influence on discussions of education ever since. The first point, by implication, is that one of the key factors in the rise of unemployment is the shortage of relevant skills, This can be called the 'skills-deficit' of unemployment. It is a model which is adopted implicitly, and sometimes explicitly, by the Government White Papers discussed shortly. In adopting this model Callaghan was suggesting that one of the key functions of education is as an instrument to provide 'necessary skills' and thereby reduce youth unemployment. The second implication is that a set of 'relevant' or 'necessary' skills exist which (if required) would make students more employable and, in Callaghan's words, provide the 'basic tools to do the job'. Callaghan made no attempt to outline what these necessary or relevant skills are—he simply implied that they exist.

Since Callaghan's speech (though not as a result of it) unemployment has risen from 1.2 million to somewhere between three and four million. This steady increase in unemployment had led, paradoxically, to a strengthening of the bonds between education and *employment.*

The impact of unemployment on education can be crudely, but usefully, divided into four sequential stages:

1. The implicit promise in schooling (i.e. 'work hard at school to get a job after it') is undermined.
2. The direction and traditional function of schooling and education are questioned.
3. Education, training, and 'pre-vocational education' are increasingly seen as an instrument to respond to youth unemployment.
4. The bonds between education and employment are tightened.

The latter stage is perhaps the irony in the influence of rising unemployment on education. It seems a paradox that the main effect of unemployment has been to strengthen the bonds between education and employment, and lead to the growth of *pre-vocational education*. This is the area where skills as educational objectives are most in evidence.

The two key White Papers which helped to develop the notion of 'pre-vocational education' were entitled *A New Training Initiative* and *Training for Job*. The former was one of the key documents leading to the YTS. The aim of the paper was to provide 'better preparation for working life in initial full-time education', a reflection of the fourth stage described above. The paper therefore aimed to ensure that 'the school curriculum develops the personal skills...needed for working life'. The reader is left searching in vain through the remainder of the paper for a clarification of which skills are needed for working life.

It (the YTS) will aim to develop basic and recognized skills which employers will require in the future.

Some mention is made in the following paragraph of specific skills: literacy, numeracy and communication skills are listed. However, these could hardly be said to lie outside the realms of general education. Nowhere in the paper is an attempt made to specify the skills required for a truly vocational education, or the skills which 'employers will require in the future'.

The question of whether these skills exist, how

they can be specified and if so what they are, is one of the issues I would like to raise in this paper.

The 1981 White Paper also contains three key paragraphs which reveal two implicit models of the *causes* of unemployment and its relation to education:

The skill shortages which have held back our economic progress in the past could reappear when the economy recovers.

For the immediate future the Government sees an increase of public expenditure on this scale as the only way of plugging the gap in the training provision required if we are to be ready to meet the skill needs of the economy as trading conditions improve and to offer adequate opportunities to the current generation of young people.

For many years now or system of training has failed to produce the number of skilled people required by a modern competitive economy.

These paragraphs are interesting for two reasons. Firstly, they tacitly rely on two models of unemployment. The skill-deficit model comes through strongly in all three paragraphs. The second model of unemployment, which can be called the 'cyclical model', suggests that an upturn of the economy is 'just around the corner and that unemployment will decrease as trading conditions and the economy recover. This model is now more than five years old but recovery is not yet in sight. Both models have been attacked by established authors since 1981. Stomer, for example, argues that unemployment patterns are caused by structural changes within society in undergoing a revolution from an industrial to a post-industrial era. Unemployment patterns are not fundamentally altered by skills shortages or by cyclical changes in trading conditions. Stonier's argument is supported by raw statistical data. Japanese labour trends indicate that structural changes are indeed occurring in their rather advanced industrial society. There has been a clear trend, which is still continuing, towards service industries and the so-called 'information sector'. The Japanese have even coined a world for it which cannot be printed here but means roughly 'servicization'. Similar, though more depressing trends, can be seen in the statistical data on Britain. Primary and secondary industry have both declined sharply while only service industries have grown.

The reliance of the 1981 White Paper on the skills-deficit and cyclical models of unemployment clearly determines its views on education and training. This comes through most clearly in its references to 'skill needs', system of training', 'skill shortages', and the suggestion that unemployment can be tackled by tightening the bonds between education and employment i.e. by 'pre-vocational education'.

Three years later the 1984 White Paper, *Training for Jobs*, seemed to be offering similar explanations of unemployment and the failure of education despite the published warnings of Stonier, Toffler and even of Daniel Bell a decade earlier. The skills-deficit model of unemployment comes through clearly:

It (vocational education) will enable many more people to be trained and improve their prospects of employment by placing greater emphasis on equipping them with skills that are currently required.

As in the 1981 paper, no attempt is made to investigate or even clarify the notion of 'skills that are currently required'. References are again made to 'skill shortages holding us back' but no suggestion is made as to which skills are in short supply. One reference only is made to the effect of new technology upon training and employment:

> The main objective of this strategy (training programmes) is to secure an adequate supply of people with up-to-date skills to meet the demands of new technologies upon which economic growth must be based.

This reference to up-to-date skills meeting the demands of new technologies will be investigated later in the paper. The main aim of this section has been to trace the rise of the rhetoric of skills, and alongside it the notion of pre-vocational education. The twin notions of 'skill' and 'pre-vocational education' will now be examined.

The concepts of pre-vocational and vocational education

The notion of *vocational* education is in itself difficult to interpret. 'Vocation' is usually associated with training so that the idea of 'vocational training' makes perfect sense. Training is linked to specific job, career, skill or vocation, when discussing training, it always make sense to ask 'training for what?' Indeed the notion of training makes no sense at all unless it is a training *as* or *for* 'something'. A person can be training as a car mechanic, training for a Judo competition, or training as an account. To say that sometime is training always begs the further question *as* or *for* what. Education is a very different concept. Education, unlike training, can stand on its own without being linked to some other aim, goal or vocation. This is perhaps why the concept of "vocational education" is almost a contradiction to certain purists. But, given the instrumentalism or 'new vocationalism' set in motion by James Callaghan it has now become increasingly commonplace to ask of education, 'education, for what?' Hence, the notion of vocational education has become more widespread and perhaps more palatable as 'education' is interpreted as 'training'.

But the notions of pre-vocational education still remains an enigma to translate. Can you imagine a teacher trying to explain the idea to a worried parent?

Teacher: Well, it's the education that your child gets before he(she) starts on his(her) vocational education.

Parent: Well, what's vocation education, then?

Teacher: Well, it's the education your child gets once he(she) has finished his (her) pre-vocational education.

The concept of pre-vocational education remains a mystery to me, and (in a most cowardly fashion) I will give up any further attempt to translate it.

Dearden, with his usual rigour and clarity, analyses the notions of vocational education and training in a valuable way (though he sheds no light on the notion of pre-vocational education, so at least

I am in good company). Dearden's main general point is that education and training are 'different but not necessarily mutually exclusive'. In other works, the same learning experience may quality to be called either education or training, or perhaps both. One such area at the intersection of the two concepts *may* be vocational education, which could therefore equally be called vocational training. This would be in sharp contrast to other experiences where the labels' 'education' and 'training' imply totally different activities. Sex training and sex education will provide totally different experiences - if the former were adopted on the school curriculum, for example, I believe it might cause far more parental anxiety than the latter.

However, vocational training could only be worthy of the tern 'vocational education' if it were 'liberally conceived', and included 'learning about the nature of work, discussing its forms and contexts: a version of careers then the notions of 'vocational training' and 'vocational education' might indeed by synonymous, and there might also be some meaning for the notion of pre-vocational education in terms of the wider, more liberal conception which Dearden describes.

In practice, however, the notion of vocation training is almost always translated in terms of 'skills' which can be specified and stated. If we use Dearden's perfectly acceptable view that education should involve 'the development of knowledge and understanding in breadth and depth' and a 'degree of critical reflectiveness and corresponding autonomy of judgment' then learning experiences involving only skills cannot possibly be called 'vocational education'. This assertion rests on the analysis of 'skills' which now follows.

The language of skills

The interpretation of vocational education, used synonymously with vocational training, is given almost entirely in terms of skills in the White Papers cited above. Similarly, the aims and content for the YTS are based firmly on a Core Skills Programme, consisting of a set of 103 identified skills. This approach is in turn based on the influential IMS report, *Foundation Training Issues*. The language of skills is also employed in the 1985 White Paper, *Better Schools*, which talks of the 'skills and attitudes needed for adult and working life' and 'the issue of how best to fit work-related skills within full-time education'. In addition, the documents of both the FEU and the MSC have relied heavily on the notion of skills in describing aims and content. I do not propose to analyse any of those documents in detail here. A detailed and rigorous analysis of the documents on which YTS is based, for example, can be found in Ruth Jonathan's.

This section will examine briefly the notion of a 'skill' and then go on to consider its father-figure, the generic or transferable skill. In so doing, I hope to show that a worthwhile vocational education can never be defined solely in terms of skills. The language of skills may be *necessary*, but it can never be sufficient.

In addition, a skill-based education may not be very valuable to employers, particularly those involved in new technology. The final sections of this chapter examine the value of the language of skills in matching education and training to the needs of employers in new fields such as information technology. My contention is that a narrow skills-based definition of education makes neither conceptual nor economic sense.

The notion of a skill

The rigid knowledge/skill/attitude division is reminiscent of Bloom's three domains of objectives: cognitive, psychomotor and affective as well as psychomotor'—the skills of literary criticism, violin playing or counselling a patient are given as examples. This broadening of the notion of skill to include cognitive and effective aspects beings the notion which nearer to Ryle's concept of *knowing how* as opposed to knowing that. Unfortunately, this broader and more acceptable notion of skill is not applied in the *Skills in Schools* document, or the previous FEU, IMS and MSC publications on which it relies. This is clear from its definition of a skill: 'A skill is the ability to undertake an action under given circumstances to a defined degree of expertise'.

That definition clearly relies on a psychomotor notion of skill and a behaviourist-based view of education. Is skill necessarily tied to action? Can skill not involve 'mental action'? There seems to be no *logical* connection between a skill and a physical action. Can all skills be governed by a 'defined degree of expertise'? If so, where does this leave the mental processes in the exercise of a skill?

The bias towards behavioural and psychomotor skills is shown in the lists of skills which are given as part a possible 'core' of identifiable skills required by school leavers. Included in the list are such skills as:

Read and write numbers	Count objects
Pull, push, lift and carry	Cut materials with scissors, shears etc.

In fairness, however, many of the 'core' skills are on a higher level and are listed as:

Give answers	Deal with complaints
Advise	Explain something
Decide job priorities	Describe or give information

But surely not one of the latter group of skills makes any sense or carries any meaning without a *context*. How can a person possess 'advising skill' which is context and knowledge *independent*? This is the first major point that I would like to propose in discussing the notion of a skill. A skill cannot exist except within a certain context, and within a framework of prior knowledge and understanding. How can a person 'decide on job priorities' without an adequate understanding of the relevant context, the necessary information and the prior knowledge of either facts or general principles?

This, in my view, is the essential mistake in the rhetoric of skills i.e. the belief that a worthwhile skill can be separated off and defined in isolation from the context of understanding and knowledge which surrounds it. That mistake is made in both science and technology education. Lists of scientific skills are given for example, which include 'observation skills', 'the ability to hypothesize', 'predicting and informing', 'controlling variables' and so on. Yet not one of these science skills has any sense or meaning in isolation from the knowledge-base, framework or paradigm which forms the foundation of science. As Popper is so often quoted as saying, observation is theory-laden. The same is true of hypothesizing, inferring, controlling variables and all the other skills involved in science. A science or technology education which is biased totally towards skills will be as meaningless and empty as one which concentrates soley on content or propositional knowledge.

In short, skills without knowledge are empty. This will be particularly true in 'new industry', as I will argue later, which is by its very nature *Knowledge-intensive*.

Generic and transferable skills

Two criticisms of a skills-based approach to education and training are:

1. That it often produces lists of skills which, although easily definable, are often trial and demanding.
2. That a narrow, and specifically-stated, skills-based approach to training is hopelessly vulnerable to changes in society and in technology.

As Ruth Jonathan puts it, 'the more specific the skills, the shorter their useful life'. These twin criticisms of trivialization and vulnerability to change have pushed forward the notion of 'generic' or 'transferable' skills. These higher level skills are 'fundamental to the performance of a number of activities carried out in a range of contexts', and are significant for vocational education because they are 'generic to a wide variety of occupations and are transferable between vocationally specific areas' (Perry and Barnett 1985)

I would like to examine some of these generic skills and show that, as with specific skills, few of them carry meaning if seen as context and knowledge independent. To hold them up as educational goals in themselves, therefore, is both vague and conceptually unsound. Lists of generic, transferable skills often include the following.

problem-solving	information handling
planning	decision-making
diagnosis	communicating

Take 'information-handling', for example. This is often put forward as one of the key skills for the future, and who could doubt this is an age where information is said to be vital resource and where the possession of propositional, factual knowledge ('knowledge that') can only decrease in importance as an educational goal. Information skills will involve the ability to collect, prepare, code and retrieve information, in conjunction with the endless capability of new information technology to process and communicate this information. But information skills, vital though they may be in *serving* education, can never provide an educational goal in themselves. Information skills alone, without ends and purposes, have no meaning or value. They cannot exist in a vacuum. Education does not involve the *passive* handling and acquisition of information. Active and meaningful education involves selecting, interpreting and transforming information according to the learner's previous experiences, present needs and purposes, and prior knowledge. Information skills are to caricature Popper, knowledge and context laden.

Similar points can be made about an equally valued generic skill, 'problem-solving'. Can such a skill be knowledge and context independent? In other worlds, can the ability to solve problems in one domain *transfer* across to another? The question of generic skills, therefore, rests squarely on a debate which is totally unsettled and indeed has occupied psychologists for much of this century: transfer of learning. This issue, like the heredity versus environment debate, is by its very nature unlikely to be decided conclusively. Perhaps the belief that skills can be transferred from one area to another is, like pseudo-scientific hypotheses, incapable of falsification. Yet the bulk of the literature which puts forward generic skills as the aims of education and training totally ignores the question of transfer.

The same question mark can be placed over the generic skill of 'decision-making'. Is there any evidence to show that decision-making in one domain, e.g. the art of Cordon Bleu cooking, is transferable to another domain, e.f. car repair and maintenance? Indeed how could such a belief ever be falsified let alone confirmed? Dearden makes a similar points in discussing 'good judgement':

> ...simply because good judgement can be exercised in both the stock market and in landing a hot air balloon, it does not follow that there is some general skill of 'good judgement' which is common to both and in which we could be trained free from any particular context.

My contention, therefore, is that the language of generic skills can be criticized on two related counts. Firstly, skills of any kind are context and knowledge dependent - skills without knowledge are empty. Secondly, the belief that there are genuine, transferable skills which are the proper aim of education and training ignores the contentious question of transfer.

A third objection to the language of transferable skills, which is based on political grounds, is given by Cohen. He argues that many of the new initiatives in training are based on 'a hidden agenda for redeploying the notion of the skill itself'. By dissociating skill from specific practices and defining it in terms of 'certain abstract universals', a pool of 'abstract labour' can be created thereby undermining the control by skilled manual workers over conditions of entry and training in their own trades. This may well be as much a consequence of new technology, however, as a political poly—a point which Cohen acknowledges:

> What 'transferable skilling' corresponds to in reality is the process of deskilling set in motion by new information technologies.

The question of the relation of skills to the problems posed by new technologies will be returned to later.

A similar attack on the redeployment of the notion of skill is given by Ann Wickham in Dale. She suggests that the notion of skill has been redefined which, in turn, has given 'training' a new meaning:

> In the past the notion of skill had been associated with craft work, with a combination of mental and physical dexterity in a particular area of work. Under the aegis of the Special Programmes Division (of the MSC) a much wider definition of skill came into use. Skill was regarded more as a way of organizing activity and involved a combination of what are now regarded as individual skills and general skills, that is numeracy, communication and practical skills, together with social and life skills, attitudes to work and a knowledge of working life. Training was ...given a new meaning which was removed from that traditionally used.

This redefinition of the term 'skill' can be seen in its recent broadening to include 'social and life skills', 'employability skills', 'communication skills', 'attitudes to work', 'preparation for life skills', and so on. It is as if the concept of skill has ascended to a new level to embrace not only competencies but also abilities, aptitudes, dispositions, and attitudes. It needs only to subsume the concepts of knowledge, thinking, understanding and motivation to have taken over as the umbrella term covering the whole of education. We may soon be talking of the skills of understanding and knowing just as we already talk of thinking skills, reading skills, social skills and even moral skills.

Hart argued with emotion against such distortion of language:

> If you don't hold out against talk of 'skills', if you don't see that 'skills' only account for part, and that the less important part, of what we learn, you are driven to conclude that there is

nothing for which a man can be held responsible or in which he can see himself mirrored.

Hart's paper makes two valuable points. Firstly, that talk of skills 'is simply a kind of incantation, by which one creates the illusion that one is actually saying something about education'. In other words the addition of the label 'skill' actually adds nothing descriptive. How, for example, does 'reading' differ from 'reading skill'? The same is true of the language launched by Callaghan's great debate. Much talk was, and is, heard of 'relevant skills'. Those terms have yet to be give any concrete, descriptive meaning. Indeed the noun 'relevance', and the adjective 'relevant', have no meaning on their own. Like the term 'skill', they are almost always used as terms of incantation, a seal of approval, having no descriptive but only emotive meaning. To describe a skill as relevant is meaningless. We need always to ask the questions 'relevant to what?' and 'relevant to whom?'. This confusion over relevance is particularly important in considering the 'skills relevant' to new technology.

Hart's second main point, as I interpret it, is that the acquisition of skills is, in a sense, an activity of tackling on of appending skills to bodies. It is largely *impersonal* process. In contrast, truely educational processes will profoundly affect and alter the person involved. This is not true of skills, as they are traditionally conceived:

...education, whatever else is involved in it, is about the individual person and his development; and it's been my contention that only that which is more than simply a skill can contribute to that development, the continual forming and reforming of the person. So that when receiving an education is conceived of, as it is so often today, in terms of acquiring skills, it is conceived of as something superficial.

This point leads in to the next two sections of the chapter. Does industry want bodies with skills 'appended' to them? Do employers in fact phrase their requirements in the language of skills? Does it make either practical or conceptual sense to discuss the needs of new technology in terms of 'relevant skills' and 'skill shortages'.

The language of skills and the needs of employers

An important article by Gilroy discusses the value of conceptual analysis in clarifying the work done in empirical research—similar points are made by Barrow in *Giving Teaching Back to the Teachers*. Gilroy implies, however, that it is not only the 'philosopher' who is 'competent to identify and resolve linguistic confusion.' There is a role of the 'empiricist as philosopher' as he expresses it, in direct contract to John Locke's under-labourer conception of philosophy.

This is surely the case in examining the language of skills. Armchair analysis may be necessary but it is not sufficient. Valuable progress can be made in my view, by interviewing employers in depth to probe their 'needs' and requirements and in particular (in this context) to examine the language in which their needs and demands are actually framed. One such study, albeit on a small scale, is reported in Wellington, and is summarized below.

It is clearly a huge task to identify the 'needs' of employers in terms of the skill which they require of school-leavers and trainees. The range of employers will be so vast in terms of numbers employed, on-the-job skills, and the nature of employment that there maybe no common ground. With this proviso in mind, a pilot research project was carried out which involved detailed interviews with a small sample of employers from service industries to so-called high-tech employers.

The interviews were conducted in a fairly unstructured way, although some specified questions were asked of all the staff involved. The person approached and interviewed was in each case the 'development and training' or personnel officer of the company. In fairness to those interviewed no specific comments and quotes will be included here—I will simply sum up some of the general principles which came through strongly, and also select some of the more interesting remarks on skills and specific training which relate to earlier parts of this paper.

The strongest message which came through in this pilot study is that the needs of these employers are not framed in terms of *skills* required of school leavers - their requirements are always stated in the language of *attitudes* and *dispositions*. This is perhaps the most important message as a response to 1981 and 1984 White Papers—they are making a basic 'category mistake' in framing the needs of employers and therefore of vocational education in terms of skills. What employers seem to be demanding of school-leavers and YTS trainees, is a collection of general attitudes and dispositions. The 'attitude' which came at the top of the list was 'interest and motivation'. This was felt to be the most important quality in a school-leaver. Other attitudes and dispositions considered important were: initiative, confidence, self-belief and maturity.

In none of the interviews were skills specifically mentioned. Each of the employers interviewed was asked which skills they required of new employers—non listed skills other than numeracy and literacy, which (incidentally) they felt were of the required standard in the young people they appointed anyway. The so-called high-tech employers were asked specifically about 'computer literacy'. Did they want their employees to be 'computer literate' before joining the company? This notion was dismissed. The kinds of 'computer literacy' (a virtually indefinable notion anyway) they might receive before employment was not felt to be of use once they had joined the firm.

One rather depressing comment was made by a national high-tech employer. they suggested that school-leavers were not likely to be taken into the high-tech side of the industry at all. Recruitment to this facet of their company would be entirely at graduate level and above. Even then (incidentally) the graduates appointed would not necessarily be in Computer Science, who were often receiving training in the wrong computer language e.g. Pascal rather than Cobol.

Some of those interviewed did comment, of their own volition, on the Youth Training Scheme. They saw YTS largely as a grading or interviewing system which enabled them to 'have a good look' at a prospective employee. They felt that it was an ideal opportunity to see if that trainee had the right attitudes and dispositions, such as those already mentioned. One described YTS as a 'year-long interview,' a comment which has since been used by many employers.

I would not suggest that this small empirical enquiry with its small sample could be used to form any definite conclusions on the requirements of employers. However, I would suggest that the study does indicate a gap between the language used in statements and documents on pre-vocational education and the language in which employers and industry couch their requirements. In particular, the study posed the following questions. Should discussions and statements on vocational education be framed in the Callaghan language of 'skills', 'relevant training' and 'tools-for-the-job'? Or should the aims and philosophy of vocational education be couched in terms of attitudes and dispositions? Is there any sense in the notion of 'relevant skills' or 'skills for the future' in a society which may be entering a new phase? If not, then what meaning does the very notion of 'pre-vocational education' hold? With an increasingly uncertain future for employment, depending more and more on the rapidly changing field of information technology, does the notion of *vocational training* make economic, let alone conceptual sense?

These questions will be discussed in the final two sections of this paper, firstly by considering the likely 'skill demands' of new technologies and then by sketching the response of Japan to the education and training needs imposed by technological change.

Skill demands and the new technologies

The 1981 campaign to install microcomputers in all of Britain's schools was accompanied by a wave of uncritical enthusiasm and a flood of rhetoric regarding its vocational significance. Kenneth Baker, the new Minister for Information Technology typified the political mood of the time:

...I want to try and ensure that the kids of today are trained with the skills that gave their fathers and grandfathers jobs. It's like generals fighting the battles of yesteryear. And that is the reason why we've pushed ahead with computers into schools. I want youngsters, boys and girls leaving school at sixteen, to actually be able to operate a computer.

That optimism for the vocational significance of the computer permeated into many of the two million or more households which subsequently acquired computers, and largely caused the unprecedented growth of Computer Studies as an examination subject. The unquestioned connection between computer education and the world of work also surfaced in the plethora of books discussing the use of computers in schools. Mullan, for example, even drew a connection between primary children's use of the microcomputer and the use of the computer in the world of work which they must experience:

If children meet the microcomputer in an exciting and pleasurable role in school then one could argue that there is a greater likelihood of them accepting it as an aid in the world of work which they must experience in the future.

The unquestioned belief in the vocational significance of information technology also affected deeply both the thinking and the publicity associated with the two key innovations in vocational education: the YTS and the TVEI. Finn writing in Dale, discusses the publicity at the launch of the YTS which 'attempted to associate it with the new technologies at the forefront of employment creation'. This publicity has continued in the same vein with the advent of the two-year YTS, a publicity drive which is analysed in the following section. Similarly, the drive behind TVEI depended to a large extent on its perceived links to new technology and in particular to IT. Dale, in discussing the background to and inception of TVEI, diagnoses one of the key factors behind the initiative as the continuing emphasis on 'high-tech' industry in the early 1980s. This in turn led to the belief 'that future employment prospects are likely to be most propitious in IT-based industry and commerce'.

This is a belief which requires thorough and critical investigation. The links between information technology in education and information technology in employment have never been fully and critically examined. There is simply an implicit and unquestioned belief in the minds of many people (parents, children, teachers and policy-makers) that IT education at any level will make its recipients more employable. That belief has provided the main impetus for much of the information technology education in schools, colleges and ITECs.

The purpose of an ITEC have been described in Smith. Their aim is:

> to provide young people with the *new skills* necessary for Britain to take a leading part in the technological revolution.

But what are these 'skills', and at which levels of education are they required? The question can be explored in two ways. Firstly, by considering recent documents and reports on the links between IT in education and industry. Secondly, by a full scale empirical investigation into the perceived 'skill demands' of employers in IT, their current recruitment patterns at various levels, and the relation of those demands to the range of IT education currently offered in our education and training schemes. An empirical investigation along those lines was launched in April 1986 at the University of Sheffield, and its findings will be published in full elsewhere. However the first method of tackling the question will be discussed briefly here, by considering two recent publications. A crucial document was published in August 1984 by the Economic Development Committee entitled *Crisis facing UK Information Technology.* This publication described the critical skill shortage in Information Technology which is apparently holding back the UK industry:

> Too often contracts are being lost, and employment opportunities lost with them, because of the lack of a few key engineers.

But at what level are these skill shortages? The answer given by this document is that the shortages occur at *graduate level and above.* For example:

> The problem is critical even before the effects of the University Grants Committee cuts have really shown in graduate output.

In other words (according to this document) the critical skill shortage holding back the UK 'Information Technology Industry' is clearly not at the level of 16- or 17-yar-old school leavers who are likely to opt for the YTS. It is at the graduate level, of a 'few key engineers'. Skill shortages at this level, according to the document, are resulting in a lack of demand for the employment at *lower* levels. This is perhaps a more *subtle* version of the skills-deficit model of unemployment, i.e. lack of the right skills at graduate level leading to a lack of demand for labour at lower levels. This more subtle version of the skills-deficit model, however, is not even hinted at in the 1984 White Paper.

The EDC report also includes a passing criticism of vocational education and training:

> The UK has a multitude of institutions and agencies engaged in education and training but then appear to have difficulty in responding to the now very insistent signals from the market for skilled people and developing a consistent response.

But what 'signals' are being sent from the market for skilled people? What skills do employers actually require, or at least *say* that they require? This is clearly a case where the rhetoric of skills and skill demands needs to be transated into reality. Clear signals are needed from employers so that education can be expected to develop a 'consistent response'. There can be no substitute for empirical investigation here.

A second key publication in predicting the 'skill demands' of new technology is the report of the

Alvey Committee on the future of IT and so-called fifth generation of computers. This vital report is given further consideration in the next section, but its major themes can be introduced here. A large proportion of the report was devoted to the education and training which would be needed to provide the human resources for Britain's advanced information technology programme into the 1990s. Perhaps the crux of the whole report for the future of education in IT is contained in one short statement: 'Information Technology is knowledge intensive'. In other words, IT industry is *not labour intensive.* The addition of skilled personnel for Britain's advanced IT programme is quantified by Alvey in terms of *thousands,* not even tens of thousands. At what level are these personnel required? Alvey suggests that 'urgent action is needed in the higher education sector':

> Restrictions on expenditure in higher education, whatever the intentions, have tended to fall across the board. It has not escaped.

So what action can be taken for students in the 14-18 range of education and training? Alvey's response is one of the most quoted sections of the report:

> ... it is no good just providing schools with microcomputers. This will merely produce a generation of poor BASIC programmers. Universities in fact are having to give remedial education to entrants with A-level computer science.

Where does this leave the emphasis on 'information technology skills' and computer literacy' at the heart of YTS schemes, the ITECs and the new TVEI? My own view, which I have argued elsewhere (Wellington 1985a), is that *education* (not training) in and through information technology should be seen as a valuable end in itself. It can enhance traditional educational aims but should never replace them. The vocational significance of IT has for too long been overemphasized or, indeed, 'hyped up' by the media, by politicians and even by parents. The best way in which education can support the essential growth of IT in Britain's economy is by providing a sound general education for all pupils. This is precisely the pattern in the education system of Britain's Eastern competitor in IT, Japan.

Lessons from the east: the japanese approach to skills and vocational education

A full-page advertisement began to appear in the newspapers early in 1986, from *The Mirror* to the so-called quality dailies such as *The Guardian*. The advert warned the Japanese of the advent of Spikey Dodds, Tracy Logan and others with names like Joe Bloggs, about to embark on the new two-year Youth Training Scheme, Spikey Dodds, for example, will 'begin his course by trying out several different skills before he chooses the one he'll train through to the end of the second year'. By the end of his course he will have 'a skill, a certificate to prove it, and a better chance of getting a job'. This may well prove true, though as yet there is little evidence to support such optimism. But the point I would like to take issue with comes in the next paragraph of the advertisement:

Our competitors in the Far East and Europe

> have been training their young people like this for years.

Presumably, one of the countries implicity referred to here is Japan. The suggestion, therefore, is that Japan's education, system has been training youngsters' by allowing them to 'try out several different skills' before choosing the *one* which they will train for and obtain a certificate in. This is patently untrue, and I will not need to exhume publications from university libraries to prove it. A series of articles on the evolution of Japan's education occurred in *Look Japan* from May to December 1983. These articles, written by leading Japanese economists and educationalists, indicate that the skills-based vocational training alluded to in the YTS advert may have taken place in the 1960s and early 1970s but has now been superseded by a totally different educational drive.

> School education now provides both general and vocational courses at the secondary level, but the general public tends to regard the former as preparing intelligent youths for university entrance and accordingly for better employment opportunities and the latter as accommodating the less intelligent who are to enter lower level occupations. Industry generally expects schools to turn out youths with a good level of academic achievement and adaptability and does not attach much importance to pre-employment training designed to prepare young people for specific occupations.

The first sentence of this paragraph gives an early warning of the potential divisiveness of vocational curricula, discussed five years later in

Times Educational Supplement articles on studies of the new TVEI. The second sentence indicated that the world's most successful industrial nation would encourage its youth to follow a general education rather than vocational training in the 1980s. This view is made rystal clear later in the document:

> ... the emphasis (in school education) is on developing general intelligence rather than specific skills.

The 1981 statements have since become reality. In 1985, no less than 94 per cent of Japanese students stayed on for 'senior high school' after leaving the compulsory junior high school.

Despite Government effort to make work-related courses more attractive to students, the vocational high schools are still generally viewed by pupils, parents and employers as being second-best. The demand for place at vocational schools has declined, and many entrants are students who have failed to gain entry to a general high school.

Such enduring attitudes are coupled (both as a cause and as an effect) with the huge growth in Japan's higher education, sometimes called its 'transfer to a higher education society'. The proportion of the relevant age-group staying on for higher education in 1985 was just under a remarkable 40 per cent compared with just over 20 per cent in the United Kingdom.

An important part of Japan's higher education in ensuring its industrial success was, of course, the high-level engineering education provided. At the start of the 1980s Japan's total output of graduate engineers was between five and six times higher than ours at about 75,000, compared with Britain's 13,000. This poor comparison still continues at a time when Britain's information and manufacturing industries are desperate for electronic, electrical, mechanical and software engineers at graduate level.

Britain's principal area of competition with the Japanese in the next decade will almost certainly be in the area of information technology. The Alvey Report indicated Britain's needs for the future:

> ... there is a requirement for a new breed of information engineer' with a wide understanding of the potential applications of IT to industrial needs. The supply of graduates with skills relevant to IT must be increased. The undergraduate output is currently some 6,500 per year. This is wholly inadequate to meet our future requirements.

How has Britain answered Alvey's plea?

The central response to the keenly felt need for IT education has been to provide every school in the country with at least one computer and some with as many as thirty or forty. Britain's populace now has the largest number of home computers per head in the world. This is in direct contrast to the Japanese approach to computer education. The 1984 *Japan Educational Journal* reported that only 0.1 per cent (i.e. on in a thousand) of its primary schools had microcomputers at that time. Less than 2 per cent of its lower secondary schools had computers, though the figure reached 45 per cent in its upper secondary schools. However, the computers in the latter area were used largely as an administrative and management tool. The motions of 'computer studies' 'computer literacy'' and 'computer-related skills' so widespread in this country, have no place in the Japanese approach to education:

> The school curricula in Japan are designed to give children a broad and basic knowledge which is necessary in order to grasp and enjoy a wide range of ideas and activities. In the field of science and technology, Japanese children are taught concepts, principles and laws of basic science and mathematics, which are the basis of industrial technology. Computer technology is not yet considered to be part of the required 'basic knowledge'.

It seems that the abacus is a more common learning tool in Japanese schools than the computer.

I am not suggesting that we should attempt to copy Japan's approach to computer education, or its education system in general. Britain's culture, its hidden curriculum and its material resources are too vastly different to make that a possibility. I am suggesting that we should radically re-think our approach to vocational education in the light of lessons learned from the Japanese, and in view of our need to compete with Japan in the development of new 'knowledge intensive' industries.

It makes little sense to base a new and expensive programme of skills-based vocational training on a view of a system 'in the Far East' which is at best out-dated and at worst purely fictional.

4 Determining Curriculum Content

Introduction

Determining curriculum content for vocational and technical education is very rewarding and yet extremely frustrating. The rewarding aspect is the final product: content that may be actually used in the instructional environment to and vocational students in achieving their fullest potential. The frustrating aspect of determining curriculum content consists of identifying that which is truly relevant to *both instructional and occupational settings.* The paragraphs that follow focus, directly on these concerned. Initially, consideration is given to the factors associated with curriculum content determination, including constraints placed upon the curriculum developer. Next, areas of concern associated with selecting a meaningful content derivation strategy are discussed. Finally, a number of strategies are presented, each of which serves as an alternate route to determining meaningful curriculum content.

Factors associated with determining Curriculum content

Perhaps it seems that one could just sit down and

decide which content is most important to include in a curriculum, but this impression is far from reality. In a typical educational setting, the curriculum developer is confronted with a variety of factors that may affect the task of determining what should actually be taught. These factors may have great impact on the direction one takes when establishing a content framework. Idealistically, the developer may have unlimited resources and flexibility to shape content in the ways he or she wants to; however, real-world considerations often dictate the scope of the content determination process. Factors such as time and dollars available; internal and external pressures; federal, state, and local requirements; skills needed by employers, academic and vocational education content concerns; and the particular level of content all have potential to affect the means by which content is determined for a particular curriculum.

Time and dollars available

Time becomes a critical element in the entire curriculum development process and is obviously a key concern when content is to be determined. The curriculum developer typically is not able to spend an unlimited amount of time deriving content to be taught. Instead, he or she is usually given a prescribed amount of time within which to establish content. This may be a day, a week, a month, or a year, but time is, nonetheless, a finite entity that affects the content determination process. A developer who is given two weeks to establish content for a curriculum will, in all likelihood, use a content determination strategy that can be executed in a relatively short period of time. On the other hand, an individual who is able to spend a year at this same effort has a variety of options available as far as strategies are concerned.

The dollars a developer has at his or her disposal to use in the content determination process can, likewise, affect the scope of a particular effort. Time and money are often considered synonymous in education, since professional salaries constitute such a large portion of the overall budget. Within this context, however, money may be considered in connection with the purchase of items such as travel, printing, postage, secretarial assistance, and the hiring of temporary personnel and/or consultants. When one is examining the ways content might be determined, money is a key factor, since the amount actually available tends to dictate which content derivation strategy is used. Some strategies require no additional funds over what may be available in a typical educational institution's budget. Others require extensive travel or mailings to gather information and, consequently, demand that additional dollars be made available. Thus, the curriculum developer must be very much concerned about time and dollars available in support of content determination activities. Each of these areas is a constraint placed upon the developer that must be dealt with logically and thoroughly as content is being determined.

Internal and external pressures

Another factor related to determining curriculum content consists of the subtle pressures exerted by individuals and group from within as well as outside the educational environment. Certain individuals or pressure groups may feel it is in the best interests of themselves or others to support inclusion of certain content in the curriculum. The reasons behind this sort of support are numerous, since local situations and personalities often enter into the process. Reasons may range from honest concern for students' welfare to quasipolitical tactics. Regardless of the reason behind such pressure, the curriculum developer must recognize that in some cases the cause supported by certain individuals or groups may not be in the best interests of students. For example, emotional concern about content that might be included in a curriculum is no substitute for systematic content derivation. This is not to say that concerns of this type should be ignored. The contemporary curriculum developer must maintain an open mind and search for meaningful curriculum concerns that individuals and groups might process.

Pressure in support of certain content might be exerted from within an educational environment by several sources. Administrators, vocational and technical teachers, academic teachers, guidance counselors, students, and placement specialists may each feel that certain content must be included in a curriculum and strongly support that conviction. A major responsibility of the curriculum developer is to sort out these concerns and determine which are valid and which are not. If this critical analysis is not accomplished, an invalid concern might receive widespread support and actually be included as content in a curriculum. When a situation such as this occurs, students as well as the school may suffer the consequences.

Pressures from outside the educational environment may emanate from areas such as businesses, industries, self-employed persons, professional organizations, unions, and advisory committees. Since every vocational curriculum must be responsive to the world of work, concerns from these areas cannot be ignored. In certain situations where pressure for specific content is applied from an individual or group outside the educational environment, the validity for a claim must be established. It might be that a particular business firm supports the inclusion of curriculum content dealing with word processing, since they have a need for competent workers in this area; or an occupational advisory committee might believe that metrication should be an integral part of building construction curriculum. In either case, such concern might be valid and should, therefore, be verified during the content derivation process. Working with the public is an ongoing responsibility of vocational educators and handling the concerns of lay persons is just one part of this responsibility. The curriculum developer must be responsive to public concerns and pressures by examining their implications and determining which claims are valid and justifiable.

Federal, state, and local content requirements

Curriculum content determination is seldom made solely by a curriculum developer or teacher group. In numerous occupational areas there are content requirements specified that serve as a basic framework for curricula. These requirements, which may already be established at the federal, state, or local level, tend to limit the extent to which a curriculum developer can become involved in the content determination process. For example, the Federal Aviation Administration (FAA) specifies the content and hours of instruction required of a person before that individual may be qualified as an aircraft mechanic. This content has been established through national surveys of people working in the occupation. Obviously, major departures from prescribed FAA content might affect not only graduates' competence but also their licensure as aircraft mechanics.

A similar situation exists at the state level with regard to certain occupations. State regulations often specify the content and hours of instruction that must be included in nursing and cosmetology programs and examinations administered at the state level tend to focus on this content. Consequently, there may be few changes one can make in curriculum content in such areas as these.

State-level content requirements may also be seen in the general education area. The specific general education courses required for completion of an associate degree or high school diploma may be contributing or limiting factors in the design of a relevant curriculum. Excessive general education requirements can limit the extent to which vocational and technical content is provided. Likewise, requirements for extensive vocational and technical content may adversely affect students' general educational development through restriction of course selections.

Local content requirements tend to parallel job opportunities in the particular geographic area. If industries in a locale are heavily involved in the production of textiles, providing relevant core content for all students planning to enter this occupational area would be appropriate.

Arrangements might be made with local unions to give credit toward the completion of apprenticeship programs if certain content requirements and met while students are still in school. The content ties between school and work not only benefit the graduate but the employer, the school, and the community. Whereas local content requirements are of a more informal nature, they are equally as important to curriculum building as state and national requirements.

Skills needed by employers

In a basic sense, much of the vocational education curriculum content is aligned closely with employers' needs. This focus exists so the educational institution may provide its students with content that is work-place-relevant. Unfortunately, individual employers may not have the most progressive view of what skills their workers need. Factors such as the evolving nature of the workplace and the time lag in knowledge dissemination cause some employers to fall behind others in terms of understanding workplace needs. This is particularly true of future worker needs since employers are more likely to focus on the present rather than the future.

Thus, in the determination of curriculum content, consideration must be given to future as well as current employer needs. This task is made easier through the use of content determination strategies such as the Delphi technique that focus what workers may be doing in the future. However, more general views of the current and future workplace may be drawn from studies that focus on entire industries or businesses or employer at-large.

These studies can provide the curriculum developer with much valuable information about current and future employer needs that may not be discovered through contacts and discussions with individual employers and workers.

One such study, conducted by the American Society for Training and Development), focused on workplace basics: skills that employers want their workers to have. It is revealed that basic skill requirements will continue to increase in a wide variety of occupations and that the preparation of skill and craft employees with better basic skills may assist America in regaining its competitive advantage. Provided in the ASTD report are descriptions of what employers want. These are organized into a hierarchy of seven skill groups ranging from most advanced to most basic. The groups include

Organizational Effectiveness/Leadership

Interpersonal/Negotiation/Teamwork

Self-Esteem/Goat Setting-Motivation/Personal and Career Development

Creative Thinking/Problem Solving

Communication: Listening and Oral Communication

3 Rs (Reading, Writing, Computation).

Learning to learn

Learning to learn is most basic to employees because it enables them to achieve competence in other skills. On the other end of the continuum workers who are skilled at organizational effectiveness and leadership can contribute more effectively to employer success in the marketplace. As the curriculum content determination process proceeds, it is important to recognize the basic skills that workers must demonstrate in the workplace. The skill groups provided by ASTD can serve as a meaningful foundation for curriculum content section and delivery.

A different set of studies presented by Bailey further supports the changing nature of the workplace. Bailey and his colleagues conducted extensive examinations of jobs in four employment sectors apparel, textile, banking, and business services. It should be noted that the nature of work *across* each sector was examined and information could therefore, be gathered about how jobs are changing and how they will change in the future. The studies strongly support the notion that jobs of the future will require greater and not less skill and that this will occur across both the service and manufacturing areas. Instead of the traditionally held notion that jobs will become deskilled, curriculum developers must recognize that future jobs will require workers to perform a broader range of skills and to demonstrate them at higher levels. Employees must be able to change and develop as an industry or business evolves. Workers of the future should expect their jobs to be more demanding. They must be able to work efficiently as members of teams "manage more-frequent and more-complex interactions with other individuals, perform a greater number of frequently changing tasks, and otherwise operate in a more uncertain and less well-defined environment'. Workers will, additionally, be required to make more individual initiative and must have a clear understanding of the overall processes, products, services, and markets associated with their employers' firms. The implications for determining vocational education curriculum content are indeed great. Information reported by Bailey as well as Carnavale et al. point to a need for aligning curriculum content with the rich context of the workplace. Thus, although specific tasks, skills attitudes, values, and appreciations will continue to be important, other capabilities that are needed to survive and grow in the ever-changing workplace will become even more critical. These workplace basics and skills of the future must, therefore, be firmly embedded in the vocational education curriculum.

Academic and vocational education content Concerns

As noted earlier, employers currently need and will continue to need workers who can demonstrate facility in mathematics, science, and communication skills, and this need will continue to grow as the workplace continues to become more and more complex. This situation, coupled with the overarching responsibility of education to prepare persons for both having and earning a living, presents educators with a thorny problem how to prepare students in terms of both the academic and the vocational education aspects of the curriculum. Concerns related to this area have evolved into the concept of integrating academic and vocational education. Integration essentially means that academic and vocational education content are brought together and taught together in such a way that the content in each area become more relevant. By providing more relevant contexts for both academic and vocational education content it is anticipated that students will learn more and at a more rapid rate than under more-traditional instructional conditions. Since it may be important to identify relevant academic content concepts during the content determination process, the curriculum developer must be aware of specific academic content needs and plan accordingly. For example, if mathematics is to be integrated into a new drafting and design program, the developer may choose to modify drafting and design content determination processes so that mathematics content will emerge instead of remaining firmly embedded in vocational education content. To accomplish this, survey or interview forms can be modified or the curriculum content focus can be broadened to embrace mathematics in a more holistic manner. Basically, the curriculum developer should recognize that when content is being determined it is an opportune time to obtain relevant information about academic as well as vocational education content.

Level at which content will be provided

A final factor related to curriculum content determination is the level at which that content will be provided. These different levels have direct impact on content, with the impact being felt in rather subtle ways. At the secondary level, students' educational needs tend to be more basic. Although some students may progress more rapidly to advanced studies in technical areas, the majority focus on developing those academic or general and technical competencies associated with the entry-level work. Instruction is general geared toward preparation for a specific occupation or closely related family of occupations or, in terms of Tech Prep programs, preparation for an associate degree in a technical field. At the postsecondary level, students are typically those who have completed high school and have chosen to pursue education beyond that level. The postsecondary student is usually older and more mature. Thus, content must focus on the needs of this type of student. In many instances postsecondary vocational and technical education prepares students for an occupational field rather than for a specific occupation. If this is the situation curriculum developers find themselves in, content needs to be identified which has high transferability to a number of occupation within a field.

Selecting a curriculum content determination Strategy

The actual selection of a curriculum content determination strategy appears simple. However, the selection process can be quite complex with the degree of complexity dependent on a variety of concerns. Of immediate concern to one who is selecting a strategy are the aforementioned factors time and dollars available; internal and external pressures; federal, state, and local content requirements; and level of content that may impact on the content determination process. Each of these factors can affect the decision that is ultimately made, and, therefore, all factors should be examined closely and information about them saved for future reference. Once the various factors associated with determining content have been examined, the developer may focus on three additional areas of concern: the educational setting, the occupational setting, and the content determination strategies available. Each of these concerns is discussed in the paragraphs that follow.

The education setting

The setting in which curriculum content will be implemented is most important to study. This enables the curriculum developer to determine which aspects of the setting may affect selection of one strategy over another. Although there are a multitude of questions one might ask about how the educational setting relates to curriculum content, some likely examples might be: What is the current educational philosophy of the school and the attendance area? What support for vocational and technical education emanates from the educational community? To what extent will teachers and administrators assist in the content determination process? How well will educators accept the results of systematic curriculum content determination? These are several questions a curriculum developer should pose.

The occupational setting

The occupational setting represents another area of concern for the curriculum developer. As with the educational setting, those aspects of the occupational setting that may result in a better strategy choice must be identified. Several of the questions one might ask about relationships between the occupational setting and curriculum content include: Is the occupation clearly identifiable or is it emerging? Can workers in the occupation clearly identifiable or is it emerging? Can workers in the occupation be interviewed by telephone or face-to-face? Will permission be granted for workers to complete survey forms and questionnaires? To what extent will businesses or industries assist with data gathering? These are the types of questions that should be asked by the developer as he or she begins to focus on the ways content may be determined.

Content determination strategies

A final and most important concern is with strategies that may actually be used to determine curriculum content. Each of the various strategies will be described in detail later in this chapter, but one must first see how these strategies are similar to and different from each other. If we were to draw a straight line and place "more subjective" at one end and "more objective" at the other, we would have a continuum along which each of the strategies could roughly be placed. The *philosophical basis* for determining content is perhaps the most subjective strategy, since a specific philosophy or set of philosophies serves as a foundation for content decisions. This strategy is most typically used to develop curriculum content in academic areas. *Introspection* is used by an individual or group to examine personal experiences and knowledge and to incorporate these into a framework for the vocational curriculum content. This strategy may be classed as quite subjective, since very little (if any) "hard" data are used in the decision-making process. The *DACUM* content determination approach utilizes occupational experts to derive relevant content. Its focus is on development of a single-sheet skill profile that serves both as a curriculum plan and an evaluation instrument. *Task analysis* focuses on the identification and verification of tasks performed by workers in a certain occupation or cluster of occupations. Its procedures enable this strategy to produce quite objective data related to worker tasks. Several other meaningful strategies may be considered by the curriculum developer. This include the *critical incident technique* and the *Delphi technique.* The critical incident technique is useful in identifying curriculum content related to worker values and attitudes. Content in emerging occupations may be identified via the Delphi technique.

The observation may be made that the more objective curriculum content strategies are, the more costly they are to use. For example, task analysis is a very objective process, but this objectivity is obtained at a high cost, since one must send materials or travel to locations where workers are employed. The philosophical approach is very inexpensive and the small investment yields a meager return in terms of objectivity. Realistically, the curriculum developer should *consider using several strategies,* since each has its own particular strengths and weaknesses. When several strategies are used, there is a much greater likelihood that the content developed will be valid.

Philosophical basis for content determination

Philosophy appears to have had the greatest history of affecting curriculum content decisions. Before more sophisticated means of determining content were established, philosophy served as the guiding light for curriculum developers. Even today, the philosophy of vocational education espoused by a particular school, school district, or community college may provide a framework for the various curricula offered. Most of the general education offerings found in our schools today are based solely upon teachers', administrators', and/or school board members' personal philosophies of education. Thus, the fact that philosophy can and often does serve as a foundation for curriculum content is quite evident.

Establishing a philosophy

A detailed discussion dealing with philosophical foundations of vocational education is beyond the scope of this volume, however, focusing on some examples of philosophy is certainly appropriate. These serve to illustrate the ways that a philosophy might be specified. One must keep in mind that a person's philosophy is basically that which he or she believes. We may say that a philosophy is composed of several belief statements, each of which contributes in some way to the overall makeup of the philosophy. Philosophy tends to vary from individual to individual and group to group just as might be expected of such a value-laden area. Therefore a group may have difficulty reaching consensus regarding some belief statements whereas other statements may be agreed upon unanimously with little or no discussion.

The establishment of belief statements is a rather straightforward activity. Various sources are examined to identify statements that might align with one's personal philosophy. Textbooks, articles, and speeches can all serve as useful sources of information. Philosophies developed by professional associations, community colleges, school districts, and similar units provide a wealth of potential belief statements. Whatever sources may be used, it is important to recognize that these statements represent a potential philosophy. Eventually, a group of concerned and knowledgeable persons must examine each belief statement and agree as to which ones will constitute a philosophical base for the curriculum.

A literature search might serve first to clarify the characteristics of vocational education. For example, a review of numerous sources that included individuals, organizations, agencies, and federal legislation served as a basis for the following statements about vocational education's character:

1. Preparation for gainful employment that requires less than the baccalaureate degree
2. Can include the development of academic skills in concert with development of specific occupational skills
3. A lifelong set of learning experiences ranging from occupational exploration and preparation to on-the-job development
4. May serve to link occupational preparation at the secondary and postsecondary levels.
5. Provides a foundation for an employment career in addition to preparation for an entry-level job

The foregoing serves to illustrate how a basic curriculum framework may. If, for example, we believe that vocational educational involves preparation for gainful employment," our belief should certainly have an impact on the curriculum that is established. Based on this belief, any vocational curriculum content that does not relate in some way to the work environment should be seriously questioned.

Belief statements may take many forms. The following represent a number of possibilities in this regard and, in some cases, serve as sources of other belief statements:

1. Each person should be educated in the least restrictive environment in which that person's educational and related needs can be satisfactorally met.
2. Secondary vocational education courses should provide instruction and practice in the basic skills of reading, arithmetic, speaking, listening, and problem solving.
3. Lifelong learning is prompted through vocational education.

These statements are but a few of the many that may be drawn from the literature and used as a foundation for the vocational curriculum. Dedication to the task of identifying belief statements such as these will ensure that a comprehensive philosophy is developed.

Philosophy as related to curriculum content

Once belief statements have been identified, agreed on, and molded into a philosophy, content may then be identified that aligns with this philosophy. As this process begins, it is almost immediately realized that belief statements are rather broad and tend to cut across several content areas, whereas the technical content appears to be more specific to the individual curriculum. This, perhaps, indicates a basic strength and weakness of the philosophical approach to content determination. The strength has to do with the way a philosophy can permeate an educational institution. A philosophy can, for example, direct the focus of curricula within a school better to meet the needs of groups such as women minorities, and the handicapped. If those who oversee the operation of a school firmly believe in the statement that "vocational education should be available to all those who can profit by it," their actions should be directed toward the establishment and maintenance of curricula for these groups. This does not mean merely providing a few token offerings but actually aligning curricula with students' needs on a large-scale basis. If it is stated in a philosophy that "a comprehensive placement service should be provided to both current enrolled and former students," then action should be taken to establish the type of service to align with each curriculum.

These few examples serve to illustrate the broad impact that a sound philosophy can have on curriculum development. However, this impact is not as great in the area of specific technical content, and here is where problems tend to arise in relating philosophy to content. The general nature of a belief statement may not describe specific competencies needed by an individual in the work environment. Thus, the curriculum developer must speculate about what the specific competence should be and hope that this speculation results in the identification of appropriate content.

Introspection

The introspection process basically consists of examining one's own thoughts and feelings about a certain area. However, within the context of curriculum content determination, this strategy may involve either an individual or a group. The person or persons engaged in introspection are typically vocational teachers who each ask themselves the basic question, "What do I feel should constitute the content of this curriculum?" Then a search is made of one's personal employment, teaching experiences, and education to identify what might be most appropriate to include as curriculum content.

The introspection process

Introspection typically begins with an examination of ongoing vocational programs and literature related to them. This serves to remind the developer of what content might possibly be included that he or she would not otherwise recall from past experiences. The examination of literature and observation of programs might include traveling to other locations and talking to those who are involved with relevant curricula or examining course catalogs and outlines from other institutions. Concurrent with this, magazines and other related sources are reviewed to identify "ideas" for curriculum content.

Once the examination is complete, the developer considers what content might be best for students, using subjective judgment as the decisive element. Consideration is given to both the education process and the result of that process from the perspective of an experienced vocational teacher. Eventually, a content outline is developed that serves on the basis for the curriculum.

Introspection often becomes a group process

where several teachers develop their individual thoughts regarding curriculum content and then need to decide collectively what form the curriculum should take. This procedure has the advantage of providing a variety of inputs from persons with differing backgrounds and experiences. Teachers who have had different exposure to an occupational area will most likely be in a better position than one individual to determine which content is more relevant to a particular occupation or occupational area. The group process can also serve as a means of keeping personal bias to a minimum. If the group must agree collectively on curriculum content, one person's biases become more difficult to be accepted—unless, of course, all group members share the same bias with this individual.

The foregoing points to a major shortcoming of the introspection process. Whereas moving the curriculum decision-making process from one teacher to a group of teachers may make these decisions more reliable, using introspection does not mean that the content will be any more valid (i.e., relevant and realistic). For example, even though a group of electronics instructors unanimously agrees that curriculum content should consist only of studying vacuum tubes, this still does not make the content precisely relevant to employment in our transistorized society.

Therefore the curriculum developer must recognize that introspection is not always the most valid content determination process. To come up with truly realistic content by this process is often quite difficult, particularly when one considers the nature of individual instructors and the scope of many occupations.

One means of at least partially overcoming this validity problem a through use of occupational advisory committees. The advisory committee is, by its very nature, supposed to be in close touch with reality Committee members should be able to distinguish between relevant and irrelevant content and provide the curriculum developer with the sort of guidance needed. A basic assumption is that committee members are, in fact, close to the occupation, can determine what content is most relevant and, therefore, should be included in the particular curriculum. However if this assumption cannot be met, the curriculum developer is not much better off than he or she would be with a teacher group.

The DACUM approach

A most useful variant of introspection is the DACUM approach, which utilizes some basic ideas associated with introspection but shares few of its shortcomings. The reason for this is that DACUM relies on experts employed in the occupational area to determine curriculum content and allows them to be guided through a systematic content determination process. Although the approach has some commonalities with other content determination strategies. DACUM will be examined in a singular fashion because of the success curriculum developers worldwide have had using this approach in content determination

DACUM was initially created as a joint effort of the Experimental Projects Branch, Canada Department of Manpower and Immigration and Genera Learning Corporation. The idea was later adopted and used by Nova Scotia New Start, Inc.

and utilized in the determination of vocational curriculum content for disadvantaged adult learners. DACUM was felt to be particularly useful for the New Start activity because immediate action needed to be taken on curriculum development and limited dollar resources were available.

DACUM may be defined as "a single sheet skill profile that serves as both a curriculum plan and an evaluation instrument for occupational training programs". A unique aspect of the DACUM approach is the way that curriculum content is displayed. A single-sheet will profile is used to present the skills of an entire occupation, thus refusing the chance of treating one element of an occupation separately from the others. The profile provides an independent specification of each of the behaviors or skills associated with competence in the occupation. These behaviors are stated in a rather simple manner so that the student can understand them and are organized in small blocks on the chart in such a manner that each can be used as an independent goal for the student. The profile can also contain a rating scale that facilitates evaluation of achievement for each of the behaviors.

The development of a DACUM profile involves using a committee of ten to twelve resource persons who are experts in a particular occupation. Employers nominate as resource persons, people who are skilled in the occupation and who are currently serving as a worker or supervisor in the area. Experiences with this approach have revealed that instructors in an occupational field *do not always* contribute effectively to the DACUM process. If vocational teachers are involved in the DACUM process, they might be best utilized as ex officio committee members and be brought in after the basic committee has prepared a preliminary or draft profile.

The DACUM committee functions as a group with all developmental activities taking place when the members are together Time required to complete a DACUM profile generally ranges from two to four days. A coordinator from outside the committee works with the group to facilitate the development process. Examples of previously deprived DACUM charts and related materials are provided to committee members so that they may see what the end product will look like.

Following committee orientation, the facilitator guides the group through a series of steps that includes:

1. Reviewing a written description of the specific occupation
2. Identifying general areas of competence within the occupation
3. Identifying specific skills or behaviors for each general area of competence
4. Structuring the skills into a meaningful learning sequence
5. Establishing levels of competence for each skill as related to realistic work situations

Once the DACUM profile has been developed, the product may serve as a basis for developing instructional content and materials that focus on student attainment of specified skill. It should be noted that teachers tend to become involved *after* the profile has been produced. This procedure has the advantage of identifying only those skills that are more relevant to the work setting. This does not mean teachers are de-enfranchised; they are recognized for their overall technical expertise and ability to organize, sequence, and detail curriculum content.

The DACUM approach to curriculum development has some distinct advantages. First, the committee procedures results in a relatively low development cost. The major expense would be payments to committed members, and in many cases, a business or industry will gladly release an "expert" from his or her duties to assist in this process. Second, the time frame for conducting the DACUM activity is quite short. Thus, in a relatively brief time, instructors may use the profile to prepare for their classes. No time is spent waiting for forms to return or worrying about nonrespondents. Third, and perhaps most important, is the way the DACUM enables curriculum content to be derived without academic intervention. DACUM's advantage over the traditional introspection process is quite clear. The process allows more relevant content to be identified and incorporated into a curriculum. At first glance, the DACUM approach appears no different from the traditional trade and job analysis process. One should note, however, that these approaches rely to the instructor to determine what the content should be with little direct consideration given to input from persons employed in the actual work setting.

Task analysis

Few content determination strategies have seen such widespread use as task analysis. This particular approach has been employed by vocational educators in varying forms for a number of years. However, during the mid-1960s, several development occurred that resulted in major refinements to the task analysis process. These refinements have enabled curriculum developers to make more objective decisions regarding content that should be included in various curricula. Of particular note was research conducted at the Personnel Research Laboratory, Lackland Air Force Base, Texas, which resulted in the development of a procedural guide for conduction occupational surveys. This guide has enabled educators to study systematically the behavioral aspects of job requirements. Further refinement and use of the task analysis process by groups such as the Vocational Technical Education Consortium of States (V-TECS) has shown this approach to be quite applicable to public vocational and technical education.

Task analysis fundamentals

Basically task analysis may be defined as the process wherein tasks performed by workers employed in a particular job are identified and verified. The worker's job consists of duties and tasks he or she actually performs. *Duties* are large segments of work done by an individual that physically serve as broad categories within which tasks may be placed. Example of duties would be organizing and planning, typing, maintaining equipment and tools, and loading and hauling.

Tasks, on the other hand, are work activity units that form a significant aspect of a duty. Each task has a definite beginning and ending point and usually consists of two or more distinct steps. Examples of tasks performed by workers would be planning menus, filing materials, computing depreciation, and winterizing vehicles. Basic to the task analysis process is the gathering of information directly from workers. Obtaining information from this source ensures that workers are actually providing input for curriculum content decisions. Just as the name "task analysis" implies, potential tasks are identified and then verified by job incumbents, with the resulted analysis serving to determine which tasks are actually associated with a particular job.

Conducting the task analysis

There are several possible ways that a task analysis may bé conducted, from the key to success lies in being both thorough and systematic. For this reason, much of the discussion that follows is drawn from procedures by the Vocational-Technical Education Consortium of States in the conduct of their task analyses. V-TECS is a cooperative among a number of state agencies to develop catalogs of performance objectives, criterion referenced measures, and guides in selected occupational areas. The consortium in administered by the Southern education of Colleges and Schools, Commission on Occupational Education Institutions, Atlanta, Georgia, Catalogs based on task analyses are completed or underway for hundreds of job titles ranging from child care to management. The experience of this consortium over the past several years has enabled V-TECS to develop a set of task analysis procedures that is extremely functional. There are, of course, other sources of information for persons who are planning to conduct task. However, most reference are, at least in part, based upon analysis Archer's work. Those interested in marketing education occupations may explore parallel competency identification efforts conducted by the Marketing Education Resource Center, Inc., Columbus.

What, then, are the basic steps involved in task analysis? Typically they include reviewing relevant literature, developing the occupational inventory, selecting a worker sample, administering the inventory, and analyzing the collected information.

Reviewing relevant literature

The first step in conducting a task analysis consists of examining literature in the occupational area. This review is useful in determining the extent to which other analyses may have already been conducted. If meaningful analyses have been completed, there is usually no reason to go any further with the analysis process. A second use of the literature review is to develop lists of potential tasks and equipment associated with the occupational area. Tasks may be listed for one or several jobs with the exact scope of the analysis being determined by the curriculum developer. Thus, an occupational area typically consists of two or more jobs in a related area or cluster. Equipment lists serve to identify the extent to which equipment is sued and, once verified serve as meaningful aids in laboratory planing and similar areas.

Developing the occupational inventory

After task equipment and work aid lists have been gleaned from the literature, duplicate items are deleted and, wherever appropriate, relevant items are added. Lists are then incorporated into an inventory that will eventually be completed by incumbent workers. The equipment list is generally placed on a separate sheet of the inventory, together with spaces for workers to check items used in the current assignments.

In order to keep track of the various jobs examined in a task analysis, standard numbers and job titles provided by the Dictionary of Occupational Titles (D.O.T) may be used. The D.O.T. classification scheme is utilized by the U.S. Department of Labour and might prove especially helpful when an instructor is eager to know what tasks are appropriate to various jobs in an occupational area.

An equally important aspect of inventory development deals with the areas marked by incumbent workers. These consist of scales to check whether or not tasks are done in the present job, and they permit the indication of time spent doing the tasks. Unfortunately, time spent on a task does not indicate that it is more or less important than other tasks. Some very important tasks take a very short time to complete. Data collected from workers are used to determine whether or not a particular task is of sufficient importance to warrant its inclusion in the curriculum contains one task-list page from an inventory for biomedical equipment technicians.

The items are representative of background information that is usually gathered. Workers' names and addresses may be needed in the event that some responses require clarification, whereas "How long have you worked in this occupational area? may be used to categorize workers' responses in accordance with their work experience. A curriculum developer using this approach is advised to keep informational items to a minimum and only include items that are absolutely essential.

Selecting a worker sample

Although, in some instances, information may be gathered from an entire population of workers, this procedure is usually not followed. Workers in a particular occupational area may number several thousand or even hundred thousand; thus, data must be gathered from an appropriate sample of that population. Sampling not only cuts costs in terms of printing and mailing, it also reduces the magnitude of data to be analyzed. Numerous references are available that describe procedures for determining the appropriate sample size. Regardless of the sampling procedure used, any sample selected must be truly representative of the population. An appropriate sampling technique will ensure that results from the worker sample can be generalized to the population.

Administering the inventory

Once the inventory has been developed and the sample selected, data can be gathered from incumbent workers. Perhaps the most expeditious approach is to mail the inventory out and rely on workers to complete and return it. Unfortunately, this is not always successful, since inventories usually contain twenty to thirty pages and hundreds of tasks. When care is not taken to follow up on those who fail to return forms, the result may be a low return rate. If fewer than 60 percent of the selected sample complete and return inventories, the generalizability of results to a population of workers may be seriously questioned. Therefore a high return rate should be secured whenever the inventory is mailed to workers. An alternative approach is to sample employers and make contact with persons at the managerial level to solicit the cooperation of their employees. By dealing directly with employers, the curriculum developer is able to obtain support "from the top" and thus encourage a good return rate. Workers whose employers support the inventory process may feel a strong personal obligation to complete and return the inventory promptly. A third alternative would be to interview workers at the job location. This is often an expensive proposition, but it may be the only effective way to gather data from workers in certain occupational areas.

Analyzing the collected information

After the data have been collected from workers, responses are typically processed via computer. This is certainly the most expeditious route to take since each inventory contains so many different tasks and items of equipment. If, for example, 200 workers each completed an inventory with 300 tasks and 75 equipment items, 75,000 bits of data would be produced!

In the determination of what actually constitutes a meaningful task the recommendation is made to establish some appropriate cutoff point. For example, this might be "80 percent of the workers perform the task." Whatever standard is eventually established, it must be remembered that the vocational curriculum typically prepares students for entry level employment. Tasks should not be arbitrarily eliminated just because they are not performed by seasoned veterans, since these same tasks may be performed by a high percentage of novice workers. By taking information from the workers' background information sheets such as time spent on a job, a determination may be made of which tasks are performed by more experienced and less experienced workers.

The critical incident technique

Even though the critical incident technique has been available for many years, its use in deriving curriculum content has been quite limited. This technique is comprised of "procedures for collecting direct observations of human behavior in such a way as to facilitate their potential usefulness in solving practical problems".

An incident is any observable human activity that enables "inference and predictions to be made about the person performing the act" and assessment of facilities currently available. While financial resources could be discussed in this chapter, this topic is treated in Chapter 5 since finances are closely linked to community resources.

The goal of this chapter is to provide the curriculum planner with the capability to conduct an internal scan of what is really happening in the school system or technical or community college as it now exists and to identify data for use in either establishing program standards or determining if established standards can be met. One of the first steps in curriculum development is to study the current program.

Assessing the current status of vocational and technical education programs

Before any curriculum-planning decisions can be made, consideration must be given to assessing current programs and developing a basic understanding about them. Whereas some curriculum planners are able to build a vocational and technical education program where none exists, most will be faced with making decisions related to the improvement, redirection, and/or expansion of ongoing programs. Thus, it is imperative that full consideration be given to the current vocational and technical education program.

Current vocational and technical programs, enrollments, and capacity

The assessment of current programs begins with identifying and listing individual courses that are presently being offered. This may seem a trite step to some, but the listing will help the eliminate some future problems and misunderstandings, especially with those involved in curriculum planning who do not have vocational education backgrounds.

The use of a form, enables the curriculum planner to produce a clear, concise picture of current vocational and technical education programs. Titles approved by the state department of education should be used in listing program areas or courses. the use of abbreviated names or nicknames will often lead to confusion and misunderstanding in communications between curriculum planners and noneducational decision makers. If the state department of education has assigned code numbers to approved courses, these could also be used and placed in parentheses after each course offering. The second column is designed to help identify the location in which a course is currently being offered. This would be of special value when vocational courses are offered in different buildings or when students are bused to different locations for their vocational and technical courses.

An example of how the form can be of assistance to vocational teachers and administrators in understanding the current status of a total vocational program. Let's assume the data represent the current status at East Central High School in December of a school year. The following observations of the data could be made.

Marketing Education

A. Classes are operating at about 80 percent of capacity

B. Courses tend to have a high degree of holding power as students advance.

Home Economics

C. Low enrollment exists with Food Occupations II.

D. Over enrollment exists with Introduction to Foods and Cuisine Foods.

E. Number of seniors enrolled is substantially lower than the number of juniors.

F. The program may be operating at near capacity with only one teacher.

ICT

G. Program could serve twice as many students.

H. Do scheduling problems exist since a high number of seniors are enrolled in ICT I?

I. One teacher could be reassigned.

Technology Education

J. Could the large number of 11th and 12th graders in Engineering Drawing be prohibiting 10th graders from taking the course?

K. Woods Technology, Metals Technology, and Construction are underenrolled to a high degree.

L. Program could serve more students.

M. There may be a high attrition of students when comparing enrollment of 10th graders to enrollment of 12th graders.

Overall Vocational Program

N. Program is operating at 77 per cent capacity.

O. Can the program do a better job of holding students?

As with these observations for East Central High School, it is evident that the use of the form and type of data would be very valuable to the teacher, administrator, and curriculum specialist in gaining a perspective of the current status of the vocational program. The data collected by use of the form would become even more valuable as data are collected over time and trends are identified. For example,someone could raise the following questions:

Is the enrollment of 120 students in Marketing Education (80 percent of capacity) good or bad?

Is the number of seniors (27) enrolled in Technology Education high or low?

Is the percentage of the student body at East Central High School who are enrolled in vocational education increasing or decreasing?

The answer to each of these questions is "That depends." if the enrollment in Marketing Education for the previous two years was 140 and 130, then a current enrollment of 120 could imply that problems exist. If the number of seniors enrolled in Technology Education has decreased in the last few years, then someone needs to take a close look at the program and/or the scheduling to pinpoint what may be causing this decrease. If the percentage of the student body at East Central High School enrolling in vocational courses for the last three years has increased from 50 to 52, and now to 56 percent, then one may conclude that the program is gaining in quality, serving more students, and operating at an increased efficiency.

It must be remembered that the data collected for any one point in time will limit the analysis that can be made. Data collected over time where trends can be identified will enhance the abilities of teachers, administrators, and curriculum planners to make the right decisions for strengthening current programs.

Determining student occupational interest

The story is told of how a new vocational program was added to a school's curriculum and the most up-to-date facility was constructed for it, but when it came to enrolling students, no one wanted to take the program. Although this story may be more fiction than fact, administrators and teachers have no doubt wondered from time to time of students were really interested in the courses being offered. Planners must take into account the occupational interests of students when measuring program standards.

Standardized tests

One approach to assessing the occupational interests of a large group of students is through the use of standardized tests. This is especially helpful if several different grade level are to be surveyed. Such tests are available to educators and can be an effective tool in curriculum planning. But it must be kept in mind that no test is available that specifically identified into which occupation a person should go. Vocational interest tests are intended to point out general vocational interests of students and should not be interpreted beyond this point.

Interest Inventories. Students will be more highly motivated to investigate occupations and firm up career decisions if they have a good understanding of themselves. Interest inventories not only help students to learn more about themselves but also aid curriculum planners in making generalizations about future program direction.

The following factors should be kept in mind by students and curriculum planners when using standardized interest inventories:

1. Interest inventories do not indicate ability. A student may be interested in an occupation but not have the ability to succeed in it.

2. Interest inventories may help students recognize interest in occupations that they did not know existed.

3. Interest inventories may help students confirm what they thought were their interests.

4. Interest inventories should never be used as the only method of assessing student occupational interests. Other factors to consider are stated interests, individual observations, and activities in which the student has participated.

Several interest inventories are currently available. Four of the more common tests are the Kuder Occupational Interest Survey Form DD (KOIS), the Ohio Vocational Interest Survey (OVIS), the Differential Aptitude Test (DAT) Career Planning Program, and the Self-Directed Search (SDS).

The KOIS takes about thirty minutes to administer and can be given to tenth graders or above. A unique feature of the third edition of KOIS is that scales are included that focus upon occupational interests as well as college majors. The inventory cannot be scored by hand.

The OVIS is designed for grades eight through twelve and requires sixty to ninety minutes to administer. This survey measures an individual's preferences on the following twenty-five interest scales: manual work, machine work, personal services, caring for people or animals, clinical work, inspecting and testing, crafts and precise operations, customer services, nursing and related technical services, skilled personal service, training, literary, numerical, appraisal, agriculture, applied technology, promotion and communication, management and supervision, artistic, sales representative, music , entertainment and performing arts, teaching, counseling and social work, and medical. This survey must be machine-scored.

The SDS is a recently developed interest test that is a reasonably short, self-administered, self-scored, and self-interpreted inventory. It reflects a person's interests and relates them to appropriate occupational groups. The SDS can be completed in forty to fifty minutes and is suitable for students age fifteen and older.

Standardized aptitude tests

Scholastic aptitude tests are also available and can give a rough estimate of a student's ability to learn from books or from tasks required in school. Several aptitude tests that may be administered are California Test of Mental Maturity, Otis-Lennon Mental Ability Test, SRA Primary Mental Abilities Test, and the Lorge-Thorndike Intelligence Test. To prevent "branding" or labeling of students, educators should refrain from using specific test scores or IQ scores. The recommended practice is to use test scores in general terms.

Another aptitude test is the Genera Aptitude Test Battery (GATB), which is administered by the branches of the state employment service. The nine factors included in this test are general reasoning ability, verbal aptitude, numerical aptitude, spatial aptitude, form perception, clerical perception, motor coordination, figure dexterity, and normal dexterity.

Standardized achievement tests

Tests such as the Stanford Achievement Test and the California Achievement Test are also used by many school systems. Achievement test measure what a student has already learned, whereas aptitude tests are used more predicting future performances.

Selecting standardized tests

With the multitude of tests on the market, the curriculum planner may wish to review current listings in the Education Index. However, he or she must eventually decide which test to administer to students. A review of the different types of standardized tests may lead the planner to eliminate some tests immediately, since the purpose for which a particular test is to be administered may not be appropriate for curriculum planning.

In addition to the purpose for which a test is tc be used, several other factors should be considered regardless of the type of test desired. Information regarding the following factors is usually found in the booklet describing each test *reliability* refers to the ability of the test to give the same results if administered to the same student at a later time; *validity* refers to the ability of the test to measure what it purports to measure. Several other items should be considered to determine if the test is practical to administer. One factor to consider is the time required to administer the test. The time should be reasonable; it is helpful if the test can be administered within a single class period. Another factor is the cost. Although curriculum planners would not want to select a test solely because it is the least expensive one available, tests that entail a higher cost per student could run into a sizable figure if administered to a large group of students. The last factor to consider deals with the ease of administering, scoring, and interpreting the results. A test would be selected only if it gives understandable and usable results.

Specialized interest scales for Specific vocational and technical program areas

Although some research and development on special interest tests have been initiated, curriculum planners will not, in general, for the foreseeable future, be able to use standardized tests to any great degree for determining occupational interests of students within specific program areas. Further research and development need to be carried out in each of the vocational program areas before interest tests can be used with any degree of accuracy for program planning.

Teacher-made surveys

Many planners have relied on teacher-made surveys for use in specific program areas. Although these surveys are not as sophisticated as standardized tests, teacher-made surveys can prove valuable to curriculum planners. Each survey must be developed with a purpose in mind. If the need arises for determining the occupational interests of students in the area of marketing education, then occupations or situations that lend themselves to occupations found in this area must be identified and incorporated into the survey.

The format and length of such surveys can vary widely, depending on the degree to which a curriculum planner desires to pinpoint occupational interests. The survey should be relatively short and easy for the students to complete. Short answers or questions that students can check or circle will aid in maintaining student interest throughout the survey.

Although teacher surveys are usually developed for specific vocational program areas and are used with students already enrolled in those areas, administration of the survey to other students has some merit. The standardized instruments discussed earlier indicate student interest in occupational groups. Teacher-made surveys, however, assist students in identifying specific interests within a certain area. To administer any interest survey or test to a certain group of students and not to others assumes that the student not provided the opportunity to express their interests do not possess occupational interests in that area. This is often a false assumption and one that curriculum planners cannot afford to make.

Administering tests and surveys

One important factor to determine is when a test should be administered. Typically, standardized tests are administered to all students in a school system to assess their current occupational interests. If a program is being planned that will go into effect two years from the time a survey is administered, instruments should be administered to students in the lower grades who will be able to select vocational and technical courses two years hence.

Obtaining assistance

Curriculum planners who are unfamiliar with the administration and interpretation of test results may want to seek professional assistance. Most colleges and universities with vocational and technical teacher education programs have personnel who can provide assistance to local schools in collecting and interpreting data related to educational decision making. Specialists in state departments of education also have expertise in this area. Furthermore private consultants are available to high school systems on a fee basis; however, the cost for this type of service may prove to be prohibitive.

5 Vocationalism and Education

Education has always been intimately connected with the world of work. Early impulses to provide schooling for the masses contain a mixture of motives but all of them take cognizance of the social reality of employment. On the one hand humanitarian instincts promoted compulsory schooling in the early years of the nineteenth century as a means of liberating children from the heartless depredations of what amounted to little more than slave labour. On the other hand, later in the turbulent years of revolutions and the widening franchise a note of 'education for our masters' was to be heard, schooling as a means of 'gentling the masses'.

In the twentieth century the ideological currents of egalitarianism, notably in the writings of R.H. Tawney, introduce a levelling function into the debate about schooling. Here for the first time in the public sector schooling is not just to follow a religous or secular social order but to act as a reforming force. The invention of meritocracy in the mid twentieth century is a dramatic step towards the fulfilment of schooling as a power of social change. In such social change what work people are to do is at the centre. Harold Wilson's concept of the comprehensive school as providing 'grammer school opportunities for all'—clearly meritocratic in itself-was a step towards a concept of a common curriculum for a common culture.

What this latter formula lacks is a clear recognition of social inequalities pervading the culture, most importantly perhaps in inequalities in access to work and its highly differentiated rewards.

It may well be doubted to what extent we have a common culture, so far are we divided on lines of class, race and region. Our recognition of these factors has been heightened by the increase in wordlessness which has been clearly patterned along class, race, gender and regional lines.

In the 1980s, therefore, we are faced with the problem of redefining the relationship between schooling and work. We are helped in this by the legacy of all the experimentations and theorizing that went on through the 1960s. At that time it became possible to articulate a concept of education which separated it from narrow instrumentalist and saw it as an end in itself. To be sure this was not new to human history for Dewey had long ago expressed the idea that the only true aim of education was more education—but in an American context where there was no doubt that schooling served a democratic social order, albeit one which was rapidly developing on competitive and capitalist lines.

The question then is not whether schools should serve society, but how? The philosophizing of the

1960s developed a purist conception of education as the pursuit of personal autonomy based on reason. This lacked a responsible account of the social and economic relations necessary for that purpose. In that way it mirrored the separation of the education service, and teachers particularly, from social audit. As economic and ideological stringency set in during the 1970s this separation broke down to the point of mistrust and disillusionment. Two political events may be seen as symbolic of these developments: the abolition of the Schools Council, which was one of Sir Keith Joseph's early measures, and the creation in 1974 and subsequent growth of the Manpower Service Commission. These two developments attacked the values held by the education service and called them to account for the part education should play in the social order.

Unfortunately this accountability, though necessary (for what democracy ought to tolerate vast unaccounted-for expenditure?), has been converted to its own ends by a narrow range of interests from the world of business. Aided by a businessman's government, business and industry have been holding education to account. The next step in the evolution of education as a public service is surely to widen the interests to whom education is to be legitimately accountable. Already, for other reasons, parents are coming to the fore and we may well be seeing the creation of counterforces to the assumption of industry.

Among these assumptions have been the following.

1. Education principally concerns the pupils' preparation for a world of work.

2. This preparation should concern itself with the 'skills' industry needs.
3. These skills are mainly technical in nature.
4. Schools have perpetuated an anti-industrial culture.
5. Schools have neglected a substantial minority ('the bottom 40 percent') in favour of an academic group of high flyers.

All of these assumptions, and more, may be called into question by the arrival of new interests on the accountability scene. Parents and governors who get to know the work of the schools intimately will certainly realize that schools can hold out the view that there is more to life than earning a living. What, after all, are we to do with the wealth created by work? As curriculum reform goes on, some of it motivated by criticism such as the above and some of it springing from other sources, the questions will be freshly formulated and we may go some way to asking on what principles an educational curriculum which is also socially responsive may be defined. A suspicion of an answer is that no permanent theory for all this is possible. Instead we should look for a balance of interests in which the recent swings of the pendulum from teachers to industrialists are held more in check by a continuous process of social negotiation in the developing institutions of schooling and government.

The purpose of this chapter is to suggest a broad set of considerations for those concerned with the development of curriculum. Its central theme is that 'education' and 'preparation for work', however broadly defined either or both may be, are not synonymous terms. It will be argued that if there are attempts to convert education to the interests of business or commerce these must be regarded with a critical eye lest other equally legitimate interests in education are consequently devalued. The critique of education from a vocationalist standpoint in recent years has been unhelpful to the improvement of the school curriculum because it has focused attention on too narrow a from. This paper indicates some broader considerations.

It is no part of this thesis any particular moves are in fact being made, nor that there is any actual conspiracy to being the education service under the control of business. Those are exceedingly difficult empirical questions which others are addressing. Equally, however, the thesis is not the purely conceptual or linguistic one that the two terms have different 'meanings'. It is not proposed that the content and structure of an 'educational' curriculum can be derived in some *a priori* fashion from an analysis of the terms involved in discussion about it, for example, by contrasting 'education' and 'training'. Though these terms are indeed used to pick out distinctions among practical activities, reliance is better placed upon ordinary human wishes for young people. It will be important therefore that curriculum planning is conducted in such a way that these wishes are not obfuscated by ideology. Centralist tendencies carry this danger and it will be suggested that curriculum planning should be devolved as far as possible to the grass roots level.

In the end, to uphold such a view of curriculum planning is to espouse a value position which has political as well as curricular implications. The message for innovators and curriculum developers will be that personal and professional responsibility demands that full account be taken of the historical and moral dimensions of their work. Relevance to 'work' or 'the economy' must be set against and balanced with the perhaps less easily articulated values contained in the preferences of parents and others for their children. The new school governing bodies—since they will contain a majority of people with a direct personal stake in the curriculum of their school-present an opportunity for this form of resistance to distant dogma.

Rather than philosophically defining terms, it is important for this form of argument to inspect the substantive ends that education may from time to time be called to serve. This is so not only because philosophical analysis tends to carry little weight in the practical world but also for two other reasons. Firstly, philosophers do not agree among themselves on the issues; secondly, and connectedly, philosophy is not value-free enquiry which, if only it could be perfected, would provide the answers to social and moral questions. The work of the philosophers of education in the dominant Peters tradition has been subject to enough scrutiny to establish that a specific educational position is contained within their endeavours. The whole form of work that this genre of philosophy of education represents goes towards reinforcing an academically oriented school curriculum.

The initial question before us in this enquiry is what alternatives may be specified as the ends of education. The bid from vocationalists has to be seen as not the only alternative to intellectural elitism; too much of the debate has been polarized between these two alone. The deficiencies of our secondary education have been exceedingly well rehearsed and practically nobody denies that the secondary curriculum needs overhauling. How far academic values are to retain their central place is, however, a matter of some contention.

A first riposte to the vocationalist thrust, one dismayingly seldom seen, would be to accept the criticism that schooling has failed perhaps the majority of pupils but to say that this is no reason for rejecting the view that school is primarily about the virtues of the considered life. Are formed, well resourced, properly assessed curriculum should be preserved with; it should be detached as far as possible from the ravages of a competitive examination system and the straightening effects of subject-mindedness. This move would preserve the centrality of mind without elevating mere cleverness as an organizational criterion, for example, by rejecting streaming and setting without good reason. General education would be reinstated as the purpose of the compulsory school years. Perhaps the most urgent challenge for such a position is to incorporate practical and expressive activities in a tradition of education which is predominantly concerned with the abstract and theoretical.

This move is perhaps too obvious to have achieved much attention yet it is something of the kind the HMI have been propounding in their various publication since *Curriculum 11-16 and A View of the Curriculum*. These documents have consistently put forward a counter view to that contained in the parallel Ministerial publications. In *A Framework for the School Curriculum* and in the subsequent more muted publication, *The School Curriculum*, for example, there resides no discernible overall view of curriculum design. They are concoctions of the obvious, reflecting only an uneasy consensus of the ill-informed and responding to the political preoccupations of the hour. As such, they are of course undefended against the next trend or moral panic to come along. It is noteworthy, too, that despite obeisances in the direction of the world of work such proposals are bereft of specific curricular ideas in that direction. This is surely because the conceptual apparatus being deployed is limited by the rather narrow educational experience of politicians themselves. It is predominately the subject-based curriculum which is assumed in such proposals and this curriculum has the greatest difficulty in articulating a coherent response to cross-curricular initiatives. There is no traditional school subject called 'the world of work' and thus no clear views are forthcoming on what it could represent in the curriculum beyond generalizations of a saloon-bar nature about 'the basics' and the 'will to work'.

As it is, then, the popular rhetoric has it that Britain is an industrial country with an anti-industrial culture; the education service does little to rectify and may even be responsible for this state of affairs. But these assertions are linked to no historical explanation why Britain became pre-eminent industrially and otherwise in the first place, nor to the role of the education system in that ascendancy. If there were some such analysis we might have more confidence in the capacity of education to contribute to prosperity as well as benefit from it. The suspicion must remain that, historically, the origins of industrial success lie well outside the education system, in factors such as maritime access to imperial markets. By the same token it might be thought that the seeds of late twentieth-century economic renewal may well lie equally distantly from the schools, for example, in the movements of international capital. If in the nineteenth century the contribution of the school was to provide a docile labour force in turbulent political times, then perhaps today's role for the schools is, minimally, in being seen to respond to economic crisis and unemployment. In regard to schools, politicians can be seen to be doing something, sometimes with the added frisson of censoriousness.

But these are big ifs and it is not to the present purpose to claim they are true. They are raised only to suggest that the relation between the schools and the economy is both multi-faceted and essentially contested. Because it cannot be contended that this relationship is clear in a causal, or in any other, way it makes little sense to claim that the schools are responsible for economic decline or that the economy can be turned round principally by education reform. Nevertheless, the educationists are in receipt of regular accusations that hey subvert the aims of industry, from pre-school to university, mainly by failing to emphasize technological subjects, by failing to foster the entrepreneurial spirit and by indulging the luxury of individualism at the expense of discipline and team work.

The effect of this undifferentiated mass of complaint is to imply that the alternative to the curriculum as it is—and we have acknowledged its defects—is a curriculum geared to the 'real' world of work. And this despite the poor theoretical background and the paucity of though going suggestions for curriculum reform—apart from spectacular but essentially marginal assaults on the system such as TVEI.

But these are not the only alternatives. Indeed, at a time of high unemployment, and unemployment among the young in particular, it would seem logical to contemplate an education for a wordless future. This, however, is plainly not a political possibility and no political party has dared to mention it. Because it is so inconceivable we have hardly any indication what such an education would look like. It would certainly not be the same sort of thing as education for leisure, for leisure constitutes a range of activities defined as such by contrast to work in precisely the same way treat holidays make sense only when there is something to go back to afterwards. A workless culture will necessarily redefine what it takes seriously as constituting the essential tasks of life and what it takes less seriously as perhaps being recuperative or playful. Since we cling to paid employment as the source of social identity, financial sustenance and personal dignity, we are unable to contemplate a workless future whether for ourselves as individuals or for us all socially. Thus education cannot be conceptualized in this dimension and is apt to degenerate into education for leisure. Education is indeed a vision of the future and curriculum plans can only be made on the basis of what we are able—and willing—to see of the future.

If education for worklessness is a more logical and education for leisure a more likely response to the modern situation we should not be ignoring other aspects of adult life for which education should be preparing. It is predictable that the vast majority of pupils will become parents. Yet despite James Callaghan's emphasis on the family at the outset of the great debate a decade ago this aspect of the responsibility of the education service has received scant attention in the ensuing rush to vocationalize. It is tempting to ascribe this neglect to some deep intuition that the family is potentially at least a centre of resistance to social engineering. What close-knit family would be prepared to see its members dispersed nation-and Europe-wide in fulfilment of the supreme imperative of work? But the family itself is in crisis, a crisis certainly in part due to an undermining social, political and economic environment. Education for parenthood ought to equip people to understand their predicament as parents in such terms, enabling them to act in defence of the family as an institution as well as in the interests of their own family as a unit. As it is of course, education for parenthood degenerates to child care without reference to its social context. It is hardly likely that there is need of a conspiracy to suppress the family in this subtle way, by reducing it to hygiene and sentimentality, when we are all in general so limited in our understanding of what the family could represent in the social structure and in our personal lives.

For much the same reason community

education also fails to gain a real grip on the mainsprings of curriculum development which remains torn between academic and vocational emphases. Much energy and ingenuity has been expended on community education but these endeavours have consisted mainly in attempts to share school facilities. There is little sense of what communities might become; and insofar as efforts remain at the technical level there is little prospect of educational action pragmatically clarifying possibilities.

As well as exercising the role of parents and as well as inhabiting a local community, all pupils will also be members of a political form of life we call democratic. Citizenship, equally with parenthood and community membership, has been much neglected and misrendered goal of the curriculum development movement in recent years. There are few attempts to relate a knowledge of the forms of government to the levers of political power. So in schools the old civics and British Constitution survives; there are pictures que role playings in the shape of school councils and moots; but the skills of participation and the exercise of personal and community rights receive scant attention. To go beyond the costly descriptive is for schools to court the charge of mixing education with politics. Here the academic tradition of neutrality is seen as a disease preventing the positive engagement of young people in the political culture. The proposal in the 1986 Education Bill to bar pupils from membership of their own school governing bodies is a symptom of that fear of political activity among young people and in or near schools that has nullified even the most legitimate of programmes such as that proposed Crick and Porter. It seems that in this most crucial of areas the fear of responsible political activity is greater than the fear of the consequences of ignorance. Political breakdown and disorder is surely a more likely eventuality than economic bankruptcy; moreover, it is an area where appropriate teaching could directly affect the quality of judgment the citizen deploys. This is certainly a more likely educational contribution to the collective quality of life than the purveying of dubious employment-related 'generic skills'.

In the closely-related field of economics it is truly significant that calls for education to prepare pupils for 'the world of work' include only nostrums of the 'there are no free dinners' variety and contain no invitation to a critical economic literacy. That there are a number of theoretical ideas about economic growth, all with different policy implications, is to be forever unknown to the majority of people who will make their political choices on the basis of personalities and slogans only. School, which for very many will be their only exposure to a critical consciousness, will have been in dereliction of an educational duty. The conflict between education and vocationalism will have claimed another casualty in the middle ground.

The educational imperatives from the family, from the community, from citizenship and from economics have all suffered neglect or suppression as a result of the vocationalist assault on the curriculum. These modern concerns threaten to go the way of those older curricular aims—Christian salvation and gentlemanly cultivation—in the struggle between ideologies. For it is important to recognize that no bid on the resources of the education system can be free of social and political assumptions concerning the distribution of power and the nature of the good life. When national economic survival is postulated as an overriding priority it will be important to ask 'survival in what form?' which distinguishable interests will be advantaged and which disadvantaged in any new settlement? Reference to Raymon Williams"s threefold classification of educational interests—the industrial trainers, the classical humanists and the public educators—may be complemented by Salter and Tapper's state bureaucrats as a basis for such enquiry. There is an urgent need for research in the real politics of educational policy. Such research, of which Broadfoot's is the best recent example, could help us to discover the centres of educational influence at national and local levels and thereby to learn how deliberation might be opened up to wider constituencies.

Such is the overwhelming strength of the vocationalist impulse that deliberation over the curriculum has been severely curtailed in recent years. It is surely now time to review the direction education is taking, and a start should be made by considering the adequacy of the forums within which educational policies and initiatives are generated.

Since the demise of the Schools Council there has been no independent body wherein curriculum development could be promoted. Despite its well documented shortcomings, its labyrinthine committee structure, its failure to produce a 'whole curriculum' policy, and its apparent lack of 'take-up' in the schools, this was the nearest we have seen to a research and development agency holding the ring between the many diverse interests in education. Its successor bodies, the School Curriculum Development Committee and the School Examinations council, are not representative of those diverse interests and respond principally from the centre to the political imperatives of the day.

The proposal in the 1986 Education Bill to do away finally with the old Consultative Committees which contributed so much intelligence to policy making over the years is perhaps another symptom of the flight from independent advice which has characterized centre over the past few years.

In this situation the professional vogue for school-based curriculum development is likely to be restricted to the realm of technique against a backdrop of structural decisions on the curriculum taken centrally. If curriculum is to be rescued from the truncations of vocationalism it can only be hoped that the LEAs will exert themselves and set up their own curriculum development agencies. These should be based on a genuine collaboration of local interests using a disciplined form of enquiry and resulting in clear statements of policy for the whole curriculum. Such statements are not to be confused with prescriptions for detailed curriculum content. It is rather a matter of establishing an agreed working rationale against which practitioners, governors and education committees themselves may make judgments on future developments in the light of experience. The power of the LEAs has been greatly diminished since local government organization in 1974 but they could surely redeem their educational souls by taking seriously their responsibility for the curriculum in concert with governors and teachers.

In doing so there would be a strong tide to swim against. The flow of events is increasingly in one direction, from central to local and then to school level. Centralization is of course a separate question from that of the desirability of the messages that are sent. In the professional mind, though, centralization is inevitably bound up with the vocational trend of recent years. Given the central government's legitimate interest in the economy and in manpower planning it is likely that only the coarser-grained messages will come through that channel. All the more reason, then, for LEAs, governors and teachers to mount their own curriculum initiatives, preferably in concert at the local level where they can be enacted, monitored and improved.

The urgency of this is not simply in defending more sophisticated and locally responsive curricula. More, it is a matter of preserving and furthering the art of curriculum making at the scene of its transmission. If teachers are not to become a mere 'delivery system' of curricular goods defined at the centre, local exertions are necessary. The new machinery for INSET will need to be used not solely for short-term system maintenance or so as to be seen to be applying central priorities, but also to research more distant goals and more adventurous possibilities. The contractual relationships implied in new forms of teacher appraisal will need to be moderated by a spirit of collegiality. Above all, the deleterious effects of rush must be minimized. Of course there is urgency; but the strongest impression left by the last ten years of curriculum initiatives is one of too many answers chasing too few questions. This form of educational inflation has depleted energies through out the system and eroded reserved of educational commitment which badly need renewal. The kind of local activity suggested here, albeit having to work against a prevailing climate, would be a means of introducing a desperately needed and greatly desired quantity of deliberation into a curriculum development process marked of late by destructive haste.

Curriculum making restored to the local level as a participatory and collaborative activity would discipline the rampant and ideological vocationalism proposed by elites for the children of others. It would achieve this by setting employment prospects in their proper context, namely as important considerations among the full range of desires we all have for our children. We wish them to become good parents, full members of the community, thinking citizens and critical participants in an evolving democracy. We wish them to be happy. Set in this context all sorts of employments themselves stand a chance of being revalued for their contribution to a well-lived life.

Appendix

A commitment to vocational education and training

The system of vocational education and training in the Federal Republic (West Germany) is one which has attracted a great deal of attention from British observers, and, as a consequence, has been frequently examined by visitors—including politicians, industrialists, civil servants and educationalists—and just as frequently reported on. The reason for our consuming interest in the Federal Republic's provision of vocational education and training is not far to seek: the 'economic miracle' which had led to West Germany raising itself from the rubble of the immediate post-war period to become the most prosperous and economically powerful country in Western Europe must surely, it is said, have something to do with its system of vocational education and training? As the United Kingdom's industrial position and prosperity relative to other developed countries have declined, so that of West Germany have increased. By 1980, for example, as Professor Prais has pointed out, output per employee in manufacturing was some 50 per cent higher in West Germany than the United Kingdom and real income per head of the total population was about a third higher. At the same time West Germany boasts a much comprehensive and seemingly effective system of vocational education and training, so that it is natural to assume that the former state of affairs derives, inpart at least, from the latter.

The Federal Republic of Germany is, of course, a creation of the decade after the Second World War. It grew out of a fusion of the three zones occupied by the American, British and French armies of occupation and became a sovereign independent country on 5 May 1955. With the exception of West Berlin, which is an outlier embedded in East Germany, its territory is contiguous and is made up of 11 *Lander*, or states: Baden-Wuttemberg, Bavaria, Berlin, Bremen,

Hamburg, Hessen, Lower Saxony, North Rhine-Westphalia, Rhineland-Palatinate, Saarland, and Schleswig-Holstein. It occupies an area of almost 250,000 square kilometres and has a population of just over sixty-one million, of whom 49 per cent are Protestants and 44.5 per cent Roman Catholics. Over four million foreigners are living in the Federal Republic at present, of whom almost half come from Turkey and most of the rest from southern Europe. The size of the population within each *Land* varies considerably, from about 700,000 in Bremen to some seventeen million, or more than a quarter of the country's total population, in North-Rhine Westphalia. Its economy is predominantly an industrial one, based on coal-mining, iron and steel, machine construction, electrical and metal products, and the processing of food stuffs.

The social and educational background

The Federal Republic today is a stable democracy with a federal constitution which lays down the division of power and responsibility between the Federal Government in Bonn and the administrations within the eleven *Lander*. Thus, the federal constitution bestows upon the latter 'cultural sovereignty' which, as far as education is concerned, gives them primary responsibility for the provision of primary and secondary schooling, with the partial exception of vocational education. Indeed, it was not until the late 1960s that a Federal Ministry of Education and Science was established. This system of government represents little change from the past as West Germany has never had a centralised and uniform education system. However, it is important to understand that each *Land* has a highly centralised power structure which applies to education equally with other aspects of provincial government.

In general, West Germany is both an ordered and orderly society in which most aspects of economic life and educational provision are determined by detailed laws. It has developed a tradition of 'consensus politics' which is based, among other things, on middle-of-the-road Federal Governments, and an elaborate body of constitutional law enforced by a powerful judiciary on both the executive and the legislative. In this context there is general agreement about the importance of vocational education and training, which has long been regarded as an integral part of West German life, and about the parts to be played in its provision by the Federal and *Lander* governments, by employers, by trade unions, and by the individuals themselves. Education is highly regarded and is seen by many as the principal means of bettering themselves.

The school system, which is relatively simple, has to British eyes, a somewhat old-fashioned appearance as, at lower secondary level, selective schools are predominant and comprehensive schools the exception rather than the rule. Although there are slight differences in organisation and structure between the individual *Lander*, the basic school system is broadly similar across the country, being divided into three stages: primary, lower secondary, and upper secondary. There are nine years of compulsory full-time schooling from 6 to 15 in most *Lander*, with ten years in a few. In addition as we shall see, all West German pupils have some form of compulsory education or training up to the age of 18. Moreover, the compulsory period of schooling is preceded for more than three-quarters of the pre-school population by attendance at *Kindergarten*, whose numbers have grown very considerably in the past twenty years. The primary school, or *Grundschule*, comprises Grades 1 to 4, ages 6 to 10 years, everywhere except in West Berlin and Bremen where it covers Grades 1 to 6, that is from 6 to 12 years. Like primary schools elsewhere, those in West Germany have not been without their problems. These include the procedures for selection for the different types of secondary school which in the past have often been very rigid, bringing pressures upon children and teachers similar to those associated with the formerly widespread 'eleven-plus' examination in the United Kingdom. However, in recent years the transition to secondary schools has become more flexible with the introduction in the first two years of lower secondary school of what are variously described as 'probationary', 'observation', or 'orientation' stages (*Orientierungsstufe*). Their function is to leave open the decision about what the pupil will do next until the end of the sixth grade and then reach this decision on a reliable form of assessment. In many parts of the country, primary schools have had to accommodate substantial numbers of children of foreign workers, *Gastarbeiter*, and many of them have been less than successful in providing multicultural and bilingual programmes for these children.

Once youngsters have completed their four years of primary school, they move on to three types of selective secondary schools: the *Hauptschule*, or roughly equivalent to the British secondary modern school; the *Realschule*, or intermediate school, and the *Gymnasium*, or grammar school. The *Hauptschule*, which caters for about 45 per cent of the 10-15 or 16-year-old age group, is a five-or-six year school which takes those children who are unable to obtain places in the other types of schools. It has been in decline for some years and inevitably finds itself, especially in the urban areas, with the most backward and most deprived West German children, including a high proportion of the children of the *Gastarbeiter*. Numerous attempts have been made by the *Lander* to revise the *Hauptschule*, for example, by means of curriculum reform and by the introduction of a school-leaving qualification which is recognised as equivalent to the *Realschule* diploma, but these have not been very successful.

On the other hand, the *Realschule*, which now caters for over 20 per cent of the age group, has expanded its position over the past twenty years as an alternative selective institution to the Gymnasium. It offers a four-year programme, from age 12 to 16, and its increased popularity is due partly to the fact that its curricular, emphasising science, mathematics and modern languages, is increasingly popular with pupils and parents who see it as a good preparation for later employment or higher education; and partly because the educational opportunities for those completing the *Realschule* have greatly increased. It has proved particularly attractive to children of working-class parents who are deterred by the more elite aura of the *Gymnasium* and who prefer the more practical curriculum available in the *Realschule*.

The *Gymnasium*, which caters for about one-quarter of the age-group, is a nine-year school, from age 10 to 19.It has changed dramatically in the past twenty years or so, both in the socialcomposition of its students and in the curriculum which it offers. Its main function has been, and remains, to prepare students for entry into higher education,principally via the *Arbitur*, the graduation certificate which entittles the school-leaver to study at university. Moreover, the changing nature of the *Gymnasium* in recent years means that it is no longer as highly selective as it once was; indeed in some suburban areas it enrols as much as 50 per cent of the age cohort. In North Rhine-Westphalia, for example, its most populous state, the school population fell from 3.4 million in 1975 to 2.7 million in 1985.

Finally, in a few of the *Lander* there are comprehensive schools, *Gesamtschulen*, which cater only for about 3 per cent of the schools population, compared to over 900 per cent in the United Kingdom. Their geographical distribution is very uneven and they are mostly concentrated in the politically less conservative states, namely those with Social Democratic governments, such as West Berlin, Bremen, Hamburg, Hesse and North Rhine-Westphalia. The reasons their supporters put forward for their introduction are similar to those in the United Kingdom: that they are a means of provising equality of educational opportunity for all youngsters, that they enable more young people to develop their full potential, and that they promote co-operation and citizenship among all strata of society. However, their introduction has aroused considerable controversy and has been held up by legal and other impediments. Moreover, even in areas where there are comprehensive schools, a Land must provide the other three types of secondary school in order to ensure that parents have a full choice; this frequently results in the 'creaming off' of the most able students into the *Gymnasium*.

In addition to the four types of public secondary schools described above, there is also a variety of Special Schools which cater, for instance, for physically or mentally handicapped children. These schools accommodate about 5 per cent of the age group. In addition, there is a relatively small private sector of education.

Before examining the provsion of vocational education and training which becomes available for yongsters after age 15 or 16, it is important to consider how far their school-leaving attainments provide a sound basis for this subsequent training. In this regard the acquisition of mathematical ability is clearly significant, and it seems indisputable that West German standars are higher than those in the United Kingdom, and that youngsters leaving all the four types of secondary schools have a greater mathematical capability than their equivalent in the United Kingdom. Moreover, about 90 per cent of all school-leavers obtain a school-leaving certificate appropriate to each type of school, requiring minimum attainments in core subjects such as mathematics, science, German and a foreign language. As a consequence, it can reasonably be concluded that the 'schooling stage' in West Germany provides a better foundation for later vocational training than its British counterpart. It also offers a broader curriculum and significantly higher levels of attainment in core subjects, for a greater proportion of pupils.

West German schools also provide more pre-vocational instruction than do their British counterparts, in the form of programmes known as *Arbeitslehre,* or Education for Work, which have been introduced into schools in all parts of the Federal Republic. However, they have been confined to the *Hauptschule* and *Gesamtschule,* and in practice are larlely restricted to children of working-class parents. They are essentially pre-vocational in character pin that, although they include a period of work experience, they are not designed to provide job-specific training. Their official aims are ambitious and include the provision of a general vocational education to enable youngsters to find an adequate profession, the promotion of vocational and professional flexibility, and making young people aware both of the nature of employment and also of their role in the home and in society at large. *Arbeitslehre* replaces former subjects such as woodwork, metal-work and needlework; however, the precise form which it takes varies from one Land to another. Unlike many school subjects, it is not tied to one related area of learning, but may be taught through several, such as engineering, economics, social sciences and home economics. In this respect, it bears some resemblance to the Technical and Vocational Education Initiative (TVEI) programmes which have been introduced into British schools in recent years. However, the latter are designed for youngsters aged between 14 to 18 of all abilities, while *Arbeitslehre* is provided for the 13 to 16 age range, very largely for the lower half of the ability range.

Arbeitslehre has been particularly well developed in West Berlin where compulsory education continues to the age of 16, and it comprises a general course in such subjects as basic work techiniques, typewriting, the reading of technical drawings, consumer information, bank accounts and family budgets; a choice of option fromamong mechanical technology, electronics, textiles, and household subjects; and career guidance, including talks by local personnel officers and visitis to local places of employment. Elsewhere, where compulsory schooling ends at 15, *Arbeitslhere* may be obligatory only for the last three years and somewhat less time may be devoted to it than is the practice in West Berlin.

Inevitably, the introduction and evolution of *Arbeitslehre* have not been without their problems, including the difficulty or organising the programmes over a range of school subject and ensuring that teachers have the attitudes and knowledge to teach them effectively; and the administrative complications of organising work placements in factories and businesses. While properly organised programmes of *Arbeitslehre*, tailored to the needs of individual students, have much to offer them—for example, in improving their motivation in mathematicss and other school subject areas-they do reauire a high degree of co-operation between those concerned and hinge upon the difficult task of properly integrating the various components of the programmes. Moreover, to work effectively they require special methods of instruction including projects, and the production of goods for sale and even services in the form of repairs and information, which in turn require specific teaching techniques from the teachers concerned and the provision of specializsed class rooms. Clearly, therefore, the implementation of effective programmes. *Arbeitslehre* will require more money than traditional school subjects. As they are patronised very largely by lower ability children in the *Hauptschule*, it remains to be seen how much public support they will command.

The provision of vocational education and training

In the Federal Republic, the vocational education and training of youngsters to produce skilled workers takes place once they have completed their general education at school. Thus, for the majority who leave school at 15 or 16, two types of vocational training are available. The first isthe celebrated *Dual System* which most youngsters of this age embark upon, whereby as apprentices they combine on-the-job-training in industry or business with part-time, compulsory attendence at vocational schools until the age of 18, and the second consists of attendane at full-time vocational schools, which have been growing in popularity in recent years.

The much admired *Dual System* is the classic way by which the majority of West German school-leavers enter into a vocational training programme. It is characterised by two major features which distinguish it from most vocational training systems in other countries, such as the United Kingdom. First, as we have seen, training is split between two instructing parties: the employer and the school. For one or two days a week they attend state vocational schools, where they combine general education with the theoretical underpinning of their vocational subject, and for the rest of their working week they acquire practical skills at their place of work. Second, as is apparent from the foregoing description, vocational training takes place to a considerably greater extent in the workplace than in school.

This system of apprenticeship, not unlike that in the United Kingdom which combines workplace experience with day-release to the further education college, though of course in a much smaller and less systematic scale than in West Germany, has very deep historical roots going back to the guilds and the master-apprentice relationships of the Middle Ages. It depends for its success on the willing co-operation of four major parties: the Federal Government, the *Lander* governments, the employers, and the trade unions.

At present, about two-thirds of all young people in the 15 to 18 age group participate in the *Dual System*, which overall caterfs for about 1,80,000 trainees. During the course of 1986, for example, over 700,000 new trainees were accepted as apprentices, 40 per cent of them girls, in no fewer than 500,000 training firms, approved for this purpose by the Federal Government. These youngsters were training for some 430 different trades in 13 broad categories, although they were largely concentrated in relatively few of them. Moreover, sexual segregation occurs so that the bcys especially patronised 'male trades' such as motor mechanics, eletricians, machine fitters, joiners, masons, painters, gas and water fitters, salesmen, bakers and locksmiths. These 10 trades accounted for no fewer than 39 per cent of all apprentices. In the case of girls, the concentration in a few trades is even greater, with 58 per cent of all female trainees following one of seven trades: hairdressers, saleswomen, offic work, business women, doctor's or dentist's assistants, bank clerks, and retail shop assistants.

The specific training programmes which apprentices undergo are usually of between three and three-and-a-half years' duration, though a large number of occupations require only two years of training, and in some individual occupations training can be completed after one year. In addition, young people with above average school-leaving qualifications, and judged to be of superior learning ability, can have their training period shortened. Subject to the successful passing of exminations, training programmes culminate in qualifications as skilled or white-collar workers. The training which takes place in the employers'premises, which as we have seen comprises the greater part, is governed by a series of federallaws and regulations. Among the most important are the Vocational Training Act of 1969 which specifieds the basic legal conditions for the provision of on-the-job training, and the Vocational Training Promotion Act of 1981 which governs the planning of vocational training and the work of the Federal Institute of Vocational Training, which is part of Federal Ministry of Education and Science, and which, in collaboration with representatives of industry, business and trade unions, determines what skills and knowledge are required for each occupation. Thus, the BIBB's role is a key one in the *Dual System* is that, among other things, it provides a kind of 'clearing house' in which the various partners in the system-including the *Lander*, the employers and the trade unions—can hammer out agreements on vocational training matters. A very important part in the system is also played by private sector autonomous bodies known as Chambers of Industry and Commerce, Crafts, Agriculture, and certain professions, consisting of representatives of employers, employees and vocational school teachers. The chambers are 'responsible agencies' for vocational trainig and are autonomous, regional organisations to which all firms must belong. The most important chambers are the sixty-nine of industry and commerce and the forty-two of craft. They are responsible, at the end of the apprenticeship, for testing centrally both the vocational elements of the curriculum which are learned largely on the firm's premises, and also those general theoretical aspects learned in the vocational school which are of specific application to the apprenticeship concerned.

The curriculum which apprentices undertake consists of an initial period of broadly-based training lasting about a year, followed by specialist training appropriate to their place of work. Regulations governing curriculla for specifc trades are agreed upon by the major parties concerned and these are revised and brought up-to-date from time to time. They always include written and practical tests and, often, oral tests as well. A form of quality control derives from the fact that most chambers obtain standard examination papers from semi-commercial bodies set up for this purpose. The awards given by individual chambers are recognised nationally and are valid throughout the country.

The bulk of the costs of training within the *Dual System* are borne by the firms with whom trainees sign a contract which guarantees them employee status. These costs include those of providing instructors, training workshop, machines and materials, and the remuneration of the trainees. In 1985, for example, industry and business spent approximately 20 billion DM on this training. In recent years the amount of money spent by firms on vocational training has risen considerably. This is due partly to the increase in the number of trainees, partly to the need to provide more and better trained instructors and for trainees to spend longer periods in workshops, and partly because an increasing number of small firms are having to send their apprentices to interplant training centres. Both the Federal and the *Lander* governments have also been spending more money in an effort to persuade industry to provide more training places, especially for young people who are disadvantaged in some way, and to improve the quality of vocational training itself. In 1984, for example, they spent more than one-and-a-quarter billion DM on special programmes for pupils at vocational schools, while the Federal Institute of Labour spent over 3.7 billion DM on promoting vocational training on an individual and institutional basis.

6 Emergence of the New Vocationalism

Introduction

In this chapter, we outline the diverse and numerous factors that lie behind the emergence of new - and the reinforcement of some old - forms of vocationalism: what is meant by a vocational orientation in the education of young people, and why it has emerged. We do not, at this stage, differentiate between the settings - school, office, workshop, specialist college or whatever - since these factors are at work in all of them, and there are aspects of the responses which are common to all. Differences of course there are; they are considered in later chapters where a more detailed appraisal is made of the main theme of this chapter.

Setting the Scene

For reasons that are primarily economic, the years since the early 1970s have witnessed a major resurgence of interest in the vocational role of education and training in the personal and social processes of formation which are governed by such purposes as preparation for working life and occupational choice, and the matching of human capabilities to labour market needs and opportunities. This interest is part of the close attention being given to the conditions necessary to sustain growth in the modern economy. In the face of massive challenges to reorient and restructure, to achieve greater efficiency, to find new economic opportunities, and, more recently, to alleviate or forestall youth unemployment, countries have increasingly turned to education and training as an investment in the future. This has given a strong functional or instrumental tone to a great deal of the contemporary debate about education, whose purposes and procedures have always included vocational preparation, albeit often indirectly, usually in conjunction with other values both personal and social, and seldom in sufficient degree. Changes reflecting the redefinition of the vocational factor, ways of making it a more explicit aim of education and the transformation of the nature and conditions of work are all evident; these are occurring within enterprises, both private and public, in schools and colleges and in public policy. Notable, too, are the so-called new growth theories which single out research and development, education and training as crucial factors in economic growth and thereby provide a stimulus to researchers and policy-makers to identify key points for intervention, including a working life orientation in schooling.

Education in general has been coloured by the increased attention that has been given to its economic and its wider social utility. Of particular interest, however, is a distinctive movement of ideas, policies and practices which has emerged during the last quarter of the twentieth century. Known variously as the new vocationalism, preparation for working life, transition from school to work or simply as vocational or technical education and training, this movement has, in Britain and many other countries, been the source of significant and frequently controversial innovations in educational structures, content, methods and funding. A major challenge to much that is established in the education system, it has generated a growing volume of analysis and research, public policy initiatives, action in both the public and private spheres of education, training and employment-and sharp divisions among advocates and critics.

The initial focus of the new vocationalism in the 1970s and 1980s was on adolescents aged 14-18-at the point of transition from compulsory schooling to working life. Increasingly, as a response to demographic change and to shorter-term employment needs, the focus is widening to include continuing education and training for mature adults including re-entrants to the workforce. The initial stage, however, remains of great importance not least because it directly connects the all too frequently separate domains of schooling and general education with specialised vocational preparation and experience of working life. It is to this initial or transitional stage that the principal arguments of this book are addressed.

The different traditions—of general, school-based education with its roots in a culture of broad-based knowledge and understanding and of technical, vocational training with its origins in specific, employment related tasks and its preparation for work through work—are converging.

The diversity of interests involved, competing purposes and programmes and the pace of change in the working world, are sources of energy but also of uncertainty and confusion.

The very terminology, of 'educational', 'vocational', 'training', 'skill', 'competence', 'working life' and so on, has become fluid: definitions need to be operational and provisional, relative to and clarified in the context of particular programmes and inquiries. While consistency is not easy to sustain, we shall, in this spirit, treat 'education' as a comprehensive term for purposive, structured human and social formation, governed by intellectual and ethical principles, directed at knowledge, understanding and their applications and informed by a spirit of critical inquiry. 'Vocational' refers to those educational functions and processes which purport to prepare and equip individuals and groups for working life whether or not in the form of paid employment. 'Training' is task specific but nevertheless, in our usage, a part of education and subject to the values, criteria and principles which govern education processes generally; even though, as frequently used, its reference is to factual knowledge and unreflective skills. Obviously, those who control education, vocational preparation and training will in both policy and practice colour the interpretation given to these functions and processes. One of the most striking modern developments, affecting the vocational sphere as much as other aspects of education, is the emergence of new forms of control: the growth of parent power, of the influence of industry and commerce and of various partnership and collaborative procedures for decision-making.

Less common until recently in school systems, the partnership principles have been long established in technical and vocational education.

As we look back on some two decades of rapid growth and change in vocational education, we can identify both the major landmarks and the tasks that must be addressed if this transformation of ideas and structures is to take effect in soundly conceived practice. Much has been achieved, as a result of immense effort during a period of change unparalleled for the scale and intensity of commitment to reform of vocational education and training. After this extended period of innovation and experimentation it is also necessary, now, that we undertake something of an educational audit. To what extent has this vocationally oriented drive contributed to our broader educational practice and values? What have we learnt about the problems in vocational education and training and how best to overcome them? Why is there a continuing sense of unease about the direction of reform, a questioning of assumptions, values and of what has been achieved? These questions have acquired a fresh significance in light of the immense changes now under way in the general secondary and higher education sectors - changes which should be informed by the experiences of reform in vocational education and training as much as they will, in turn, impact upon it.

The rationale for the national vocational drive in Britain since the 1970s is multifaceted, but its main purposes have been clear and stark; to create and consolidate a comprehensive system of vocationally oriented education and training for all young people; and to bring education and training at the mid-adolescent stage into line with perceived requirements of the work environment. In turn these purposes reflect concern - concern about the state of the economy,its competitiveness, adaptability and potential for growth, concern about the capacity, unaided, of schools, colleges and undergoes substantial changes, and an overriding concern about the inadequacy of an education system which, for all the changes, remains unduly stratified and exclusive.

Education and training are, it has been proposed, to be perceived instrumentally and from a particular standpoint. Notwithstanding the efforts made, the resulting achievements, and the clear and valuable corrective provided by this national vocational drive, there is still risk of a cramped vision and an inadequate understanding of the place of the vocational dimension in a wider philosophy and system of universal, lifelong education. It is in the nature of a reform which, its full potential yet to be realised, runs the risk of over-determination by its narrower rather than its broader purposes and values. In Britain, at least, this is the contention of the critics who have been quick to seize upon the values underlying major government initiatives even more than the change strategies that have been adopted.

Major central governmental initiatives both within and outside the formal schooling and further education sectors have been the key factors in the new vocational drive. Industry and commerce have in varying degrees co-operated and there have been a number of joint ventures, but there is no doubt about the prime mover. A considerable diversity of patterns is evident in Britain as among the other industrialised countries and the British experience both contributes to and can be better understood - and perhaps better directed - when seen in this international context. Key elements in the newer British approaches are also more clearly seen and appreciated when set against a background of national history. The new vocationalism is unintelligible unless it is situated or contextualised in this way.

Vocationalism and the restructuring of employment

Vocationalisation of education includes, but goes beyond, training for a job or paid employment. On the one hand, it is a dimension of education for life, for living, of which work in some form is an all but universal attribute: 'vocationalism' is a process or activity, the imparting and the acquisition of broadly defined skills and knowledge believed to have a discernible relationship with the capabilities needed for productive work and required or expected of workers, now and in the future. This aligns 'vocationalism' with a philosophy of purposive activity designed to accomplish results and render service. On the other hand, vocationalism is a function, whereby the education system services the workings of the economy, deriving its purpose and rationale from some assessment of economic need and requirement, such as trained manpower for the labour market. Both dimensions draw attention to the fundamental importance of vocational education in any society. In doing so they remind us that a critical problem for Western societies has been the persistence of dualism-a disunity rather than a unity of relationships: mind and body, head and hand, leisure and work, theoretical culture and utility, superior and inferior occupations.

From its foundation, systematic, popular or public education has always had a vocational content and function, even if it has not been recognised as such. The new vocationalism is a critical movement - radical in the sense that new foundations are being put in place and new structures erected on them. The issue is not whether education should be vocational, but what vocationalism means in contemporary terms, what could count as adequacy or quality of vocationalism, and how well the vocational orientation is balanced with other purposes and values of education.

Even though some industrialised countries seem reasonably satisfied with their provision of vocational education and its orientation, the new vocationalism as an educational force has not been an isolated trend, limited to economies in trouble or those moving into what is now frequently, if rather loosely, described as the post-industrial era. Societies throughout the world are aware of a lack of synchrony between, on the one hand, human, societal and economic needs and, on the other, the processes of production and distribution of wealth. A classic example is the unresolved environmentalist debate between conservation and exploitation of natural resources. Another is the apparent inability of many governments, in both the industrialised and developing countries, to solve the chronic problems of large-scale youth and adult unemployment. Every central government and educational planner is, to at least some degree, concerned with the matching of manpower, or, rather educated and trained people, to the drive for economic growth. This is a drive which entails structural adjustment—that is, a restructuring not only of jobs but also of industrial and social relations and organisation.

Such restructuring necessitates an overview of the whole territory of vocational education and is perforce resulting in several different kinds of fusion. The number of fields of vocational and professional life has been reduced through job restructuring; professional associations and unions have amalgamated; the number of training 'lines' has been reduced through regrouping. As work itself becomes more highly organised globally and not only locally and nationally, more dependent on research and on advanced knowledge and refined sensibilities in workers more interactive in terms of both structures and relations, so do the domains of 'work' and 'education for work' become interactive. The corollary to the 'vocationalisting of education' is the 'educating of work'—its transformation into an educative culture. We are still at an early stage in this revolution, practice falling far short of what is technically and organisationally possible, let alone of advanced ideas.

Significant long-term, rather than short-term cyclical, changes in the nature and structure of jobs in industrialised countries have occurred over the last two decades. These long-term structural changes, as exemplified in the case of Britain, are acting to decrease the number of unskilled jobs available for young school-leavers, especially males, reduce full-time jobs generally, make greater us of sub-contracting, increase part-time temporary jo..s, demand multi-skilling of the existing labour force, and provide jobs requiring higher-level skills - that is, a more educated workforce. These structural changes in recent years have worked in the same direction as the cyclical downturn of the economy, exacerbating unemployment, especially among youth. Such long-term changes indicate that even the smaller youth cohorts of the next few years, allied with any significant upturn in general economic activity, will not fundamentally ameliorate employment prospects for the young unskilled.

The widespread development of global markets, especially, has changed the terms of competition in many product markets, notably those of large-scale manufacturing industry. Companies with strong national bases from which they export to other national product markets are being transformed into transnational companies with the world as their market and no particular national allegiance or single base. As a consequence, production can be transferred between or cascaded across countries, weakening the link between the level of product demand in a national economy and established levels of demand for labour. This trend has led to the lose of many unskilled and semi-skilled jobs in manufacturing in Britain as in other industrialised countries. Technology and economic globalisation pose a profound challenge to established national practices in allocating and organising work.

In parts of the service sector in Britain, particularly in the distribution, hotel and catering areas, increasing industrial concentration has occurred, with the consequent larger national and international companies adopting different systems of labour management and utilisation from those of the older family firms displaced in the process. A drop in full-time and increase in temporary part-time jobs has been quite marked in this sector in Britain. Employers have sought recruits with good interpersonal skills, as quality of client contact has become of key competitive concern.

In commerce the introduction of information technology, and in manufacturing information technology and advances in machine design to produce computer numerically controlled (CNC) machines, robots and flexible manufacturing systems, have worked to enable a smaller number of more highly skilled individuals to achieve a given output. From its retrospective review of member country labour markets in the 1980s, the Organisation for Economic Co-operation and Development (OECD) drew one basic conclusion: 'that more training and retraining will be required'. The issue is, however, not only a quantitative one, important as that is for an under-educated country like Britain, but one of form, content, relevance and quality.

Vocationalism: A worldwide trend

A broadly defined vocationalisation has been a common thread which runs across the education and, increasingly, the employment policies of every country, whatever its level of development, political system or geographical location. In the post-war era, it has been advanced under many shapes and forms depending on the ideology and economic system of each country, through such concepts as unity and diversity in the curriculum, career guidance and education, polytechnic and polyvalent education, work experience, multiskilling and pre-vocational and further education and training. Since the early 1970s there has been a powerful impetus as well in most, if not all, OECD countries towards vocationalisation of the curricula of basic and post-compulsory schooling and towards a multiplication of vocational training measures designed to bridge perceived gaps between educational provision and social and economic needs.

Such developments are not confined to the major industrialised economies. Many less industrialised countries have long been concerned with enlarging and updating the vocational dimension of the education systems they inherited from the colonial past, Strenuous efforts continue to be made to orient primary and secondary education towards meeting the perceived needs of adult working life and to adapt them to local and national development requirements, both economic and social, nowadays usually under the rubric of 'human capital formation' or 'human resource development policies'. At higher levels, the aim has been functional education within the framework of established development plans, again with the goal of raising the competence of the citizenry to the highest possible levels. Surveys and consultation meetings carried out under the auspices of the Commonwealth Secretariat, and under the Commonwealth of Learning, which has been established to foster and strengthen international collaboration in distance education among the 40-plus members of the Commonwealth of Nations, confirm the very strong interest in reshaping the education of the 14-16-plus age group to bring it into line with national development needs. Unesco, too, has sought to give a fresh impetus to its long-standing involvement in technical and vocational education by launching a project for the creation of an International Centre for Technical and Vocational Education. The language of 'enterprise culture' and the competence required of effective workers in such a culture has, too, emerged in the Asia-Pacific region of Unesco.

In the era of planned economies of the former COMECON countries, a commitment to the principle that labour is the fundamental source of human value was part of the declared ideology. The human capital theory in some form or other has indeed long and widespread support across political and ideology. The human capital theory in some form or other has indeed long had widespread support across political and ideological boundaries: Adam Smith and Karl Marx had much in common. The theme of education and training for productive work has for long played a significant part in the Central European countries as it has in other parts of the world. How far this will remain a focus following the recent and continuing political changes in these countries remains to be seen. Given the necessity and the widely declared aim of restructuring their economies, it is to be expected that the development of education and training in these countries will retain a very strong vocational flavour, albeit on somewhat different ideological promises.

The new vocationalism in several of the Western industrialised countries belonging to the OECD may be said to be rapidly following a direction which some other countries, from a variety of value positions, began to pursue many years earlier. Put in simpler terms, this may be expressed as a recognition of the fundamental importance in educational provision during the compulsory years of schooling of an explicit element of 'preparation for working life' and of the necessity for all youth, beyond the compulsory years, to have the opportunity of systematic training and of continuing general education.

It is important to realise that we are not witnessing an isolated phenomenon, one that has the fragility of a particular, transitory set of politico-economic circumstances. Dissatisfaction by certain employers and employer groups with the performance of the education system in some of its basic functional tasks may seem to be the immediate cause of this change, but to treat the trend as a mere reaction to what are often conflicting and somewhat superficial criticisms is to misconceive the fundamental transformations that are taking place.

The distinctively late twentieth-century global combination of economic growth, technological change, structural transformation of the workplace, democratisation and the universal quest for material betterment are among the factors of over-riding importance. How these factors are perceived—whether as deterministic of or interactive with educational values and processes—and the extent to which their importance is assessed by the different actors,both nationally and internationally, provide the dynamic for action, or, just as frequently, inaction or confusion. Thus whether or not employers perceive a skill shortage or inadequacy may be as much a function of work organisation and of other structural features such as financial management and industrial relations as of the outcomes of schooling. Moreover, there are wide differences in the employment sector with respect to technological applications and hence in the perceived need for 'technological literacy' and other skills. There is also the question of whether policy for vocational education is best directed-as much of it has been in Britain - at the lower skills echelon, the early school-leavers, or at the middle and higher skill levels. A greatly improved dialogue between the actors and more refinement of the categories of analysis used in research, interpretative literature and policy-making are necessary conditions for achieving more coherent and effective policies.

During the immediate post-war period, continuous economic expansion and full employment came to be considered normal in OECD countries, allowing for the cyclical fluctuations of the business cycle. In recent years they have remained stated objectives of national policy if muted by the determination to maintain a balance at the macro-level between potentially contradictory and destabilising trends. There is a growing recognition that countries do not merely trade their way out of difficulties or 'fix' their economies at the level of macro-policy; they must increasingly assure themselves of highly trained, flexible workforces. Moreover, these trained workforces need outlets for their talents, competence and energies: they need jobs. This is indeed a key element in the move towards the complementary micro-economic policies of structural adjustment. 'Structural adjustment' means, in effect, the reform of the socio-economic structures which inhibit or reduce the capacity of countries to pursue longer-term development goals and to relate to one another in mutually beneficial ways in the international environment of trade and exchange. Education and training are central to any programme of structural adjustment for the very obvious, if sometimes neglected, reason that it is upon the educated and trained capacity of the actors-the people-that the ability to restructure and to gain from its benefits depends.

We have, belatedly, entered the era where, as Bruce Raup and his co-workers long ago put it, 'the improvement of practical intelligence' is coming to be recognised as a primary policy goal. In this respect, we have indeed entered a new era. Whether conventional, full time, paid employment for all or practically all youth and young adults will continue to be delivered by the advanced economies is a moot point. It does not, however, vitiate the claims being made for ever higher levels of education and training, with preparation for work as one of the primary policy objectives.

This new 'education era' is characterised not only by a recognition of the need for what the OECD Ministers of Education referred to as a high quality of education and training for all. Comparability and transparency of credentialled knowledge and skills across national boundaries assume greater importance than even before in the new Europe; globally the spread and transferability of technology, of industrial and commercial organisations and the moves to establish agreed 'rules of the game' in international markets and trade are among the factors that are leading to a reappraisal of the vocational content and structures of education. Moves towards mutual recognition of qualifications throughout Europe are bringing additional pressure for both breadth and a restructuring of vocational qualifications in Britain. The age of self-contained national systems of vocational education and the attendant qualifications and certifications processes-however adequate they may have been in their own terms - has passed. While these propositions may receive assent in principle, their practical consequences are, however, far from clear.

Rising expectations of basic schooling

The forces for change-scientific, technological, economic, social, cultural-call for a renewal of policies for education and training, yet there is far too little understanding of the actual dynamics of these forces and agreement over just what changes in education are most needed. Nevertheless, in pursuit of long established goals relating to universal literacy, social participation and equity, Western countries, Japan and many developing countries have invested massively in education, throughout the whole of the post-Second-World-War era. This expenditure has assumed that economic benefit and other social goods would accrue in the short and the long term, although not necessarily directly.

From the inception of public education systems, the economic argument has been clearly reflected in investment in vocational education and training, however impoverished provision may have been in practice. Other predominant notions, dating back to the Enlightenment, have been that education is crucial in the formation of culture and the maintenance of social order and that it can contribute significantly to equity, social justice and material advancement. Nowhere is this doctrine more tellingly advanced than in the writings and actions of the eighteenth-century polymath, Benjamin Franklin. For Franklin, as for many who have followed him, the quest is for betterment of the human condition, and have followed him, the quest is for betterment of the human condition, and this includes the economic condition. But, in the particular rendition of the concept that Frankling gave, betterment has of necessity a component of universal, practical education whose utility was no less social than individual, no less material in its effect than intellectual and moral. Franklin's own life experiences and his benevolent utilitarianism naturally led him to incorporate preparation for gainful and socially useful employment in his educational schemes.

The new vocational thrust in Britain may seem a far cry from the reform schemes of Franklin and other philosophical minds of the Enlightenment. Of all the major, system-wide trends in contemporary education, it is potentially, if not actually, the most revealing in its contemporaneity and its messages for the future development of policies and programmes for the education system as a whole. Yet it is part of a living tradition in education which extends back, beyond the doctrines of the eighteenth century, to antiquity. The debate about vocationalism is a debate about the nature of education and the directions of the culture. Thus it is of far wider significance to all parts of the education system and for the future of British society than may seem the case at first glance. This is evident if we consider what has often been regarded an unduly narrow educational concern: job preparation.

One of the most serious problems in many countries is matching people to jobs, and jobs to people: positive labour market policies which address not only aggregate skill levels but identify targets for employment growth and ways of achieving those targets which include but cannot be confined to comprehensive education and training policies. Measures are needed to stimulate both demand and supply. The ability in industrially advanced countries to place young people in jobs, in the years up to the first oil crisis in 1973, meant that, on the quantitative side, there was no glaring mismatch between educational provision and social and economic needs. Inefficiencies in enterprises including poor selection and training policies and deficiencies in the quantity and quality of education were widely, if unwisely, tolerated. From the point of view of the individual and the state, failure at school was not necessarily the end of the line, because a person could always get an unskilled job and hope, may be, to progress from there. This is not to any that there was great public or professional satisfaction with education systems, but the job placement function of schooling, always a latent consideration, has become increasingly problematic.

In some parts of the community and in many countries. Even in times of high youth employment, there was a justifiable concern that school and colleges did not offer the type and quality of education which was relevant to the concerns of everyday life and working people. This may be a quantitative problem-insufficient numbers of candidates qualified for particular jobs, as has been the case in Germany-or a qualitative one-inadequately trained or prepared people for whatever jobs are available. In the United States, for example, as early as the late 1940s, advocate of 'life adjustment' education were critical of schooling for its failure to prepare young people for jobs and social participation. While this dissatisfaction and related concerns about schooling have not been ubiquitous, they have become powerful enough to generate major changes-of which the modern vocational movement is itself an example. The critique has extended with labour or employment ministeries adding their assessments of schooling to those made by the educators and the employers.

How have schools and educational policy responded to these critiques and to the challenge to reform? Among the OECD countries, educational reform has become a constant theme, not, to be sure, just as the consequence of economic concerns. In secondary education, for example, reforms have included extending the period of compulsory attendance, school structure. and organisation (for example, comprehensive schools, non-selective entry, mixed ability grouping), curriculum restructuring and renewal, improvements in teacher education and the monitoring and assessment of performance. Issues of social justice, equity, efficiency and a refined sensitivity towards children's needs have featured in these reforms. But so, too, has a quite definite understanding of the changing needs of the world of work.

In some countries, new structures of secondary education have been erected, with proposed vocational streams and qualifications that have equal status with the established academic stream. France provides a striking example, at least of the intention of equality. In other countries, previously separate vocational schools or streams have been integrated into mainstream schooling in the junior high school years, if not beyond. This move has, however, had the unintended consequence of disadvantaging students in the new practical and vocational stream at schools because of a tendency to assimilate that stream to the general, academic model of the traditional secondary school rather than to rethink the whole basis of secondary education.

In the face of these concerns, universal secondary education, charged with educating the entire population, has been challenged to excise traditions based on progressively weeding out those identified as unsuitable, rather than nurturning them; it has been expected to make itself attractive to all of its clients and to excite their interest. The consequence has been demand for a more effective curriculum, for learning more closely in tune with patterns of growth and the world in which the children live. Dissatisfaction with the perceived results of the attempts made to respond to this requirement was the first stage in the development of the current drive for relevance, of which the new vocationalism is a part. It was thus the move, first, towards a mass and then a universal system of secondary education which radically changed preconceptions about what this level of education was for. Thus was provided a dynamic for change internal to the education system whose effects are now strongly felt. This historic move, therefore, may be regarded as satisfying several of the conditions necessary for the emergence of the new vocationalism. It cannot be said, however, that secondary education in Britain, or indeed in other industrialised countries, has reformed itself to the extent needed.

Thus, not only exogenous factors in the wider society and economy but also factors internal to the school system at the secondary level have played a significant, if generally overlooked, part in the emergence of the new vocationalism. For a fuller account, however, we must consider the *interaction* of factors external and internal to the school. Several of these have already been noted, but to be reminded of the heterogeneous nature of these factors, in a country whose reform policies and strategies have had a worldwide impact, it is instructive to look back to events following 1957 when the Soviet Union launched the first Sputnik and triggered a wave of alarm in the United States, where the comprehensive secondary school had been the norm for decades.

'Life adjustment' education had been tried, as a way of making the comprehensive secondary school more relevant to its universal membership but had not produced the quality of performance expected. Many Americans felt threatened technologically, economically, militarily and even ideologically by the then Soviet Union - much as increasingly throughout the 1980s they felt a Japanese threat. In both instances, education was seen as having much of the responsibility and, as a result, became the object of substantial, external pressure for change.

It had seemed axiomatic that the best system would produce the best technology and Americans tended to assume that educational reform was a key to both. the role and quality of mathematics and science teaching in particular were targeted for attention. While international studies of school performance did not conclusively demonstrate that the American systems of education and training were interior to those of the then Soviet Union, they did, in addition to showing the extreme difficulty of comparing the objectives and performance of different education systems, give rise to considerable anxiety. It became evident, also, that while large-scale public education is financially onerous, it is extremely difficult to tell how cost-effective it may be. Whatever may be the conclusion on this point, criticism of the performance of American schooling has continued; reform has been set as a major goal of national policy and a vast industry of comparative educational analysis is developing. The American reform agenda extends to reversing the decline of the always marginal territory of vocational education.

Other factors in some Western countries, Britain included, led to the effectiveness of educational provision being questioned. That mass education systems were unable to eradicate inequality significantly in a short space of time was of particular concern in countries with large disadvantaged minorities and/or strong social democratic governments. There was and is consternation about rising levels of violence among young people. Should-or could-the mass education systems have prevented this from happening? With the expansion of secondary education to cover all age groups in most industrialised countries, numbers of youngsters appeared to derive very little advantage from it. When the world economy slipped into recession in the early 1970s, the incapacity of cash-hungry education systems to pay off in economic terms appeared to be completely confirmed, at least to the satisfaction of crusading interest groups and political parties. Economic recovery in the 1980s and the sustained growth cycle of that decade brought about not so much a restoration of confidence in education as a growing sense of the need for qualitative improvement and greater relevance to socio-economic demands. Anxieties previously in the background now came to the fore in the public mind. What was significant, however, was a vastly increased weight of public feeling and emphasis on accountability and tangible, measurable outcomes.

Effective preparation for the labour market can to rank high among such outcomes but, ironically, this occurred during a period when the youth labour market in many of the industrialised countries entered what is now widely believed to be terminal decline. It was not the mainly American concern about technological slippage but unemployment consequent on recession in the early 1970s, and now chronic in many countries, that intensified the demand for relevance and through this led to the demand for more and better vocational training, among other developments. The dream of full employment was shattered and this had much greater meaning to the average voter than the relative strength of the techno-economic systems of West and East. Though the shortage of jobs relative to demand was only indirectly, if at all, attributable to education system; failure at school now meant losing the chance of participating in the labour market, a real factor in everyday life. Monetary inflation was accompanied by qualifications inflation. The value of the currency slipped, not uniformly to be sure since business cycle and market iuctuations have at some times benefited engineers or builders, at other times the tourist and finance sectors; but even the university degree steadily lost its commanding position.

In many sectors, employers pick and choose and, with increasing frequency, a basic standard of 'relevant' education is a necessary, if not a sufficient, condition for any kind of employment. At the same time, a constant refrain from employers is the need for a high level of skills.

Even though, in many occupations, there is no close link between the content of qualifications and the tasks to be performed in the workplace, the screening function of the qualifications process remain active.

Socio-economic systems have come to be perceived as having failed youngsters, as much as the other way around. Such failure was one symptom of a growing malaise compounded of crime, violence, poverty, family break-up and urban decay. What could education do? The mismatch between youth expectation, wants and demands fuelled, if not generated, by material plenty in high growth economies and the readiness and ability of youth to be gainfully employed was reduced to a 'skills gap'. Close the gap, and by a feat of astonishing simplification, many of the social ills would evaporate. From another perspective, it was necessary to make substantial changes to the education systems so that they became attractive to young people. Not least for political reasons, youth needed to be kept off the labour market but in a constructive way, through a form of tutelage which would be redesigned to prepare them realistically for new adult working roles and a generalised social responsibility. Educational institutions, therefore, have felt obliged to rethink their mission, strategies, organisation and curricula.

A skilled workforce for the future

Future economic prosperity and social 'health' and stability have thus come to be seen, as never before, depend on a putative labour force that in its entirety is educated, skilled, motivated and aware. Upon the foundations of a strengthened basic education, a superstructure of vocationally oriented, work-preparatory education and training needed to be erected. The debates on technological change, on international competitiveness and social order, have moved from the fear of job losses to the new kinds of employment opportunities that are being or need to be opened up-to the educated and trained, not the unskilled. The structure of everyday life, being transformed mainly as a consequence of the impact of new technologies in information, communication, production and distribution, is being seen as a kind of lodestone. the emergence of new industries. notably in the service and high knowledge-base sectors, together with the growing acceptance that conventional, full-time, paid employment of youth will not form part of the future employment pattern of industrial countries, indicate that education and training need a new direction. Training for a specific occupation or even clusters of occupations is being supplanted by strategies for 'generalisable skills' or general transferable education, a theme on which there has been a great volume of discourse.

Changing levels of expertise and work organisation in industry, commerce and the public services call for a dynamic and competent population. Yet, in most of the industrialised countries there is a necessity-not always acknowledged—to face up to the harsh realities of competing from a base which is underdeveloped in relation to the new technologies and to the capacity of some trading partners. Disenchantment with economic theories of full employment and optimum growth has accompanied a questioning of the modern mechanism to maintain satisfactory levels of wealth and distributive welfare. Education and training, among other areas, naturally have come under scrutiny. Both old-fashioned and futuristic ideas have been readily examined for seams of sense. The results have not always borne witness to either common sense or a depth of understanding. Interpretations of the classical thinkers have at times been extremely one-sided: Adam Smith's economics, for example has been grossly decontextualised with a resulting '[im] balance between the sacred and the secular'.

In the most general sense and in an age when the sacred is co-opted, compartmentalised and packaged, a highly secularised education has come to be regarded somehow as able to help overcome unemployment and pull the economy out of recession. In other words, education has to show what it is 'good' for in purely instrumental terms. But it is reasonable to ask whether the 'remedies' satisfy even the instrumental and secular requirements, let alone the need human beings and societies have for the moral, intellectual and spiritual riches of the 'sacred'. In seeking greater relevance and utility, more precision and applicability, educators must confront the charge of reducing the complex processes of human growth and development to instruments in the service of limited and ephemeral ends, or of powerful socio-economic interest groups.

This risk is perhaps most apparent in educational responses to technological change. These often appear as adaptations to inexorable forces rather than intelligent and creative use of a resource. Technological advances are a consequence of the 'push' from the progress of science and the 'pull' from growth-based economies. The consequence are manifold if very uneven as between countries, regions and different sectors of the population. The 'pull' becomes ever more salient as 'policy' concerns dominate the funding of scientific research and economic globalisation proceeds. 'Technological innovation has been a key weapon of international competition'. Among the most significant of these implications for a system of universal education has been that fewer people are required in the manufacturing process and of those fewer people, the need for the unskilled—a traditional resource for manufacturers - is evaporating as micro-electronics-based technologies become ever more pervasive. Robots are replacing the unskilled on automobile assembly lines, while the skilled minds and hands of specialist print workers are being bypassed as wholly new technologies are brought on stream. Innumerable school-leavers find themselves unemployed, not only because of fewer jobs, but also because they are not adequately prepared for the work that is being done on the shop floors and in those service and knowledge-based industries where some expansion is taking place. The quasi-permanent surplus of labour which rapidly emerged in most countries during the world recession of the early 1970s has been thus aggravated by technical progress including the globalisation of business. This has given yet more force to the vocationalist thrust, fuelling a perception in some quarters that education systems are failed or inadequate instruments which do not meet their clients' essential needs. The felt need for highly trained people has grown concurrently.

In the recent years, the effect of demographic change, to which we have already aluded, has brought a new element into the situation. Smaller age cohorts in most industrialised countries are now moving through the secondary schools; and the late 1980s witnessed an important shift from concerns about youth unemployment as such, a 'manageable cost', to greater competition by employers for the skilled worker, hence greater interest in the skills that are required and in the skills-jobs matching process. Demography is a dynamic major factor in the new alignment-of education, training and employment-not only with respect to the fluctuating proportion of school age students but with reference also to an ageing population.

Uncertainty about national economies and institutions in the region of the Pacific basin has been, since the 1960s, a growing source of concern in Western societies. Japan constitutes a serious challenge to all the other industrialised countries: its economic growth scarcely checked by recession in the 1970s, having ridden, seemingly with ease, the new technological tide, and in the 1980s amassed enormous trade surpluses which in the 1990s are, while still growing, placed in investment projects around the world. the rapid economic progress of the group of newly industrialising countries of Singapore, Malaysia, Korea, Taiwan, Hong Kong and Thailand, is further evidence of the vitality of this major world region. Many countries, not least Britain, are fearful of sliding into a state of relative, long-term under development, from which it would be difficult to climb back. There is no doubt that, even as the Japanese economy seems to falter, this sentiment of losing the race-much more powerful, but similar to that felt in the United States after Sputnik was launched, in the late 1950s-will continue to spur nations to seek reform of their education and training systems, to set goals for them and to pursue these energetically. Although the challenge of the new ponds and economics of Eastern and Central Europe is still in the form of a massive dependency relationship with the Western economies, in time they, too, will become a significant part of the internationally competitive environment. With strong - if historically distorted - education and training systems, these countries will, in the future, be part of the international process of standard-setting, the outcome of which no country will be able to ignore.

A reconstructed system of work-oriented education and training, broadly defined, forward-looking, relevant to perceived social and economic needs and grounded in international as well as national socio-cultural realities, means greater emphasis on things operational or perceived as such: the technical, the scientific, the productive, the instrumental, the relevant and the practical. Education of this kind is expected to 'produce the goods', to be accountable, many of its outcome measurable and its particularities concerned in the experiential domain of the everyday world. Concrete and effective, with specific stress on employable skills and the work ethos, such a form of education might seem to have an easy passage to the heartland of national policy-making and finance. This has indeed been the case in Britain since the 1970s. It is reasonable, however, to ask just what it means to be 'relevant' and 'practical' in an age of increasing scientific, technological and more generally intellectual sophistication. Moreover, it a age of ever closer ties between nations where the context of 'application' and 'relevance' is the product of a vast interplay of dynamic forces. High levels of cognitive development, of social knowledge and competence and the ability to function effectively in complex, changing life environments will better serve the demands of 'relevance' and 'practicality' than tradition notions of technical skill.

Practical relevance in schooling

The new vocationalism in the developed world has some of its deepest roots in this ideal of practical relevance: applicable knowledge and skills. 'Applicable', however, is ambiguous and it is frequently unclear as to whether this is intended to mean 'here and now' or general applicability in a fluid situation whose future is scarcely predictable. 'Practical' has innumerable connotations and is always relative to ends and purposes and to the state of material development. Since educational ends and purposes relate the performance of specific tasks to such criteria as the testability of knowledge, critical reflection and the growth of understanding, the 'practical' and the 'relevant' are neither self-evident nor uncontestable.

In a generic sense, however, to be practical is to be capable of performing the task at hand - whether that task is designing a micorchip, planning a scheme of urban transport or carving a scroll to replace a decayed capital in a medieval cathedral. Whether such capabilities are 'relevant' is a question whose answer takes us beyond an analysis of the immediately presented end to a consideration of the significance and value of the enterprise being undertaken. From an educational standpoint, 'practical relevance' refers *both* to quite specific capabilities and to principles of procedure, concepts, ideas and skills that are generalisable, capable of application in varied and changing circumstances and able to be built upon, developed and extended through acquired knowledge, experience and further systematic studies.

Standard academic education usually claims the latter, more general qualities. Historically, it has, in considerable measure and for particular groups of students, lived up to the claim. As an instrument of universal education, let alone specific training in the first sense of 'practical relevance', it is, nevertheless, from this perspective seen to be founded on disciplines and methods which are adapted neither to the needs of large numbers of individual children, nor to the general requirements of society and the economy. This is not surprising; the academic is part of foundation of universal education and makes no claim to address all of the elements of a comprehensive system of education and training. Traditional academic schooling, structured according to theoretical disciplines of knowledge and regulated by a narrow regimen of tests and examinations, is, however, overly geared to developing only that slice of the pupil population which happens to respond in the right way at the appropriate time. Mass primary and secondary education are frequently accused of not stretching children enough. On the one hand, academic elitism and its social-cultural correlates are too exclusive; on the other, attempts to produce a truly universal system of basic schooling have been only partially successful. Schooling is on the march: it is not yet clear about its new destination.

These changes reflect a variety of pressures for curricula and approaches to teaching and learning which, at one and the same time, prepare effectively for adult and working life and are reasonably demanding forms of well-structured general education for every individual chiid. Most British teachers and educators, harking back to the 1944 Education Act, would probably argue that these objectives have long been intended to be an integral part of provision. We can agree that they are, but the debate is-and for a long time has been-about the extent to which they have been, and how best they can be, achieved. What kind of person is it who is well prepared for active adult and working life, how are the necessary qualities to be developed and who is to be in control of the process? The language of the debate may be new, but these are perennian questions. It would be a mistake to suppose that educators have avoided them. It is, more than anything else, the rapid change in the wider socio-economic and cultural environment that accounts for the tensions and the difficulties in finding new solutions. Addressing these tensions and the attendant difficulties, educators and other analysts have identified competences—such as a broad range of 'entrepreneurial' qualities which set new targets for curricula, pedagogy, assessment and certification. We discuss these in greater details subsequent chapters.

Much of the emphasis on practical relevance is directed towards improving basic competence. 'Competence', like 'practical relevance', is a term that lends itself to an excessive preoccupation with the immediacies of the work environment. The competence we have in mind is of a more strategic nature: an ability to meet the immediate requirements of the working world, coupled with flexibility, openness, creativity and the capacity to identify and solve problems, to manage change and to continue learning.

Can we infer that society in its demands for a more practical and relevant education is well informed or that the media accurately reflect considered public perceptions? We are doubtful and point to a divergence of opinion about just what kinds of competence are of most value. Movements in most countries aim to identify the skills that are deemed to be essential to master and to ensure that these are learned at school. But 'skill', in splendid isolation - or compounded with 'multi', 'flexible formation', 'transferable', 'generic', 'high level', etc - is yet another of those ambiguous, question beging terms which abound in the policy statements, programme plans, innovative projects, conferences and the literature of vocational and, increasingly, the whole of education. It has the seductive quality of appearing logical - an outcome of precise analysis of, for example, the relationship between preparation and manufacture and the roles of designer and operator in precision engineering. 'Skill' is, therefore, 'practical', 'relevant', a means of linking schooling/training tasks with real work, with life, of focusing action on the attainable and the measurable. But, apart from the dysfunctions that occur in the manufacturing process, new technologies must be integrated, work organisation changes are needed, industrial relations issues affect task definition. 'Skill' needs to be contextualised and analysed with relation to other qualities both active and dispositional, such as 'knowing', 'valuing', 'intending', 'willing'. Attempts to enumerate skills, to describe and articulate and to teach and acquire them independently of content, context and relations represent a chimera, the pursuit of which is costly and frustrating.

More mature and informed assessments of the needs of youth and society are needed to replace the shrill and often naive advocacy of 'skills' in vocational education and 'the basics' in the earlier years of schooling. They call for a reformulation of the curriculum of primary and secondary schools around a well-constructed 'core' of fundamental and essential learnings with the aim of making school attractive and stimulating to the intelligence and aptitudes of its primary clients, the children. We shall argue, also, that the continuance of a framework of broadly defined core learnings into the years of late adolescence is more appropriate than the quest for either specific or generic vocational skills.

Young people are not, of course, oblivious to these debates and discussions. Closer attention needs to be paid to their views and aspirations. Educators accustomed to expression, find it difficult to listen, to inform themselves. Youth tends to feel that education is not preparing them for their future, whether in the narrower or the broader sense just defined. An influential OECD publication reported a follows:

Young people are especially critical of the relationship between school and work. They believe that the schools are divorced from 'life' and 'life's occupations', and that they are mostly concerned with the next level of education. Secondary school-leavers, therefore, get short shrift.

Being divorced from 'life', of course, is not the same as 'failing to prepare for work'. Preparation for work is indeed a function of schooling, but it is not the only one and nor is it reducible to narrow, task-specific training whether work- or school-based. While many studies indicate an alienation of youth from the prevailing mores and values of society, it is not sensible to pigeon-hole youth as a disaffected generation which will, ultimately, 'settle down'. There is a gap between the perceptions and values of youth and those of society at large which should be a source of concern. Employers' views vary more from enterprise to enterprise than from country to country. In areas where they have few links with the education system, many tend to complain that young people are inadequately prepared either to step into jobs or into induction programmes. A majority of employers across the world seek to take on personnel with ever high educational qualifications. In its forward-looking 1989 report, the Confederation of British Industry's taskforce on vocational education and training, for example, set 'world class targets' for Britain's skills revolution:

> The practice of employing 16-18 year old without training leading to nationally recognised qualifications must stop. These national attainment targets... would make qualifications at craftsman, technician and their equivalent levels in service industries the norm.

The tendency to prefer the more schooled concords, of course, with observations that the educational qualifications of those holding jobs seem to be influenced more by the supply of qualifications than by the needs of jobs. Taking the uncertain link between jobs and qualifications along with the informal preferences for the universally increasing supply of the more schooled yields an expectation that the formal minimum qualifications for jobs will inexorably rise, independently of changes in the nature of jobs. As so it has been found in virtually every country examined, industrialised or developing.

These assertions are, nevertheless, debatable. That they are being made at all indicates that there are indeed problems of both content and form in newer vocational educational initiatives which have their repercussions in the multiplication of credentials. The very fact that universal basic education in the developed world is now taken for granted has raised expectations about the 'raw material' of the labour market and set new requirements for the next stage: upper secondary, apprenticeship, on-the-job training, and so on. It is, of course, entirely reasonable that the huge expenditure on compulsory education and the many hours spent in the classroom should be justified by satisfactory levels of skill, ability and understanding among the vast majority of young people. It is also obvious that public authorities must develop policies, deploy resources and otherwise foster action to strengthen and improve the quality of education at this next stage. However, there are still far too many employers who resist the idea that they, too, have a responsibility for the training and education of their workforce, thereby reinforcing the all too prevalent belief that education and training are a cost but not an investment.

The demand for a relevant school curriculum, with an established central body or core of learning, cannot of course be illegitimate. Nor can there be objections, in principle, to the building of a superstructure of qualifications and credentials. What is contentious is what is to be deemed relevant, what that core should be, how and where it should be taught, how it should be encoded for purposes of assessment and validation, who should decide and who should pay, and what pathways into further and higher education, work and adulthood should follow. These questions have set a large part of the agenda of change in education in recent years. High up among the answers is a set of these about vocational education and training both within and beyond the school.

7 Vocational Initiatives for Schools and Colleges

Introduction

Although the Youth Training Scheme (YTS) has been the spearhead of much of the employment-led rethinking of pre-vocational and vocational education, it was part of a larger and wider reappraisal. The more far-sighted, and not only among the vocational educators, had for decades recognised the inadequacies of provision and its increasing disjunction with the changing needs of young people and society at large. It was not only the Manpower Services Commission (MSC) which identified the need and took action. Ideas and proposals for the reform of curricula and examinations for upper secondary and further education (FE) have been abundant. Likewise in the latter part of the compulsory period of schooling the vocational thrust has been a powerful force for change at the level of the schools themselves.

Starting with the activities of the Further Education Unit (FEU), which has been the leader of the further education as distinct fro the industry employment wing of the reform movement, we consider next a series of initiatives and propcsals for strengthening the vocational role of the school and further education systems. These and other developments demonstrate the scale and diversity of activity proceeding under the banner of new vocationalism. Whether, taken together, they constitute the coherent and adequately comprehensive reform that is needed is, however, questionable. The outstanding, unresolved issue is the future of a system of secondary education, the pinnacle of which is the unreconstructed A level examination. The FESU brought considerable influence to bear on the new vocationalism, as the MSC freely acknowledged. Its ideas were, however, based on rather different presuppositions from those of the MSC. The FEU, established in 1977 by the secretary of State for Education and Science, was charged with the task of making possible a more co-ordinated and cohesive approach to curriculum development in further education. It soon began to publish documents designed to stimulate discussion and policy and to participate in a number of demonstration projects. Clearly identified with the established further education sector (schooling model), although lacking power or resources to commission pilot projects or national schemes on the scale needed, its impact on policy, strategic thinking and practice has been considerable.

In June 1979 the FEU published its influential and often reprinted report, *A Basis for Choice*. This seminal work surveyed the range of full-time pre-employment courses available for 16-plus pupils who were entering further education after leaving school but without specific vocational or academic commitments. The FEU concluded that the existing provision lacked both co-ordination and a nationally recognised framework, an observation which, while it caused to great surprise, was widely endorsed as highlighting a major weakness in the national system. In order to promote the rationalisation and effectiveness of the numerous existing and proposed courses, the report recommended a unifying curriculum structure in the new form of a set of criteria which present and future schemes might satisfy. The objectives were defined as flexibility, transferability and currency, themes that were to recur throughout the 1980s. The real importance of *A Basis for Choice* is that, in quite simple terms, it provided policy-makers and practioners alike with a clear sense of the directions that should be pursued to overcome the widely agreed deficiencies.

Many of the ideas it advanced were taken up in the design of the YTS. Its weakness, or rather that of the system of which it was a part, lay in the inadequate policy and power structure for effective decision-making in post-16 education in Britain.

The schemes envisaged by the FEU were, like the YTS, intended for a wide range of ability but the FEU had in mind a distinct, school/college-based target group. It recommended provision.

> for young people who enter further education after leaving school and who something other than CCE studies or programmes preparing them for specific occupations.these mainly one-year courses are intended for young people of averageability and attainment who may be vocationally uncommitted at the start but who wish to develop an informed orientation while keeping their employment and further education options open.

The FEU astutely pointed straight towards one of the principal weaknesses in national policy and provision.This target group might be thought of as a parallel to the YTS trainees, but with this major difference: that they could continue a form of general education, within the environment of the formal education institution. These were among the students the authors of the Newsom Report, *Half Our Future*, had in mind when, in the 1960s, the effects of longer periods of full-time schooling for all were being debated nationally. They were to be the target the numerous proposals and initiatives to reform the middle and upper years of secondary schooling and curriculum and assessment procedures for use by schools and college.

One purpose of the proposed new course was to offer provision positively designed for the needs of the target group. The authors of *A Basis of Choice* drew attention to the number of post-16 one-year O level courses which, in spite of an apparently high failure rate, continued to attract pupils without a definite job or job destination, presumably because of the perceived usefulness or 'currency' of the General Certificate of Education (GEC). While the then prospective substitution of the General Certificate of Secondary Education (GESE) for the GCE promised to reduce wastage in the form of outright failure, it was seen as likely to render one-year repeat courses an even less fulfilling activity. As Pauline Green put it in 'A new curriculum -....., the concept of a new course could be

> seen as an exciting opportunity to provide educationally worthwhile experiences of students informs expressly designed to meet their needs, rather than:

— their repeating earlier 'failure'(re-take CSEs)

— attempting academically unsuitable courses which had never been designed for 'them' (O level) or:

— being 'dumped' into low-level, unrespected courses which delimited future opportunities.

The FEU report does not, in any global way, examine an age group, or deal with national provision. It puts under a microscope the existing arrangements for a defined clientele - that is, non-specific vocational preparation for 16-plus students with limited but varying academic success and inclination. This is a clientele that has always fallen into the interstices between the categories and differentiated schemes that have formed the staple of national policy and provision. A merit of the FEU thinking is the recognition of a specific target group whose needs command attention by virtue of past failures of policy and yet can be clearly addressed. By way of caution, however, it should be recalled that the aim of the post-Second-World-War reformers in implementing the 1944 Act was to provide, through separate secondary modern and technical schools, an alternative of equal value to the grammar schools. Eventually, this system of separate and supposedly equal strands was abandoned in favour of comprehensive schools. We have already said, but it bears repeating in this context, that one of the crucial, unresolved issues in the 16-plus debate is the quality and acceptability of the several alternatives now offered to those not proceeding through the GESE to A levels. Due in very large part to the legacy of separate elements and the status monopoly enjoyed by an A level system which is quite explicitly tailored to meet the needs of a small minority, Britain as yet lacks a coherent framework of education for those aged 16 and over. Especially in relation to the A level issue, policy, while clear enough, is inadequate in relation to requirements for the majority.

To return to the endeavours of the FEU, we can, with them, acknowledge the undesirability of simply adding to a plethora of existing courses. The FEU objective has been to substitute something more useful (functional) in the eyes of students, parents and employers. In view of this objective it was necessary to provide a balance between something general (because uncommitted to a vocation) and something regarded as useful in a future job; and between something nationally recognisable as a qualification and locally appropriate, and which took into account labour market characteristics. This sensible approach required a combination of national criteria and local flexibility, to easy in practice to achieve. Most important for the longer term, the FEU, unlike the MSC, accepted that the existing structure of further education institutions should be the starting point and provide the framework for action. This is a fundamental point. The MSC in advancing the YTS, started with a deficiency model - deficient content and pedagogy, deficient structures - and sought to remedy both by setting up its own, new programmes which would be (largely) independent of the existing school/college system. The FEU, however, took as its starting point the experience and potential of the existing system and argued for evolutionary change with that system as the base of operations.

Acknowledging its limitations and defects, the FEU nevertheless has consistently taken the view that reform from within was the more desirable course to follow.

In many ways, the FEU's assumptions were realistic and cost effective, and better grounded in the deep structure of assumptions about what is appropriate provision, than the grand strategy of the MSC. On the other hand, without that grand strategy, neither the penetrating critique nor the necessary mobilisation of resources that have characterised the new vocationalism would have occurred.

In the FEU proposals, colleges would determine the curriculum on a local basis with the help of agencies such as the Careers Service, MSC Area Boards and local education authorities. The need for focus would be met by a common area of studies, to be too job-specific would be inappropriate, so various combinations of common core, vocational and optional studies would be made available. They could be achieved is a number of ways. Colleges might group courses around their existing departments such as 'hotel and catering', 'building and construction' or 'the caring professions'; or around groupings of skills cutting across these divisions; or around local industries.

While the FEU was not concerned with a full-blown national plan, it stressed the advantages to be gained from rationalisation of courses and in particular from national validation. Mention was made of the argument contained in the report by Garnett College, *One Year Pre-employment Courses for Students Aged 16-Plus: a Survey of Provision in*

Colleges of Further Education, that the proliferation of courses is one of the major factors working against their recognition and perceived usefulness to students. Emphasis was to be placed upon assessment and the provision of a nationally recognised award available to students who successfully complete a validated course. This is a sign of the spread of the determination, already discernible in the MSC and the Department of Education and Science (DES), for clarification, rationalisation, centralisation and hence control of qualifications, which appears to be an essential feature of the new vocationalism. The important issue, still unresolved, is whether this will result unsterile tidying up, a further large concentration of power at the national level, or in increasing recognition and currency for a range of useful qualifications.

The quest for new 16-plus qualifications

This is not the place to recount the long, frustrating and still in conclusive saga of proposals and attempted reform of curricula and examinations for 16- to 18/19-years-old remaining in full- or part-time school or college education. There have been many studies of and commentaries on this unedifying episode of contemporary educational history. The continued dominance of the GEC A level examinations, designed for a small minority of the age group and geared towards the single subject and joint honours degree programmes of the British universities, have been one factor but not the only one, militating against a fundamental restructuring. The Schools Council for Curriculum and Examinations, the Committee of Vice-Chancellors and Principles, the DES and the examining bodies have been among those essaying major reforms. The successful combination, at 16-plus, of the previously separate routes of GCE O levels and Certificate of Secondary Education, in the form of the GCSE, is one of the few examples of a major reform in this arena that was carried through to successful implementation and even it has been under attack for allegedly 'jeopardising standards'.

Among the key reference points in the establishment of new 16-plus qualifications is the construction by the National Council for Vocational Qualifications and General National Vocational Qualifications. The NVQs and GNVQs are the source or expression of criteria for accrediting qualifications to pre-determined levels. Although not in themselves qualifications, the NVQ/GNVQ frameworks are designed to have a powerful impact on courses and qualifications. The cases of the Certificate of Pre-vocational Education and its successor the Diploma of Vocational Education, are interesting in this respect.

Certificate of pre-vocational education and its successor

The FEU has not been without influence in the quest for new qualifications that respond to changing realities. In response to *A Basis for Choice* the DES took a decision in favour of a new 17-plus qualification, the Certificate of Pre-vocational Education, thereby declaring its intention to make headway in one of the most intractable areas of British educational polity, namely the territory that lies between O level and A level. This qualification, as it emerged from the thickets of educational practices, policies and politics, soon too on a form both narrower and more instrumental than the FEU seems to have envisaged in its consideration of alternatives. It and its proposed successor, the Diploma of Vocational Education, are part of a lengthy, inconclusive saga dating to the Crowther Report which enshrined the specialist, academic subject as the key to post-16 school curriculum and examinations.

In May 1983 the joint Board for Pre-vocational Education was set up by the Business and Technician Education Council and City and Guilds of London Institute at the request of the Secretary of State for Education in England and Wales. The Board was 'to establish a system of pre-vocational education on a national basis including a 17+ qualification' and to have new schemes introduced in schools and colleges from September 1985. The proposals, circulated to all those concerned as *The Certificate of Pre-vocational Education: Consultative Document*, aimed to meet the needs of about 100,000.

16 year olds of all abilities who would benefit from a further year of full-time education but who require a programme of learning and development neither conventionally academic nor purely vocational to help them prepare for adult life and work.

The courses should be 'demonstrably relevant to the needs of young people is emerging adults and prospective employees' and the curriculum should facilitate

Not only the acquisition of knowledge and analytical and critical skills, but also constructive and creative activity which involves putting ideas into practice, making, doing and organizing.

The CPVE programmes, as described in the document, should incorporate features which by then were becoming staple inputs in school and work-based vocational innovations:

— a balance of core, vocational and additional studies;

— learning through practical experience;

— planned work experience;

— provision for careers education, guidance and support;

— involvement of young people in the planning, organising and assessment of their learning.

The framework for the certificate contained three major components: the common core; the vocational studies; and the additional studies. Intended to take up 60 percent of course time, the ten defined core areas were: personal and career development; communication; numeracy; science and technology; skills for learning, decision-making and adaptability; practical skills; social skills; and creative development.

The vocational studies were to be based upon clusters of activities which have a common purpose and related learning objectives and were included because they:

(i) are relevant to young people and may therefore enhance motivation:

(ii) provide the focus for the development of the required core skills;

(iii) provide for development of broad vocational skills to appropriate standards;

(iv) provide an important basis for progression into employment, further education and training.

Standards of attainment were to be linked with these nationally agreed for entry into employment and initial and continuing training, with assessment based on a variety of performances.

The additional studies 'provide encouragement and opportunity for young people to complement their core and vocational studies with other activities relevant to their own particular interests, capabilities and aspirations'. The additional studies were an optional element, to use up to 25 per cent of course time, designed to meet individual needs and interests within the curriculum and might lead to additional qualifications.

The first CPVE programmes started in 1985 and the first certificates were awarded in 1986. The envisaged character of CPVE as a curriculum development can be explored in intentions expressed in various public documents. In government White Papers *Training for Jobs* and *Education and Training for Young People*, its is referred to in passing under the heading of developments within education which play a part in equipping young people for work. *Better Schools* stresses the tiding up role of the CPVE, which

> is intended to replace a range of existing courses including the pre-vocational courses of

the CGLI, BTEC and the Royal Society of Arts, and the Certificate of Extended Education offered by most CSE and GEC Boards.

To think of CPVE merely as 'tiding up' is, however, to overlook its relationship with the principles outlined in *A Basis for Choice* are a reminder of the strong conviction, during the period when the YTS was attracting substantial resources and publicity, that education and training, general and specific preparation for working life and adult roles can and should be combined with in comprehensive post-16 programmes in which formal education can collaborate closely with the workplace. As school participation rates rise, the impetus for a separate, YT type of training diminishes and the A level system retains its hold, the need for the thinking and planning that resulted in the CPVE will become ever greater, but it will need to be considerably developed beyond the rather circumscribed limits of the initial formulation.

A Basis for Choice did not attempt to address the full range of educational opportunities available to all 16- or 17-year-olds and the CPVE was limited in its potential audience. Neither was part of an explicit, overarching policy designed to clarify structures and co-ordinate provision.

The authors of *A Basis for Choice* 'considered that a common core of learning was an important ingredient for courses and recommended a core which it described as not new but...derived from knowledge of existing good practice'. Recognition of the value of courses would, in their view, require an identifiable core of learning in and between courses, which was nationally validated, recognised as educationally sound, and which guaranteed certain levels of competence in basic skills in those who gained a certificate. The criterion of transferability carries implications for the nature of these core studies, as does the need for flexibility and the desirability of a vocational focus.

The claim for a link between the acquisition of competences needed for survival in an increasingly technological but ill-defined work context and a broad framework of common core leanings is exhibited in the Technical and Vocational Education Initiative, YTS and CPVE alike. In the CPVE, the common core contribution is described in terms of objectives, learning opportunities and methods of approach to teaching and learning. It is based mainly on the apparent advantages of blurring subject boundaries and avoiding jerky transitions and/or unnecessary repetitions and on the much stressed integration of core and vocational studies. At its inception, the CPVE as a whole—core and vocational studies—was intended, among other things, to 'assist the transition from school to adulthood by further equipping young people with the basic skills, experiences, attitudes, knowledge and personal and social competencies required for success in adult life including work'.

As in the YTS, its was also expected to promote the acquisition of 'process skills' such as 'those of analysis and problem-solving, social skills, personal qualities such as resilience, autonomy and responsibility'; and the capacity to transfer competences from one situation to another. Again, as in YTS core skills, the common core was intended to be used as a checklist against which the performance of individual young people must be matched in order for starting points and learning programmes to be agreed.

Throughout the Consultation Document, emphasis was placed on personal attainment recorded in individual *profiles* together with certification for all who completed the course and combined with validation to national criteria. Thus the award aspired to embody achievements in 'core and vocational studies with an indication of their highest levels reached where appropriate, together with a statement of the context within which the skills were demonstrated'. The blueprint contained all the then 'acceptable' elements - reflection of individual needs, recording of achievement, certification for all who complete - yet it promised to offer levels of achievement, quality control and recognition and currency for the award.

From this overview of aims and structural features, it is clear that the plan for the CPVE, while locating it firmly in the heart land of the new vocational thinking, envisaged a broad range of educational values and procedures. It was to be, in a sense, the education system's vocational showpiece for the 16-plus age group. It is not our purpose to attempt to assess the efforts made to implement the CPVE and the various kinds of resistance both direct and indirect that it encountered. Despite proving popular with staff and students, less than a decade after its introduction it had suffered the fate of many other initiatives lack of significant uptake and lack of credibility among employers and the academic community. Moreover, its alleged lack of rigour and limited screening functions have made it appear in some quarters as unduly accommodating educational values that rest uneasily with the more recent approaches through highly stratified, output-based assessments.

In 1990, the Minister of State for Education announced that from September 1991 schools could offer BTEC First courses - effectively providing direct competition to the CPVE from one of its existing joint sponsors. Subsequently, the CGLI was given sole responsibility for the CPVE, with a brief to bring greater rigour into is assessment and ensure clearer progression routes for students. The CGLI proceeded to produce a new qualification, the Diploma of Vocational Education (DVE) to replace both the CPVE and foundation programmes. Yet again, a new qualification containing valuable ideas seems to have vanished beneath 'structural reform', in part no doubt because of inadequate preparation and lack of consensus between the several parties involved or likely to be affected.

The DVE, in the line of descent from the CPVE but with close linkages with the new structures for general and vocational education, will cater for a wider age range (14-19 years) and be taken at three different levels. Like CPVE, the DVE will have a hybrid quality. The genuine educational objective of putting form and purpose into what has been called a 'pot-pourri' of 16-plus activities will continue to be combined with a sweep of the new vocational influences—the world of work, emphasis on qualifications, short-term employer versions of personal development. A fairly prescriptive curriculum including a common core of the familiar studies and studies with 'vocational clusters' will be a feature of the DVT. Thus, the DVE will, like the CPVE, maintain a strong orientation towards further, vocational specific training or employment.

Alongside the DVE is to be another new qualification, the Technological Baccalaureate, launched in 1991 and piloted, significantly, in several City Technology Colleges and schools and other colleges. The Technology Bac is tailored to the framework of key stages and levels to permit successful candidates, according to the degree standard attained, to proceed to higher education, advanced further education, or further education and training (NVQ3). It is thus a typical case of the adaptiveness—or opportunism—of the examining authorities.

Orienting the secondary curriculum towards work

The general educational foundation of preparation for work and adult life have long been recognised and claimed by the schools, but the meaning of vocational education in the current 'new vocationalism' context involves certain ideas which embody or imply criticism of schools and general, liberal education.The challenge to schools has been: first, to establish closer links with the workplace - that is, work experience, simulated work experience, learning more relevant to the pupils' future lives, links between teachers and local industry, etc.; second, to deploy more practical, problem-solving, initiative-building teaching methods; and third, to give greater attention to the acquisition of concrete, measurable, testable skills and competences.

This functionalist strand of educational philosophy has been evident in policy-making and in practice in some schools for many years, certainly since before the establishment of the MSC or the FEU, though it has been strengthened and accelerated in the 1980s. It can be clearly identified in the literature, appearing from time to time over the last 150 years or so of English education. Moreover, the functionalist and instrumentalist elements do not tell the whole story, since the progressive movement in education in the late nineteenth century and well into the twentieth provides many antecedents to the current emphasis on student-centred education, practical and experimental learning and so on.

Government policy for schools throughout the 1980s was increasingly influenced by the new vocationalism. The *New Training Initiative* which, outlined proposals for a better trained and more flexible workforce and introduced the YTS, also stressed the need for better preparation in schools for working life.

The last two years of compulsory education are particularly important informing an approach to the work of work. Every pupil needs to be helpful to reach his or her full potential, not only for personal development but to prepare for the whole range of demands which employment will make. The Government is seeking to ensure that the school curriculum develops the personal skills and qualities as well as the knowledge needed for working life,and that links between schools and employers heso pupils and teachers to gain a closer understanding of the industrial, commercial and economic base of our society.

This is noteworthy as a clear statement, at the beginning of a decade which witnessed more changes in educational policy than any previous decade, or the responsibility of schools for economic performance. What is interesting is not so much that government wished to stress these objectives - what government faced with declining economic fortunes would not? - but that it was felt necessary to adopt a strongly interventionist stance to do so.

In 1984 another White Paper, *Training for Jobs*, again primarily concerned with developments in the YTS, stressed the contribution of the schools. It itemised arrangements for the CPVE; for increasing links between employers and schools and colleges, and for introducing the TVEI. But the first item was the school:

> The school curriculum is being developed for this purpose. Objective have been set for mathematics and will shortly be set for science teaching. National criteria are being established for the improvement of the 16-plus examinations and their syllabuses. New programmes are in operation for micro-electronics education and for pupils for whom the 16-plus examinations are not designed.

Many other statements aimed at fostering close links between the secondary curriculum and work appeared throughout the 1980s. However, perhaps the most decisive action was that taken by the KSC in launching the TVEI.

The technical and vocational education initiative (TVEI)

The MSC's involvement in preparing young people for working life was taken a step further when the government diverted money from the DES to the MSC and that organisation embarked upon youth training and entered the schools system. This was with the acquiescence of the DES and resulted in the introduction of the TVEI into the curriculum for 14-18-years-olds. It was a momentous decision, signifying the largest ever curriculum development project funded and administered by central government with consequential developments in schooling in all parts of the country. The aim was simple, direct and audacious: to change the curriculum for the 14-18 age group by giving it a more practical and applied character and drawing out its function as a bridge to the world for work.

On 12 November 1982 the Prime Minister announced the government's intention to launch an initiative to stimulate the provision of technical and vocational education in the schools, beginning at age 14. The MSC was invited to establish some ten pilot projects

> of full-time general, technical and vocational education in England and Wales in association with the DES and through local education authorities.

Programmes, although broadly work-oriented, were to be within the education system with LEAs bidding and being bound by the contracts awarded to deliver specified programmes. The lessons from the early, pilot projects were intended from the start to provide a basis for lasting educational developments for 14-18-years-olds. At the sometime, like the YTS, the TVEI had no established syllabus; aims and objectives were not narrowly defined and through pilot projects, evaluations and a great deal of debate and discussion, a considerable variety of practice and approach emerged across the country. As with the YTS, the TVEI was to be directed by national guidelines allowing considerable local flexibility. In order to obtain MSC support, programmes had to fulfill criteria defined by a National Steering Group. Although there was no overt mention of a core of skills as such to be learnt, all programmes had to include a common or 'core' element; and the characteristics identified for the content of the programmes, as we see below, included areas common to other vocational innovations. The TVEI 'includes general, technical and vocational elements; "'vocational education" is to be interpreted as education in which the students are concerned to acquire generic or specific skills with a view to employment'.

Since the purpose of each project, and the TVEI as a whole, was to explore and best programmes of genera,, technical and vocational education for 14-18-year-olds suitable for replication, a series of very different projects was deliberately launched. Within the overall framework, the goals of the individual projects were numerous and varied, ranging from the introduction and development of new practical/vocational courses through building links with work and adult life to improving examination performance. What those projects had in common was a definite content orientation:

Each project should comprise one or more sets of full-time programmes with the following characteristics:

(1) Equal opportunities should be available to young people of both sexes and they should normally be

educated together on courses within each project. Care should be taken to avoid sex stereo typing.

(2) They should provide four year curricula, with progression from year to year, designed to prepare the student for particular aspects of employment and for adult life in a society liable to rapid change.

(3) They should have clear and specific objectives, including the objective of encouraging initiative, problem-solving abilities, and other aspects of personal development.

(4) The balance between the general, technical and vocational elements of programmes should vary according to students' individual needs and the stage of the course, but throughout the programme there should be both a general and a technical/vocational element.

(5) The technical and vocational elements should be broadly related to potential employment opportunities within and outside the geographical area for the young people concerned.

(6) There should be appropriate planned work experience as an integral part of the programmes, from the age of 15 onwards, bearing in mind the provisions of the Education Act 1973.

(7) Courses offered should be capable of being linked effectively with subsequent training/educational opportunities.

(8) Arrangements should be made for regular assessment and for students and tutors to

discuss students' performance/progress. Each student, and his or her parents, should also receive a periodic written assessment, and have an opportunity to discuss this assessment with the relevant project teachers. Good careers and educational counselling will be essential

Students would normally be expected to obtain one or more nationally recognised qualifications, according to ability; and they would be issued with a record of achievement. Industry and commerce were to be involved as partners in design and delivery and not merely as recipients of the finished 'product'. All of this has a most familiar ring: the TVEI has been part of the wider strategy whose assumptions and major elements we have seen in the different settings of the new vocationalism.

In September 1983, fourteen LEAs started the first year of TVEI programmes. This involved 4,315 pupils in10 school. A further forty-eight LEA pilot projects began in 1984. Scotland joined, but later; the reason offered by one commentator is interesting:

'Caledonian caution', a concern to ensure that participation in the initiative would not compromise Scottish educational developments, or breach educational principles which had been established in Scotland as a result of the experiences gained in attempting to introduce vocational elements into the curriculum of Scottish schools during the 1960s.

These experiences led the Scots to abandon the idea that the schools curriculum might be built around 'the vocational perspective'; rather, a balance was required between the vocational emphasis and the broader curriculum of the schools.

In its first phase, the TVEI catered for a small percentage of the relevant age group. But in the light of initial experience, and the willingness of most local authorities to co-operate, plans were announced in the summer of 1986 to extend the TVEI as an option for the entire 14-18 age group by 1997. Funding per school was to be lower than during the expensive pilot phase. Twelve LEA projects began in 1985, twenty-one in 1986, eleven in 1987 and the remainder in 1988. In 1990, budgetary cuts meant new schools would have less than half their anticipated funding, leading a new schools would have less than half their anticipated funding, leading a number to threaten to withdraw from the scheme. Nonetheless by 1992, the TVEI had become available UK-wide with, for 1992-93, over 1,000,000 students involved, 5,000 schools participating, and all LEAs involved. Responsibility for the TVEI has remained with the MSC and its successor agencies, although the Training and Enterprise Councils (TECs) have shown strong interest in the now 900 million/year activity, as indeed has the DES/DfE.

The TVEI, like the YTS, was a favoured child of the new vacationalism movement. Viewed in one light, it is at the cutting edge, a leader among a series of national initiatives to improve preparation for work in life through education and training; in another light, it is part of a series of arrangements devised to impose central government policies on education and training organisations by cash and directive. Its introduction implied dissatisfaction with the exiting curriculum in the schools. Like the YTS, it appeared to be designed to meet a specific utilitarian objective - to provide for employers' needs.

The DES in *Better Schools* gave a lengthy resume of what the TVEI, at that time, was seen to offer:

> The TVEI embodies the Government's policy that education should better equip young people for working life. The courses are designed to cater equally for boys and girls across the whole ability range and with technical or vocational aspirations, and to offer in the compulsory years a broad general education with a strong technical element followed, post-16, by increasing vocational specialisation. The course content and teaching methods adopted are intended to develop personal qualities and positive attitudes towards world as well as a wide range of competence, and more generally to develop a practical approach throughout the curriculum. The projects are innovative and break new ground in many ways, being designed to explore curriculum organisation and development, teaching approaches and learning styles, co-operation between participating institutions, and enhanced careers guidance supported by work experience, in order to test the feasibility of sustaining a broad vocational commitment in full-time education for 14-18 year olds.

The form and content of TVEI pilot schemes during the early, creative phases recognised the need for more active learning methods, to meet the challenges posed by changes in industry and the rapid development of technology. Assuming the need for pupils to learn through experience, and to solve practical problems requiring the use of initiative, team work, etc., as a preparation for work, the TVEI's objectives were:

> first to widen and enrich the curriculum in a way that will help young people to prepare for the world of work, and to develop skills and interests, including creative abilities, that will help them to lead a fuller life and to contribute more to the life of the community; and second, to help students to learn to learn, to enable them to adapt to the changing occupational environment.

Specific guidance on how to achieve these methods of learning was not given at this time.

The TVEI did not define a core, list core studies or identify essential core skills, though all the first fourteen TVEI pilot projects included some core elements which can be seen as, in practice, constituting a 'TVEI core': for elements which can be seen as, in practice, constituting a 'TVEI core': for example, careers education and planned work experience, incorporating preparation and follow-up in school. The balance between 'core and 'options' depended very much on local decision,but the first projects, either through core or options, tended to offer broadly similar set of learning opportunities - for example, variety of vocational experience, technology, design, computers, business studies and science. Given the provenance of the TVEI and the purposes it was intended to serve, matters could hardly be otherwise.

The administrative and financial arrangements for the TVEI were innovatory. While in some ways they were more directive and inflexible than the financing methods used by the MSC and its heirs in the YTS, they at the same time offered schools a certain freedom to experiment. Local education authorities were responsible for the formulation and delivery of project proposals. These needed, however, to satisfy centrally determined criteria. The TVEI as a whole was initially administered through a small unit in the MSC, in liaison with the DES over major policy matters. Elaborate involved the MSC, Her Majesty's Inspectorate (HMI) in the DES and the LEA s themselves. Funds available to support the TVEI were normally allocated to meet costs of additional staffing, premises and equipment. In principle, teachers with TVEI allowances might be required to justify receipt of them by their performance, while the percentage of pupil time on the TVEI and the content of activity differed considerably from project to project. In practice the MSC funds potentially offered much needed encouragement and momentum for schools and teachers confidently to explore what they may already have been striving to offer or trying to develop piecemeal. In the words of the TVEI *Review* of 1984, MSC funding

> enables LEA s to broaden and enrich their existing provision,so as to explore and develop technical and vocational education within a framework of general education for each student involved. In general term, TVEI activities are broadly based in order to prepare students for a rapidly changing world and to avoid premature specialisation. Thus the changes in the curriculum as a result of TVEI go beyond only narrow definition of technical and vocational education.

At the same time LEAs operating TVEI were instructed that

> Each programme should be part of the total provision of the institution(s) in which it takes place so that the students may take part with others in the life of the institution(s). (The education offered in the institution(s) to those not on the programme should continue to contain technical or vocational elements as appropriate and those not on the programme should not be adversely affected by the conduct of the programme.)

The exploration, innovation, and experimentation supported by TVEI and MSC money were from the outset intended to be set firmly in a broad general education context. In terms both of the national structure supporting it and its thematic orientation, the TVEI suggests a strategy that posited age 14 as the terminus of serious endeavours to sustain a fully comprehensive education for all. With the apparent move in many 'extension' schools, however, away from seeing the TVEI as a separate course and towards a broader enhancement of many existing curriculum areas for all pupils, this object may not be achieved.

As Roger Dale points out, the early outlines of the TVEI explain little about why it was set up in the way it was; in order to reach conclusions about its real intentions it is necessary to examine the problem it was created to solve. This is not,however, so difficult. Government statements, as we have seen, have tended to define the problem mainly in terms of making good the schools' lack of preparation for successful acquisition of, and performance in, a job. Indeed David (now Lord) Young, as Chairman of MSC in 1982, believed when introducing the TVEI, that it would lead to young people becoming 'highly employable' by the item they left school. But the TVEI as it has come to be organised inpractice need not be viewed only in more functional vocational terms. It is equally possible to emphasise its role in developing communication between schools and industry and its potential as a catalyst in the 14-plus curriculum. Much depends on three factors: local circumstances, including pre-existing school-industry links; how it is introduced and managed in individual schools; and the qualifications with which it is associated.the strategy that envisages a parting of the educational ways at age 14 would be aborted were the schools themselves to build the TVEL into the heartland of the curriculum for all.

The effect of the TVEL in any school and its power attract and keep pupils over a wide ability range depend at least in part on each school's interpretation of the guidelines, but most of all on what Dale describes as 'the salience' of the scheme within the schools.This in turn depends on a number of factors; how the scheme is publicised to staff, pupils and parents when selecting options for 14 plus; whether it is developed through existing subjects taught with a new approach or through a series of new subjects and courses; whether it is offered openly to a targeted group, defined by ability, or implicitly by the a subject options which it is associated with; the calibre of the teachers and so on.

Early studies of the TVEL suggested that it son attracted some A level students and boosted staying-on rates at school. In 1986 in Solihull, for example the percentage if the age group staying on in schools after 16 was ·10 per cent; but among TVEL students entering their third year, the retention rate was 50 per cent. Moreover, the TVEL began to infiltrate A level courses. Sixth-form college A level students getting experience of the TVEL for the obligatory non-GCE work found it a challenging option.

These assessments refer to the early, more innovative phases in the development of the TVEL, when it attracted a good deal of positive interest notwithstanding anxieties about the in roads being made by an essentially employment-based agency (MSC) into the school system. Extension, following the joint DoE/DES White Paper, inevitably meant greater consistency and an attempt to sift from the diverse experiments of the pilot phase approaches that seemed to hold greater promise for a national policy. The national curriculum was being developed concurrently. From one point of view the prescriptive character of the national curriculum undermined the diversity inherent in the TVEI and together with other factors weakened its impact: 'The status of TVEI was gradually being undermined and marginalised by displacement by other educational reforms and the diminution of its funding'. From another standpoint, however, the TVEI succeeded precisely because of its incorporation into the new curriculum policies and structures. The frequency of change is not, however, justified by such incorporation. Is the TVEI yet another vocational initiative introduced without due thought being given to its implications and likely consequences for these system as a whole?

For schools, the TVEI has been a central strand of the new vocationalism because of its aims, its explicit work orientation, its method of introduction, and financial arrangements. It has the familiar form of compulsory criteria coupled with curricular flexibility, itself a curious if increasingly accepted combination. Unlike the YTS, its pilot and evolutionary stages have not been rapidly followed by greater prescription and reduced flexibility; however, in the extension phase, the TVEI was broadened to the whole curriculum and linked with other initiatves, inevitably with the national curriculum for schools. It is still the individual interpretations of local authorities and the freedom of teachers, if they care to exercise it creatively in whatever they teach, which will decide the shape of the programmes. What the TVEI has to offer for replication nationally is its individual appraoch to curriculum planning, grounded in the work orientation stated in its first set of aims, rather than a standard package, together with potential as a catalyst for the 14-plus curriculum. The initiative has had a number of positive results, the method of financing has ensured the establishment and not only the design of new courses; nor practical and applied work is observable in classrooms; links with local employers have been established.

The advent of the national curriculum posed a real challenge for successful expansion of the TVEI to all schools, not because it would of necessity exclude it but because of the need for teachers and authorities to recast their approaches in the new curriculum framework. As yet it is not clear how it welfare, given that the TVEI is still a programme for some, not all students. However, the TVEI has been credited, by HMI, with a role in the development of GCSE and in the evolution of cross-curriculum themes in the national curriculum.

While specific studies of the TVEI, such as those by researchers at New castle and Leeds Universities, and more general appraisals of policy and direction including those cited above, give rise to rather diverse conclusions, two points are clear. First, the TVEI has been a highly innovative and dynamic national programme witch quickly made visible several of the main themes in the government's commitment to and understanding of the new vocationalism. Second, as a funded initiative designed to grow attention to one of the elements in a shifting, evolving set of national policies and programmes, the TVEI would eventually be assimilated of closely related to the emerging foci of concern in those policies and he subject to the common pattern of innovation funding whereby start-up expenditures are progressively reduced. With the reservations noted above - that is, the too rapid succession of new initiatives - the TVEI legacy will be the impetus and reinforcement it has given to the central vocationalist idea that schooling should, among other functions, orient young people towards work and actively assist them to prepare for working life.

Enterprise culture and partnership

While the most obvious features of the new vocalionalism in the developments and specific programme innovations discussed in this chapter are summed up in the terms 'vocational' or 'work orientation', direct work preparation or vocational training have to be put in a much broader context. On the one hand, the foreshadowed distinctive vocational culture and separate administrative structure have gradually been assimilated to the general education system specifically of schools and further education colleges. On the other hand, the urgency of the youth unemployment problem has diminished: it is an acceptable and 'politically bearable' problem; the youth labour market has virtually evaporated except for part-time and certain low paid jobs and the informal labour market. For these reasons, changes in the formal educational structure, in curriculum, teaching and learning and relations with the wider environment, must become the central concern of policy-makers and developers, whether specifically identified as 'vocational' or 'general', 'training' or 'education'. Attention must, once again, be focused on the fundamental challenges to schooling - broadly defined, and away from specific, particularly non-school-based, preparatory courses for adolescents with employment in mind.

Many of the ideas and practices which emerged in the more specific work preparation programmes have become of recognised value in schooling - as we saw in discussing the TVEI. One of them, school industry partnerships, has long been a feature of vocational and technical education institutions and programmes. Another, enterprise skills,is closely associated with changing practice in work organisation and with the attention labour market and employment policy-makers have been giving to the skills needed by people who will gain employment by setting up their own businesses or in small-scale enterprises. 'Partnerships' and 'enterprise skills' are likely to gain considerable support in schooling, at all levels, since they coincide with long-established educational ideals and practices: school-community relations and the fostering in schools of initiative, creativity, independence and the ability to work with others.

A large number of projects and programmes under the banners of 'partnership' and 'enterprise education' have sprung up within the orbit of the new vocationalism with, on the ground locally,often considerable interaction between the projects and programmes. The most common forms of school-industry links in English secondary schools have been: work experience placements, curriculum development involving industry and problem-solving projects specifically with industry. The development of such school-industry partnerships has also been widespread since the 1980s among other industrialised countries, with the key emerging pattern being that 'the vast majority of partnerships are small,local and basic'.

There are, in effect, two definitions of, or approaches to, the work 'enterprise' and the practice of it. One approach, which can be termed a 'narrow' one, regards enterprise as business entrepreneurialism, and sees its promotion and development within education and training systems as an issue of curriculum development which enables young people to learn,usually on an experimental basis,about business start-up and management. The second approach, which can be termed the 'broad' one, regards enterprise as a group of qualities and competences which enable individuals, organisations, communities, societies and cultures to be flexible, creative and adaptable in the face of, and as contributors to, rapid social and economic change. What is significant about the implications of the broad approach for educationalists is that it requires changes in education methods and pedagogy towards what is termed 'enterprise learning' rather than changes in the curriculum.

School-industry partnerships and compacts

The recent activity in school-industry partnerships in the UK is traced by Lawlor and Miller to the Schools Council Industry Project, established in 1978 soon after James Callaghan's Ruskin College speech. Involving the Confederation of British Industry, it emphasised from the beginning local solutions to local problems, work experience, the development of simulations and case studies, and has pioneered mini-enterprise in schools. The launch of the TVEI in 1982, as we have seen, gave a strong impetus to variety of school-industry contacts, during both its pilot and extension phases. Industry, Year, designated in 1986 by the Royal Society of Arts, proved a concerted attempt to raise the esteem in which industry was held, through bringing together into local committees people from education and industry, to organise at least one activity or event in every school and college during the year.

In September 1988, the Enterprise and Education Initiative was launched by the Secretaries of State for Trade and Industry, Employment, and Education and Science. The initiative was to encourage.

more employers to become involved with their local schools. In particular, a network of advisors on enterprise and education, mainly based in the private sector, is being established to help employers link up with schools in their area. They will work closely with all those involved in business and education link activities in their areas and will contribute to better co-ordination at the local level. Specific objectives include ensuring that enough employers are involved so as to provide work experience for every pupil before leaving school and for 10 per cent of teachers a year.

Initiatives in the higher and further education sectors were also outlined at the same time.

In 1990, another grand initiative, the Education Business Partnership Initiative, was announced by the Secretaries of State for Employment Education and Science, and Trade and Industry.

Partnerships between education and business offer opportunities to make education more relevant to life and work; to raise standards and levels of attainment, to raise enterprise awareness and industrial understanding amongst teachers and students, and to inform and develop advice and counselling so that individuals are better placed to build and use their skills.

A number of demonstrable outcomes were expected from partnership activities, including:

— increased business involvement with; and support for, primary and secondary education;

— improved opportunities to assist students in school and college in the transition work;

— increased volume, relevance and breadth of information and guidance offered to students by careers teachers and the Careers Service;

— increased numbers of young people staying in relevant and appropriate full-time and part-time education;

— improved access to, and participation in, further and higher education.

The partnership, which was to be developed locally by the then newly established TECs, thus had very ambitious and wide-ranging goals, with the expectations that activities in each locality would vary.

Of particular note among the plethora of school-industry link activities has been the development of compacts, modelled on the Boston, USA, compact of the early 1980s. The 'London Compact', launched in March 1987, was essentially an agreement between schools and employers in an area of high social and economic deprivation, with a history of mistrust and hostility between employers and educators. The agreement guaranteed offers of local jobs to pupils at participating inner-city schools if they fulfilled their side of the compact. This meant students attending 85 per cent of lessons, meeting nine out of ten deadlines for all assignments, completing a school record of achievement and satisfactorily completing two weeks of work experience. Ainley notes that in reality,

> While they do not explicitly guarantee employment, employers undertake to give priority in job offers to those school-leavers who achieve the educational targets. This can mean a guaranteed

interview or a reserved place on a company-run Youth Training scheme. Participating employers also support school-industry links with the schools involved, by offering work experience, work shadowing, holiday jobs and teacher-industry exchanges.

Run by the London Education Business Partnership, the scheme initially involved the now defunct Inner London Education Authority and a consortium, of companies, among them Whitbread, whose communist programme director, Richard Martineu, was the moving force behind the initiative. One of the compact's main initial objectives was to encourage continued education in schools and colleges and increase the level of training at work. Employers would give day-release for school-leavers to continue studies and improve their qualifications. In the London pilot schools, teachers reported a dramatic growth in pupil retention at school after 16, where the compact's guarantee of a job held good until pupils were aged 18. Other effects to do with positive orientation towards work and becoming better qualified were reported.

The first year of the London Compact was seen as so successful that in 1988 the government adopted the idea and launched the compact initiative nationally, in the context of its Action for Cities Programme. For the national initiative,

> A Compact is an agreement between employers, young people, schools and colleges. Employers guarantee a job with training, or training leading to a job, to at least YTS standards, for

every participating young person who has achieved a set of agreed personal goals and objectives. And every school and college involved undertakes to support and encourage young people in the achievement of standards and competences. Eventually, employers may wish to encourage young people to go onto further and higher education in order to meet their skills shortages at professional, managerial and technical level. This encouragement could include individual sponsorship, work experience and either full-time release.

In the first year of the programme, the government funded compacts in thirty areas of the country, and by 1989 it had become a 17 million programme of the Department of Employment. Subsequently, new forms of compacts were initiated in which higher and further education institutions guaranteed places on programmes to local students if they met previously agreed criteria. In at least Birmingham and London,there has been considerable productive interplay between compacts and the TVEI in local schools.

The interest of the compact initiative is in the positive - and formal - support seen to be given by local industries and employers to the mainstream education system; expensive new initiatives of the CTC variety, discussed below, are not part of the approach. Compacts are practical, unostentatious and something which could feasibly be - and indeed have already been - generalised to many areas of the country. Experience of combats has shown that the idea of a deal between schools and businesses linked to student performance and recruitment can indeed help generate enthusiasm, but needs to be handled with care. Inevitably, comparisons are drawn between the CTC and compact initiatives and employers have generally had to choose which to support, given the limitation on resources.

New kinds of schools

Consistent with its intention to reintroduce into a putative comprehensive system firm distinctions between different routes,whether to higher education or to a restructured technical - vocational system, late in 1986 the government announced plans to establish, as part of its Action for Cities Programme, twenty independent City Technology Colleges in selected inner-city locations. Each was to take between 750 and 1,000 11-18-year-old students across the full ability range. it was intended that the first colleges would open in 1988, and the full twenty be in operation by 1990. While progress has been less rapid than anticipated in these optimistic forecasts, the CTCs are yet another manifestation of the national endeavour to build bridges between education and employment.

Their purpose will be to provide a broadly-based secondary education with a strong technological element there by offering a wider choice of secondary school to parents in certainties and a surer preparation for adult and working life to their children.

To be established first on a pilot basis, with the hope that their influence would spread, they were expected to adopt the best practices of the TVEI and successful secondary schools generally. Their status was to be that of registered independent schools, subject to inspection by HMI but charging no fees, and functioning alongside existing secondary schools. While they would obtain financial assistance from the DES, a substantial part of their cost was to be met by 'promoters', a return to the voluntary principle, but a pious hope as subsequent events proved.

CTCs, despite the moderate success thus far in attaining the targets set by government, are of significance at this stage insofar as they signal strategies that go far beyond the institutions themselves. Behind the fundamental policy objective of government to interest the private sector in funding, and thereby to revive the dormant tradition of voluntary provision, lay another purpose, namely the weakening of power of local education authorities, a policy since pursued with great vigour and on a number of fronts.

It was initially intended that CTCs would be established in twenty-seven designated inner-city areas, either purpose built on vacant sites or through purchasing redundant schools. A shortage of suitable sites bedeviled the scheme from the start, and, despite the initial intention of their serving deprived inner-city areas, there has instead been a first come first served approach to their approval, depending on available sites and sponsors being found. There appears, now, to be no geographic plan behind identifying potential CTCs, with three of the first fifteen close to each other in the outer London are.

Sponsorship was much slower than anticipated, with the government by 1991 moving from the position that 'the principle of funding will be that the promoters will meet all or a substantial part of the capital costs' to one which saw 'private business and industry...providing substantial [sic] proportion - at least 20 per cent - of the capital funding for each of the colleges'. Recurrent funding is provided by the state. Because of the high-tech approach to resourcing the schools, individual school set-up costs have been very high, leading to situations such as that in Nottingham where some 9 million was spent on building the new CTC as against the city's entire annual capital expenditure on all its schools of less than 2.5 million. It is thus hardly surprising that the CTC programme has engendered resentment among many working in the less resource favoured state sector, especially at a time when parents are being encouraged to choose schools. While CTCs officially have a non-selective in take, the government-stipulated criteria are seen to be unworkable and there appears no doubt about their taking a disproportionate percentage of the more motivated students, if only because of their preferring those who agree to remain until age 18.

City Technology Colleges are certainly now under way, although the bold plans of twenty CTCs by 1990 was rather drastically revised downwards, with some fifteen to be operational by 1993. Even when the ultimate goal of twenty pilot schools is reached, however, they constitute a very small group in relation to the nation's 4,000 secondary schools and their impact must be awaited. With a few exceptions, industry has been relatively slow in supporting them, reportedly in many cases because of jeopardising existing links with local schools where productive school-industry partnerships exist.

They are more substantially government-supported than anticipated and also in some instances have generated considerable local parent and community antagonisms, especially where existing schools have been closed down to be sold as CTCs. Disquiet over the impact of CTCs on the offerings, morale and intake in neighbouring schools has been of concern to many education authorities schools and for opting out by main stream schools has been mentioned by some commentators; this point could be more persuasively made if the government's growth targets for CTCs has proved in any way realistic.

Plans for a new network of voluntary-aided CTCs—utilising part of the 1944 Education Act compromise on the then dominant religious question - were announced in 1990. These plans would enable an existing LEA school to apply to become a voluntary-aided CTC—as long as the school could raise 500,000 from sponsors. The government would provide further funds for refurbishment. The CTC Trust hopes also to find a way of enabling grant-maintained schools to gain CTC status.

The CTCs are to be treated as independent schools with no statutory requirement for them to comply with the national curriculum. National curriculum goals are, ever: so, expected to be influential in the different schools developing 'characteristic identities', and early indications support this.

Early indications, again, suggest that the learning programmes CTCs offer their pupils are innovative, and potentially challenging, drawing on much of the TVEI curriculum development of recent years—hardly surprising in a well-resourced, high profile new endeavour. Keeping up the momentum and establishing a well-structured 11-18 programme will prove a considerable challenge in years to come.

The form and content of the CTC curriculum as originally proposed by the DES put equal emphasis on technological content and on standards and attitudes: 'There will be a large technical and practical element within the broad and balanced curriculum...up to the age of 16. The importance of doing and understanding as well as knowing will be emphasised throughout'. Indeed, cross-curricular approaches based on projects and themes, mixed ability teaching and an emphasis on 'open' learning, backed by good investment in information technology have become the early trend.

Jones argues that

Increasingly, in CTCs, as elsewhere in secondary education, the emphasis is shifting from the discrete post-16 curriculum to planning for 14-19 education and training. For the majority of young people this will mean a continuum rather than a cut-off point at 16, guided vocal choices beyond 14 leading to increased specialization towards 18 or 19, and a culture which takes for granted that education and training will continue throughout life.

In particular, CTCs are contributing to developments in: integrating post-16 education and the world of work; broadening the curriculum developing new vocational routes which have parity of status with academic progression routes to higher education; developing new curriculum methodologies (by piloting credit transfer schemes, developing modular curricula).

Following the Continental pattern, CTCs operate longer school days, and on more days in the year, than most state-maintained schools. This is to allow for more enrichment activities and a more varied curriculum, and appears to have strong student, parent and teacher support.

It seems probable that CTCs and other schools which take the opt-out/specialist route, with favoured treatment financially and selected pupils, will have sufficient vitality to general their own values and learning patterns. This is to assume that the whole scheme continues to make progress, a subject upon which there has been much debate. We are still at the stage where policies have been declared and initial progress made but not to the point where it is clear that the lines set in the early stages will become embedded in the educational and training system.

The establishment of independent CTCs takes a stage further the administrative device introduced by the intervention of the MSC into the secondary schools with the launch of the TVEI. In November 1982, the then Chairman of the MSC, David Young, observed:

> Much has been made in the media...that the MSC has the power and the authority to open its own establishments, so let me say at the outset that we have no intention of doing that as I believe and hope we can work as partners with the local education authorities. If that did not prove possible, them we might have to think again.

In practice, local authorities have been willing to bid for resources with which to experiment with the TVEI. We have seen some LEAs willing to bear the brunt of parent and community opposition to closing existing schools, then selling them to open as CTCs. But we have also seen only a handful of major sponsors coming forward to endow CTCs, and the government needfully committing vastly greater funding than initially planned to the project.

In common with most of the initiatives under the new vocationalism, for the CTCs there is a variety of ostensible objectives: to prepare children for jobs with a high technological content ; to give parents greater choice of school and slow responsiveness to criticism of existing schooling; and to help fight inner-city decay. As with other new vocationalism policies, it is important to examine very carefully the real, sometimes hidden, objectives. The published material about the CTCs makes it clear that although the organising principles and pedagogy of the education likely to be offered in CTCs bear marked similarities to the YTS and TVEI, the real point of CTCs, as far as governments concerned, lies in their broader new vocationalism characteristics and in the potential of CTCs, in consort with the other developments, to weaken the ideology and to restructure the framework of all-through comprehensive education. The CTC initiative, like its forebears, increases central government power, at the expense of the local authorities. This is the DES/DfE version of the instruments used effectively by the MSC for rapid construction and change - mainly the disposal of substantial sums of government money.

The CTCs also form part of the government strategy of offering choice to the parent - the shopping basket of schools. Parents, keen to choose new publicity-conscious schools which appear likely to increase the pupils' job prospects, could well be attracted by the standards of discipline, the emphasis on attitudes and the acquisition of qualifications. But many parents appear reluctant to do this at the expense of losing existing schools.

The most likely pattern of development is the establishment and successful operation of a relatively small number of CTCs. These will act as development and demonstrations ties for both official and unofficial ideas about more practical, applied, work/industry-related education. Their influence on the national system is likely to be quite moderate overall, but on specific topics - for example, project-based teaching, school-industry partnerships, advanced technology teaching - some of them may serve a lighthouse role. It is for these reasons, not the scale of the innovation, that the CTC project deserves closer scrutiny and its development will be watched with considerable interest by the whole education community and not only those with a particular vocational bent.

A not unrelated development is the Technology Schools Initiative (TSI) which was launched in December 1991 by the then Minister of State Tim Eggar. It aims at establishing a network of secondary schools committed to providing technology and associated courses of a strong vocational nature. Eventually the experience of these TSI schools should be disseminated system-wide. The initiative allocated capital funding for equipment and building work, totaling some 50 million, to 222 schools over the first two years.

8 The Need for Change

Education and society

Education has always embraced vocational elements and aims. It has always combined eternal values and cultural objectives (achieved by the study of literature, science, history, mathematics, art and music) with the need to respond to the social, economic and industrial demands of the age.

There is a school of thought which suggests that somehow, out of the muddy waters of life, we have distilled that essence which is called pure education. This, it is suggested, represents the knowledge and experiences which every developing human should have, and that these are eternal, unrelated to environment or society, and untrammelled by the shadow of a later need to earn a living. Indeed, the extreme expression of this viewpoint comes close to arguing that the more useful the knowledge and experience, the less reputable they must be. Such a curriculum exists only in people's imaginations. It does not exist in reality. It is not available to be defended.

Schooling in medieval England was determined by the needs of the church and the demand for clerks and scribes. The study of the classics from the sixteenth to the twentieth centuries was based on the belief that such a curriculum produced better statesmen, administrators, colonial governors and army and naval officers. It was not based or the desire of Elizabeth I, Disraeli or even less the man in the twentieth century street that young people should appreciate the style of Cicero, the humour of Catullus or the historical writings of Tacitus, even though many have. In recent years, it served the specific purpose of gaining admission to Oxford and Cambridge Universities. Once this requirement was abolished, the decline of classical studies occurred rapidly because their vocational prop had been removed and no-one had worked out a justification for their inclusion in the curriculum on other grounds. The decline in Latin should not be attributed to the advance of state comprehensive schools, for private schools are also rapidly dropping the subject, as is clear from *Curriculum Census 1984*. Similarly the prominence of French in the curriculum is attributable from the eighteenth century largely to its function as the language of European diplomacy-an outdated-vocational reason for almost all children aged 11-14 to spend about one tenth of their schooling trying to obtain proficiency in it.

These arguments are not an attack on the worth of medieval, classical or French studies, but they do illustrate our inability to consider the curriculum *de novo* and our acceptance of vocational criteria for including elements in the curriculum provided that these criteria are out-dated, no longer relevant and unacknowledged.

All major advances in educational provision have followed changes in the nation's industrial and commercial needs.

1870 - the foundation of the first state schools coincided with the ends of a period of great prosperity, the beginning of the challenge by Germany and the USA to our industrial supremacy, and the realisation that industrialisation required a literate work force.

1902 - the Balfour Act followed humiliation in the Boer Wars, the belief that this was linked to technical decline, and a need to compete more successfully with Germany.

1944 - Butler's Act was related to the need for post-war industrial regeneration, led to the opening of higher levels of secondary education to non-fee payers and introduced grants for university under-graduates.

1960s the comprehensive re-organisation of secondary education occurred at a time of labour shortages.

1980s large-scale provision for vocational education (whether in schools and colleges or, through YTS, for those who have left school) is a response to the collapse of our traditional manufacturing industries and our failure to compete with more technologically and commercially advance nations.

Whatever the controversies caused by each of the first three developments, they all improved the general standard of education and widened opportunities. Reforms in the 1980s are intended to do the same and because they are taking place within the comprehensive school and are intended to change the curriculum of all pupils, they can be carried forward without the divisiveness of the earlier measures. The aim of a better and more broadly educated school leaver is one which all teachers can embrace.

The sadness of the stance taken by those who think that they are defending education against the inroads of vocational training is that they understand neither. The irony is that what they are defending is the out-dated vocationally-determined curriculum of yesterday. Education has always reflected the social and economic needs of the country or of a particular arrangement of society. The reform to promote overt technical and vocational studies for all pupils is both a response to the country's commercial needs and an enhancement of the comprehensive school curriculum.

Industrial upheaval and the management of educational reform

Britain is currently in the throes of industrial upheaval. Reform of the curriculum to embrace technical and vocational elements, at the behest of government, is education's contribution to the management of complex industrial change. It is one part of the picture. Others are:

(a) Youth Training Scheme, for those who have left school at the age of 16 when compulsory school ends, has a 1984-5budget of $875m.

(b) Certificate of Pre-Vocational Education, which has developed from the long-standing concept of a one-year course leading to a public examination of general education at the age of 17 into one of pre-vocational studies.

(c) Promotion of micro-computer applications and training for them by the first appointment of a Minister for Information Technology, the establishment of ITECs throughout the country, the Micro-electronics in Education programme (MEP), and Department of Trade and Industry (DTI) schemes to subsidise the acquisition by schools and colleges of micro-computers and allied equipment.

(d) British Schools Technology programme, organised by the DTI in consultation with the Manpower Services Commission (MSC) and the Department of Education and Science(DES), to promote technology as a school subject, with a a three-year budget of $2.5m.

(e) Open Tech Programme which aims to provide opportunities for adults to re-train and acquire skills at technician and supervisory management levels, with a 1984-5 budget of $15.3m.

(f) College Employers Link Project (CELP) started in eight local authority are as to study relations between further education and employers, in order to improve the supply of adaptable highly-skilled young workers.

(g) Government White Paper, *Training for jobs* to increase government control of courses in non-advanced further education.

The main impetus for reform of the curriculum in schools has come from the Technical and Vocational Education Initiative, announced by the Prime Minister in November 1982 and started in 14 local authorities in September 1983. In less than a year the decision was taken to extend the scheme, and in 1987 the extension of TVEI to all secondary schools began. It is run by the Manpower Services Commission for which the Secretary of State for Employment is responsible, with the co-operation and support of the Secretary of State for Education.

TVEI differs from the other initiatives in four respects it:

(a) covers the age range 14-18, bridging the divide of 16+public examinations and of compulsory and voluntary education.

(b) changes the mainstream school curriculum by:

(i) inserting new courses and skills:

(ii) encouraging a coherent approach to education-industry relations, work experience, visits to industry commerce teacher secondments to industry commerce, but particularly co-operative planning of courses:

(iii) changing teaching styles and learning methods.

(c) is still largely controlled and led by educationists since it is based not only on national criteria approved by the Manpower Service Commission's National Steering Group. Which is representative of all interested contributors, but on a very wide variety of local responses to those criteria. The ground-rules are national but the planning within them is local. The national-local agreement is sealed in contracts between MSC and local education authorities. All projects have to offer guidance to other parts of the country on how the curricular changes can be implemented elsewhere. They are pilots, not experiments.

(d) is a development of existing trends in the schools themselves. Its chief contribution is not novelty, but coherence and impetus.

Unemployment and changing patterns of employment

For more than two years the U.K. has had more than three million people registered as unemployed. The national figure masks regional variations(e.g. 15.3% in the North West. 15.15% in Wales. 17.5% in the North), local variations in otherwise relatively-favoured areas.

The overall figure also masks the high proportion of young people in the total.

The problem of youth unemployment is massive and international. Britain has one of the highest totals in Europe, although the proportion of under-25s unemployed is similar to most other countries.

The figures for 16-year-olds in 1983-4 show how recent measures have reduced the number of school-leavers registered as unemployed to 14%. Whilst the number in employment is only 21%.

Britain in the 1980s is not only suffering from unemployment. It is also experiencing major changes in the pattern of employment. The microchip, robots and automation create new jobs requiring different skills from those taught at present. The major job losses are amongst manual workers at both operative and craftsman level.

Notes on Fig 1.3 (all figures still in thousands). The interim figures between the two dates show distinct trends, up or down, with only minor discrepancies, except for;

(i) electrical engineering, office equipment and electrical instruments;

(ii) hotel and catering, which peaked at 1947 in September 1979, fell to 1814 in December 1982 and have increased to 1841 since then;

(iv) education which peaked at 160 in March 1980, and has kept within a range of 1565 at the March calculation each year between 1981 and 1984.

(v) the number of self-employed, which fell steadily from its peak in 1971 to a trough of 1903 in 1978-9 and has risen consistently since.

Clear trends are evident. All losses are in production, construction and manufacturing. All gains are in service industries, such as wholesaling, retailing, hotels, catering, banking, finance and insurance. Despite a strong commitment by government to reducing public employment and the achievement by December 1982 of a reduction in public administration of 133000 jobs, the number subsequently rose by 27000. Other major sources of public employment, education and health, haves seen increases in their numbers of employees.

Although the number of people who are self-employed has grown by 292000 in the period and all of the increase has occurred since the present government, committed to such growth, can into office, there had previously been a steady increase from 1966 until June 1971, the years of Harold Wilson's government. A detailed study suggests a rough correlation between the figures for growth in unemployment and self-employment and that when people lose their jobs a small proportion of them become self-employed. We should hesitate to see evidence in the figures for pinning too much hope on an increase in self-employed entrepreneurs as the solution of the problem, and should bear this in mind when considering the curriculum.

The trends in levels of education and skills required

It is also evident that it is the unskilled and low-skilled jobs which are disappearing, and posts which require a more highly educated applicant which are increasing in number.

One of the education service's responsibilities is to produces students with the basic skills which industry and commerce can develop. Schools cannot train workers. The match between what schools can do and the nation's future manpower needs, which are difficult to forecast, cannot be precise. The data in for example, is extracted from information already subject to modification, because it was based on assumptions which by the end of 1984 were considered to be optimistic. There is, however, a need to respond to major changes in the patterns of employment.

Decline in manufacturing industry apprenticeships

The early 1980s have seen a rapid decline in the number of apprenticeships. These figures are for all manufacturing industry except ship-building;

Both a decline in demand for traditional manufacturing skills and a revolution in training are revealed by the figures. Schools can no longer expect their leavers, with either out-dated skills(of little use to industry or to the individual) or a wholly theoretical education, to find placements.

Britain had by far the lowest percentage of young people in full-time education or training. A comparison of Britain with the USA and Japan is equally unfavourable to Britain. The current reform is concerned with increasing the number of young people who continue their education beyond 16. It is promoting a *de facto* raising of the school/college/ training leaving age. It cannot do that without changing the nature of what is taught. In the USA a 'drop-out' is someone who leaves full-times education below the age of 18. That concept is being promoted in Britain.

Space and status for technology

Technical studies had no place in the selective grammar, a lowly place in the secondary modern school, and have been struggling for space in the comprehensive school. Their low status has not been the fault of its specialist supporters. The achievements of adviser, teachers, industrialists and the National Centre for School Technology at Trent Polytechnic are all the more remarkable when viewed against the conditions in which they have been made. The force opposing them has been institutional.

The history of secondary education from the Hadow Report in 1927 to the comprehensive of the 1960s and 1970s was dominated by arguments between those who believed that quality could be achieved only by a minority and those who were concerned with the universality of education. Technical education did not find its place in that controversy. It flowered briefly in 1944 when the tri-partite system of grammar, technical and modern schools was formalised but that arrangement represented defeat for the technical education spokesmen in the planning of the 1944 Act. They did not make up their minds which way in the argument to go and, apart from creating a few short-lived bi-lateral grammar-technical schools, they settled for the second level of ability. Technical colleges were set up after the war, usually for those who had failed to gain admission to the grammar school. Technical education was thus equated with the second best in a system founded on selection. It could not survive. In the words of Professor Judges, when describing the state of the tri-partite system in 1953, '..one of the thing's three legs is frequently under-developed or atrophined and ..it is only in men's imaginations that the true triplex formation, with a real place for organic development on the technical side, is to be found.'

Technical education fared no better in the comprehensive reform of the 1960s and 1970s. These have been aptly described by Professor Lister as 'reforms of assess'. It was very rare for a whole area to become comprehensive at one time. In most places comprehensive schools were founded in competition with remaining grammar schools. This was particularly true in the London Country Council area, which was one of the pioneering authorities. It was possible in those years to visit an LCC comprehensive school in which many aspects of the current vocational education movement were being strongly promoted. Forest Hill School was one. But the public were convinced of the need for change, not by pioneering curricula, but by the ability of comprehensive schools to do for the ablest child what the grammar school could do: The argument was not won by convincing them that a comprehensive curriculum was better, but by the success of pupils of comprehensive schools such as Tulse Hill in winning Oxbridge classics scholarships. Technical education had lost again.

When institutional change and curriculum reform are divorced nonsenses are likely to occur. The irony is that high quality technical studies, scuppered in the division between grammar and modern schools, sank almost without trace in the comprehensive school. Those who successfully refloated the s wreckage and have brought technological studies in schools to their present level have had to face extraordinary difficulties. Without their long haul and success the present curricular reform would have had to be promoted on a much weaker foundation.

It has been the politics of the comprehensive reform which has debased the role of technological, business and vocational studies, and has ensured that a curriculum, established largely for nineteenth-century aristocrats, has passed almost unscathed through the grammar to the comprehensive school. At each stage the new institution has had to justify itself in comparison, and often in direct competition with the old. The results have been major institutional changes and a great widening of opportunities, but only very slow change in the range of what is learned. Thus it is that towards the end of the twentieth century only a tiny minority of young people in Britain undertake any systematic study of technology at any time during the period of compulsory schooling.

Current moves have to break this mould and establish technological as well as other vocational studies as essential elements in the curriculum of all children, covering the full range of ability. Without the impetus of government-supported change, we shall continue to direct the ablest away from technological studies and in the direction of what we mistakenly think of as untainted, pure education. The reform aims to enhance the curriculum by including elements which are essential but have not hitherto been admitted.

Modernising the curriculum

Inertia, despite evidence of the need for change in the curriculum, is attributable to several factors:

(a) the effect upon the curriculum of the struggles between those favouring selective schools and those favouring comprehensive, as outlined above has been perhaps the biggest obstacle to change;

(b) training of teachers as single-subject specialist, without an overall view of the curriculum and with grossly inadequate opportunities for re-training;

(c) inadequate resources for studies, some of which are intrinsically expensive in both capital and revenue terms;

(d) parental choice of secondary school, whatever its other merits, can require the innovatory school to take great risks, especially if the most prestigious school in the area is also the most traditional in its view of the curriculum.

We may reach some conclusions about the view which schools take of various subjects and the reasons why they attach importance to them, by noting their relative positions. We may also question some assumptions.

If physics an essential part of a rounded education. Why is it that almost three times as many girls studied biology as took physics and that almost as many studied cookery?. This can be seen, of course, as the result of sex-stereotyping and prejudice, but it also calls into question the integrity of the claim that a science course which is specifically physics, as distinct from one which is broader, is an essential element in the curriculum. Almost a quarter of boys who take mathematics do not take physics and two thirds of girls who take mathematics do not take it. In many schools there is a vague feeling that all pupils ought to take a physical science, and that either physics or chemistry will do.

There is evidence to suggest that French owes its high place to the notion that one needs an O-level in modern languages for future applications rather than for its intrinsic worth. It certainly drops down the list in post-16 studies at GCE A level, falling behind History. Art, Economics, Chemistry and Geography for the totals of boys and girls.

There are some subjects which have not found a traditional justification for their place in the curriculum but have nonetheless successfully claimed space in the timetable, for example sociology. British constitution and geology. The category of sociology in fact covers some broader studies more commonly thought of as social studies, but, that apart, these 'new studies' have two noteworthy aspects. They all stem from the enthusiasm of teachers within the schools who have been trained in disciplines to which the subjects are allied, i.e. history, economics and geography, and in this sense represent specialisation alongside the more fundamental study. They are all quite cheap to introduce, not requiring markedly different accommodation or expensive equipment. They are not evidence of our ability to bring in new studies and new skills when those two conditions are not to hand. Whilst they have worth in themselves, it is difficult to see their role as specialised studies in the context of a broad, liberal curriculum. They look more like the last throes of a movement which had as its highest goals an increase in the number of options and ever-greater specialisation.

The poor place of music, despite the obvious importance of all kinds of music in our daily lives and of the exciting practical and successful new approaches promoted by Professor Painter and other, seems evidence of our failure to support it in an adequate curriculum framework. Art, which is on a par with history, chemistry and French in popularity, is justified often on the vocational basis that it is useful for many careers and essential for some. Music has no such justification, except for a very small number of pupils. This suggests that criteria based upon cultural needs and eternal values are not enough to gain a place in the traditional curriculum. We may suspect that literature would not be strong if it were not tied inextricably, in the persons of its teachers, to English language. The promotion of technical and vocational studies is not an attack on music and literature. By more honestly identifying the reasons for the inclusion of studies in the curriculum. It may strengthen the position of these subjects.

The low position of economics is the more serious because the start of optional courses at 14 is, in most cases, the first opportunity which pupils will have had to study the subject. It illustrates two points;the difficulty of getting new studies into the 14-16 curriculum if there is not a member of staff already on the premises to promote and foster it, and the straitjacket of the single-subject, option - based curriculum which allows subjects in only if they occupy and can justify occupying about half a day a week for two years. Thus economics has to compete, perhaps, with languages, humanities or a second science, as an alternative study. It is not easy to see the rationale of this. The Economics Association Project report, based on a survey of one in five of all secondary schools in England and Wales, showed that very few students have any kind of study in economics in the common curriculum 11-13 and that two thirds have none either in the core or options of the 14-16 curriculum. In 1977 HMI asked. 'Can we leave this task [teaching economics]to mere chance, probably depriving vast numbers of people of an understanding of the very processes and issues which affect their lives as citizens and workers?' In 1984 the fifth European conference on economics education at Manchester University called for economics to be brought to the centre of the curriculum. The fact that the call is still necessary is evidence of our curricular inertia.

Numbers taking subjects, carelessly categorized as craft, are illuminating clearly cookery cannot claim to be in the curriculum for vocational reasons or academic reasons. It would seem that a vague notion of preparing girls for housewifery is the actual justification, at least in the eyes of the choosers.

Those subjects which are most closely related to engineering and construction-technical drawing, woodwork, metalwork and design and technology - show support which does not accord either with the needs of industry or with the thinking of advisers and teachers of the subject. Technical drawing has for years been academically the most respectable of these subjects and has promoted disciplined study and accuracy, but most current thinking does not see a major role for it as a separate subject at examination level. Yet in 1982, the year when TVEI was announced, four times as many candidates were presented for O level examinations in technical drawing as were presented for design and technology. The numbers for metalwork and woodwork were similar to those for design and technology. Perhaps the justification for woodwork should change from that of relevance to the construction industry to one of contributing to the aesthetic, self-help and confidence building elements in the curriculum. Wood is the material which we can all work in our homes without expensive plant.

As with these subjects, the current emphasis in most commercial studies courses is vocationally out-of-date. The difference is that developments have been under way for some time in the CDT field and the current reforms are a means of rapidly pushing forward along a route which already charted. This is not the case with commercial studies.

Computer studies is the one subject which has arrived suddenly in the curriculum, but it is the one swallow which does not make a summer. It is not evidence of our ability to adjust the curriculum quickly. Most syllabuses are condemned by those working in industry and commerce as out-of-date. There is a policy debate going on about whether the subject should be examined at all at 16+, and a widely-held view that it should be a basic element in learning skills courses for all pupils;the distinction between computer studies, which may be for the minority, and information handling for all is often muddled. Many schools are conscious of the need to have many micro-computers, but less clear about what use to make of them and how to integrate the facility into their learning schemes. The arrival of computing in schools is unique experience in curriculum change. It shows how schools, largely caught unawares, have responded in an incoherent and ill-prepared way to the enormous up-surge of public interest in and possession of home micros. The comment from many teachers about their pupils knowing more than them is not a joke. The generalisations under-value the work of those in the Micro-electronics Education Programme and those who have taken the initiative locally, as at Milton keynes, to develop appropriate courses in association with business and information technology centres. My general point-that education has had to respond to outside pressure rather than lead the admission of the micro into the school-remains true. A diverting account of one school's being led by parents is given in Hounsell and Martin's *Developing Information Skills in Seconday Schools*, British Library. The sequence of events was:lukewarm interest from head, meeting of heads of department with only the mathematics department interested, parental pressure to extend the development of information skills across the curriculum. The arrival of the micro is an interesting example of public pressure on the schools, not an example of our ability to lead change in the curriculum.

If we look beyond the subject labels and have regard to content, the picture is still more alarming. A paper issued by the DTI's Industry/Education Unit, *Improving the significance of GCEE O level and CSE examination papers for the requirements of modern society* concluded that, of 4100 questions set in physics, chemistry and mathematics examination in 1981-2, only 4% had any relevance to the technology of the last fifteen years, and the proportion relevant to technology which has had an established place over a longer period averaged less than 5%. Most questions were based solely on the recall of knowledge. Almost half of those questions in chemistry which did involve industrial applications relied on recall and were tests of memory not understanding. Pupils still do wrought-iron work in school metalwork shops. when they have never seen a computer numerically-controlled machine. They type on manual machines, never having had access to electronic typewriters, word-processors or micro-computers. The theory of electricity is widely taught but an understanding of electronics is seldom given, whilst practical experience of using components and making circuits is quite rare. Schools need to up-date the skills which they teach.

What is required of the schools?

Plans for reform of the curriculum need to be based on these factors:

(a) We are in the midst of industrial change as great as that of the early nineteenth century;the management of change on such a scale is highly complex, and an uncharacteristically rapid response from the education service is needed. Curriculum reform has not happened in the past without strong national and local leadership. It is happening now because the leadership is there.

(b) Business and industry require a better-educated work-force with the ability to adapt its understanding and skills.

(c) There will be significant increase in employment in the human services, which require a well-educated work-force.

(d) Britain has made significantly worse provision for education and training in the period after compulsory schooling than most countries in the European Economic Community, with the lowest combined percentage in the late 1970s of young people of post-compulsory age in any form of full-time general or vocational education or apprenticeship.

(e) Schools must take note of those types of employment which are declining and those which are expanding, recognise the long-term trends which point in certain directions ensure that basic skills with a future are included in the curriculum and design the curriculum with facility of change as a criterion.

(f) Schools must provide courses for all pupils which offer a continuum of education and training to 18, and face the challenges to existing curriculum models and teaching methods which this makes.

(g) There is a realisation that the 11-16 curriculum for most children and 16-18 curriculum for the ablest students have been dominated by the abstract and theoretical, with an under-valuation of practical experience an useful knowledge.

(h) The justification for the inclusion of subjects in the curriculum is not always as pure as we like to think, and is often out-of-date;the balance of subjects remains largely unaltered because of the difficulty of change, not the absence of a need for change.

(i) There is little evidence to suggest that the new skills or aspects of study are admitted to the curriculum unless there are teachers already on the staff who wish to promote them, or unless, as in the unique case of computing, there is such a surge of public interest that schools have to respond to demand.

(j) Technological studies have not been accorded adequate status and time in the curriculum; and economic and industrial studies have not been followed at all by the majority of young people during the years of formal education.

(k) Changes in CDT at O level show how slow is the process of change, especially when it involves taking up the time of ablest pupils, even through the promotion of technology nationally and through local authority advisers probably more supportive of change than is the case in any other subject the absence of the proper curricular framework may be the problem.

(l) Both the education service and industry appreciate that the gulf which has existed between them is incompatible with the need for young people at some stage to move from one to the other.

(m) Those aspects of detailed planning, which must follow the setting of national or local authority frameworks, need to be done by groups of schools;few schools are likely to have the resources or courage to tread the path alone.

(n) There may be a contradiction between nationally-led curriculum change and the promotion of increasing parental control over school, unless parents are convinced that the reforms, seen to be nationally essential, are also in the immediate interests of their children.

(o) Business, which wants change, must make it clear that it will welcome the products of change.

(p) Curriculum reform is not cheap. If pilot projects are intended partly to cost the extension of the reform to all schools, there needs to be evidence before long that extra resources will be available from the government.

(q) Changes in curriculum models need to be accompanied by changes in the teaching styles and examinations and teachers need enormously increased opportunities for re-training.

9 Approaches, Definitions and Criteria

Common elements in vocational studies

Any curriculum which embraces vocational considerations will include these elements:

(a) work experience;

(b) industrial visits;

(c) careful vocational guidance before admission to and throughout, the courses;

(d) problem-solving and the practical application of skills and knowledge;

(e) a relationship between the courses and employment opportunities, locally or nationally;

(f) new courses and assessment methods.

Different definitions of vocational elements

Apart from these common elements here are different definitions for the vocational elements in the curriculum. Although a subtle approach can combine some of the advantages of all and few of the disadvantages, curriculum planners have to make an initial choice about which route to follow.

1. One occupational family

Definition: the vocational elements in the curriculum are related to one of the 11 occupational families:

(a) administrative, clerical and office services;

(b) agriculture, horticulture, forestry and fisheries;

(c) craft and design;

(d) installation, maintenance and repair;

(e) technical and scientific;

(f) processing;

(g) food preparation and service;

(h) personal service and sales;

(i) community and health services;

(j) transport services.

Advantages

(i) good for motivation of students who know what they wish to do;

(ii) can be provided on a scale related to local/national employment needs;

(iii) coherent and simple for timetabling and staff deployment.

Disadvantages:

(i) prescriptive-the school arranges, the students accept;

(ii) requires a major and early vocational decision by students, which most cannot take and most should not take;

(iii) incapable, because of heavy commitment of resources to single purposes, of responding with sufficient speed to changes in local employment patterns in an age of unexpected plant closures;

(iv) no scope for changes of minds by students;

(v) difficult to involve the ablest students.

Tasters or carousels

Definition: several (usually at least three) of the eleven occupational families are sampled in rotation.

Advantages:

(i) students have substantial experience of several occupational families;

(ii) the disadvantages of following courses based on one occupational family are reduced in scale;

(iii) a major contribution to career choice, much greater than is possible by any amount of careers guidance its greatest advantage.

Disadvantages:

(i) as a proportion of time devoted to studies related to specific occupations, most of the disadvantages of 1 remain, albeit to a lesser degree;

(ii) there are doubts whether several of the occupational families span the full ability range—and a consequent need to relate occupational families to students' assessed abilities;

(iii) problem of whether the ablest students will be willing to forego 20-30% of the curriculum for courses which may be difficult to examine at 'O' level/CSE.

Skill-based single subjects

Definition: skills chosen for relevance to employment (e.g. information technology, electronics, manufacturing technology, industrial studies) but delivered within the format of normal school options, that is each taking about 10% of a week, lasting for two years and capable of being validated in a subject-based public examination.

Advantages:

(i) can be absorbed into the curriculum without stratification of the age group by ability:

(ii) not specific to occupational families, ie.e 2 or 3 'subjects' can cross several occupational families and not limit eventual career choice.

Disadvantages:

(i) danger of the vocational emphasis being lost or not appreciated by the students, because it is not explicit;

(ii) if the vocational relevance is not appreciated, the advantages of student motivation will be reduced.

4. Skill-based modules

Definition: as 3, but with the skills taught in short courses (perhaps one term) with regular teacher counselling and student choice of modules.

Advantages:

(i) student commitment is to a short course, with regular opportunities for re-direction;

(ii) student can build on success and forget failure, by continuing with the second stage of some courses but dropping others;

(iii) student can repeat a course;

(iv) quickly adaptable - new modules can be introduced at short notice;

(v) all the advantages of the 'credit' system, that is, short-term goals, a prompt assessment of attainment, the opportunity to build up success in stages;

(vi) greater student responsibility for his/her own studies.

Disadvantages:

(i) puts a heavy responsibility on the counsellor, who needs to be well-trained and experienced;

(ii) could be abused by the dilettante student conscious of the negotiating rights available to him/her;

(iii) there may be difficulties in convincing some examination boards that the modular arrangement is compatible with academic rigour.

Projects

Definition: several projects, lasting perhaps half or a whole term, are planned by teachers with industrialists, in order to encompass chosen skills and experiences.

Advantages:

(i) all the advantages of project work (motivation sustained by the interest of the project, group work, greater use of students' initiative and imagination, greater apparent student control, satisfaction of producing something in a short period);

(ii) experiential learning is promoted to the fore, and skills are acquired because they are seen by students to be needed in order to achieve an objective

Disadvantages:

(i) difficulty of validating such work by a public examination system which is acceptable to students at all levels of ability;

(ii) the initial acquisition of skills may be less rigorous, because it is perceived to be incidental to the main objective; the skills may not be practiced regularly over a long period and students may not retain then or gain confidence in them;

(iii) expensive in resources, requiring the availability of a wide range of facilite and of teachers with a variety of skills, and also requiring much teacher/industrialist time in planning projects;

(iv) difficulty of matching the ideal of student control (with its concomitant of uncharted routes to the set target) with the need to ensure that certain skills are acquired or experiences had.

Permeation

Definition: the objectives of vocational education are not achieved by discrete elements in a student's programme, but by an emphasis on the vocational relevance of all studies and a rigorous promotion of the common elements above.

Advantages:

(i) vocational education becomes part of the powerful 'hidden curriculum', that is, it is implicit in everything the school does;

(ii) a much greater emphasis on the process of learning.

Disadvantages:

(i) very difficult to achieve because teacher/school attitudes are difficult to change unless necessitated by changes in subject matter or teaching method;

(ii) the vocational relevance of some subjects is slight because their justification for inclusion in the curriculum is not vocational. For example, students do not study history in order to become archaeologists, statesmen or civil servants, and, if the school does embrace whole-heatedly and pervasively the importance of vocational relevance to all of its activities, the result could be the denigration of some studies;

(iii) could be the refuge of the humbug who wishes to pretend that the curriculum is changing when it is not.

Preparing and approving new courses: a checklist

When major new elements are admitted to the secondary school curriculum, they need to be assessed by two sets of criteria. We needed to judge whether the new studies will satisfy the objectives of the reform on which we are embarked. We also need to ensure that the new studies are accommodated in a changed curriculum which is balanced and co-ordinated. Below is a checklist which may be used by group planning the new technical and vocational elements to assess whether these will meet the objectives of the reform.

1. Are the skills which are to be learnt modern and needed by business?
2. Are they to be presented in a sound context of theory?
3. Will there be planned opportunities to apply skills/knowledge to solve problems?
4. Are these problems and applications modern and of the kind likely to be met in work or adult life?
5. Will it be possible to forge links with employers, to include:
   (a) discussions about content of courses;
   (b) joint development of course material;
   (c) employer involvement in assessment;
   (d) work experience
   (e) visits and speakers?
6. Is the development of the course best done on the basis of:

(a) one school;

(b) a group of schools;

(c) a local authority area?

7. Is the course, or elements in it, available to:

(a) the full ability range;

(b) both boys and girls?

8. Has it been decided on the structure of the studies:

(a) modular (that is, short course, with student choice);

(b) unit (standard two-year course, but short units of study with end-of-unit assessment);

(c) single-subject?

9. Has the possible influence on the lower school curriculum been considered?

10. Is it desirable/possible to draw up admission criteria (for example, essential background knowledge or skills)?

11. Has a means of managing the new courses been agreed:

(a) one person to have administrative responsibility;

(b) a planning group?

12. Have arrangements been made for guidance staff to be fully briefed on the nature of the course:

(a) a formal presentation by work planners;

(b) a written description;

(c) both?

13. How will new courses be presented to parents and students:

(a) by a direct special presentation;

(b) by inclusion in school's normal 4-5th year course booklet?

14. Is counselling during the course necessary?

15. If yes, has the amount of teacher/careers officer time been assessed and allocated?

16. How is student progress to be assessed:

(a) continuously (if so, what format):

(b) end-of-term;

(c) course work;

(d) final examination?

17. Is a record of achievement to be issued?

18. If yes, have course assessment methods been related to it?

19. What formal public validation will be sought:

(a) GCSE;

(b) B/TEC, GGLI, RSA, CPVE, etc;

(c) local;

(d) combination in order to embrace mixed-ability groups?

20. How will the course relate to post-16 opportunities:

(a) direct to employment;

(b) B/TEC;

(c) City & Guilds of London Institute, RSA;

(d) London Chamber of Commerce;

(e) Institute of Linguists, etc;

(f) CPVE;

(g) Youth Training Scheme?

21. Have the resource needs of the course been assessed in terms of:

(a) equipment;

(b) staffing;

(c) consumables;

(d) subsidies for visits;

(e) residential experience?

22. Can any of these be obtained at low or no cost;

(a) shared use of school facilities;

(b) use of further education resources;

(c) coaches, equipped for the course, to visit several schools:

(d) use of employer facilities/training schools;

(e) equipment from employers?

23. Have the in-service training needs of participating staff been agreed and, if necessary, arrangements for training made?

24. Have arrangements been made to monitor the course, ie. assess the achievement of objectives?

This is a demanding list of decisions to be taken. Some criteria are more readily met than others. Failure to satisfy some of them should not be a reason for not proceeding. Destructive critics might be asked to assess their existing courses by the same standards.

Integrating new studies into a reformed curriculum

Technical and vocational studies have been denied space and status in the secondary curriculum.. Now, with the backing of government and the enthusiastic response of local education authorities and teachers, they are forcing their way in. TVEI is a curricular thug, forcing other subjects to acknowledge its demands. But the week cannot be lengthened and the consequences for the whole curriculum have to be faced.

No solution is possible within a curriculum arrangement based on a small core of English, Mathematics, Physical Education, with a free choice of five or six other subjects from a list of perhaps twenty. If the twenty is increased, say to 25 or 30 by the addition of technical and vocational subjects, we shall have put further strains on an indefensible option system without having secured every young person's right to have these important elements included in their studies..

There is widespread agreement in Britain that we should be moving away from options and looking towards a common curriculum to the age of 16, or at least a major increase in core studies and reduction in options. To succeed, any solution must be based on the avoidance of student stratification. Plans which give vocational studies to 14-16 year olds, on the basis of selecting some pupils at 14 for courses which will not provide routes to high level jobs or admission to higher education, will undermine a major objective of the reform—the need for all students, including the ablest, to have such studies.

Three main routes towards a common curriculum have been charted in recent years, and it will be useful to consider how technical and vocational studies can be embraced by them.

HMI red books

Between 1977 and 1983 Her Majesty's Inspectorate, five local authorities, 41 schools and the advisers from these local authorities worked together to examine their thinking about the curriculum. The three *Red Books* which resulted ought to be studied by any school or group of schools attempting to inegrate technical and vocational studies into their revised curriculum. My references to them are selective and must, for reasons of space, ignore many other aspects of their enquiry. The study started in 1978 by HMI postulating eight areas of experience:

1. aesthetic and creative;
2. ethical;
3. linguistic;
4. mathematical;
5. physical;
6. scientific;
7. social and political;
8. spiritual

These were offered as one way of encouraging coherence and balance in the overall curriculum of individual pupils'. It will be noted that technical and vocational areas of experience are not included, although they may be considered to be covered by 1, 4, 6 or 7.

Thirty-five schools provided the information in the tables below and the 1981 review found significant variations between the schools.

Percentage of time given to English and Mathematics

	Average	*Highest*	*Lowest*
English	14.9	20	12
Mathematics	14	20	10

Number of option blocks offered (=size of non-common curriculum)

Number of schools	3	1	2	17	11	1
Number of option blocks	2	3	4	5	6	7

These two tables indicate a wide variation of practice, but two distinct tendencies:

1. Almost a third of the week (29%) on average was devoted to English and mathematics.

2. The core was very small in most schools, which allowed a choice of five or six subjects, with some constraints.

The 1983 final report of the partnership noted the difficulty of avoiding the alignment of the eight areas of experience with existing subjects and the ease with which teachers can justify their subjects under a number of the areas of experience. They also, however, rejected the notion of aligning option blocks with the eight areas of experience, thus:

Many schools attempt to achieve a balanced curriculum for their pupils in the fourth and fifth years by ensuring that among their options there are those which offer, for example, aesthetic/creative and scientific experiences. To do this, they identify, sometimes under faculty headings such as humanities or communications, groups of subjects in which each subject is thought to offer a similar kind of learning experience. The enquiry suggests that this assumption is unwarranted. For example, it cannot be assumed that geography, history and religious education offer similar learning experiences. It is necessary to examine fully the similarity and the differences of the learning experience in practice offered to and received by pupils. Similarly in music and art, two subjects which are commonly linked within the 'creative' studies cluster, teachers should ascertain whether each does in fact provide similar experiences for pupils. The ways in which the scientific experiences involved in a study of physics, chemistry and biology at this level complement and contrast with each other, also need careful consideration. The working assumption that for the purposes of achieving 'balance' in the curriculum, subjects within identified clusters may safely be treated as interchangeable is no longer tenable. This view is supported by the discrepancies which some schools found when they monitored the learning experiences which pupils actually received.

This conclusion is important and, if 'experience' is used in the sense of learning as monitored in the classroom, entirely convincing. However, it does provoke four comments:

1 It arises from the attempt to assess experience apart from content and 'subjects', but there is now no reason to suppose that the national system of public examinations at 16+ will allow us that freedom.

2. Music and art do provide similar experiences, in the sense that students use knowledge, skill and technique, use their imaginations, are creative and have aesthetic experiences. The medium through which they do this is, of course, different. Under existing option arrangements the choice might not be between art, music, dance or drama, but between art and French or music and chemistry. There is again from ensuring that every child has some aesthetic and creative experience by having an option block solely for the purpose.

3. Physics, biology and chemistry do offer different experiences and a random choice between them is a nonsense. Much work has been done to eliminate the need for this choice. We need to talk of integrated science only because science has become specialized, but there is such a thing as science. In Hertfordshire, for example, the advisers and science teachers have developed a syllabus which allows science to be studied as a single subject for a 16+ examination for those unlikely to specialise afterwards in physics, chemistry and biology, with a second supplementary course for those who are likely to do so. This allows all students to follow a

common science syllabus, supplemented for the minority, and reduces the space demanded by science from three to two or one options.

4. The humanities subjects-geography, history and religious education—are a difficulty, for there is little similarity of learning experience, and efforts to integrate them usually result in either an abandonment of systematic study and content in favour of a topic or method approach, or a purely administrative linkage for examination purposes with options, within one syllabus, which tend to be history or geography-based. There seems to be no obvious way forward.

The most important conclusion of the enquiry for our purposes is that 70-80% of the time available between 11 and 16 years of age should be devoted to the entitlement curriculum and the remaining time allocated for optional components.

Dr David Hargreaves was Reader in Education at Oxford, led a Committee on the Curriculum and Organisation of Secondary Schools in the Inner London Education Authority which reported within one year, and is now Chief Inspector of ILEA. It is unique in English educational history that an academic with a high reputation, having clarified his own thinking on the curriculum, should be invited to lead an enquiry into al aspects of a large education authority's schools and then be appointed its Chief Inspector and be in a position to help in the implementation of reforms which he has helped to devise. His curricular thinking is outlined in *The challenge for the comprehensive school: Culture, curriculum and community* and in *Improving secondary schools.*

In this book Hargreves proposed that:

1 16+public examinations should be abolished, in order to allow the reconstruction of the comprehensive curriculum.

2 11-15 year-old pupils would follow a core curriculum, taking half a pupil's time and embracing all existing school subjects and some new ones, with two central elements:

(a) an integrated course in community studies, not subject based although taught by subject specialists, in blocks of time lasting at least half a day and involving inter-action between community and school;

(b) expressive arts, crafts and sport, including conventional lessons, a critical study of the mass media, the production of plays to be performed publicly in the school and in the community, and music and art festivals.

3 The other half of the pupils' time to be given to options of two types:

(a) remedial options for pupils time to be given to options of two types:

(a) remedial options for pupils at all levels of ability, some formalised, others individualised;

(b) interest options, based perhaps on traditional subjects, but more likely to be specific and shorter topics e.g. 'the Victorian novel' rather than English literature.

4 Selection at 15 for A levels (three years instead of two) or for vocational courses for

those who intend to leave school at 16 for work, with an emphasis in the last year at school on preparation for school-leaving.

These proposals follow a long critique of what is done in schools at present, and a discussion of culture and the community. You should note that only those conclusions which relate to the problem under consideration have been referred to here. Dr Hargreaves' book contains many thoughts besides those outlined, which are important for any study of the 14-16 curriculum.

Improving secondary schools is not, of course, the work of Dr Hargreaves alone but the combined recommendation of a very impressive enquiry into the schools of Britain's largest education authority. The thinking in his book is evident, however, although modified to acknowledge that his main premise - the abolition of 16+ public examinations - is not on offer by the government, and that, as a consequence, we have still to think in terms of subjects. The report recommends an allocation of time for core studies of 62 1/2%, which is rather lower than that recommended in the *Red Books*, and puts into the optional category subjects traditionally part of the core, e.g. physical education. It allocates 25% of time to English and mathematics—somewhat less than the schools in the *Red Book* enquiry on average. The division is:

1 Core subjects—English (12 1/2%), mathematics (12 1/2%), science (10%), personal and social education and religious education (7 1/2% in all).

2 Constrained options—at least one aesthetic

option (10%) and at least one technical option, defined as craft design and technology computer studies (10%).

3 Either additional periods in compulsory subjects or free options or a combination (totaling 37 1/2% of time) from classical and modern language, history, geography, economics, commercial and business studies, physical education, additional science subjects, additional aesthetic subjects, additional technical subjects, additional English and mathematics.

The features of these proposals which concern us are:

1 The rather narrow definition of technical as CDT/computer studies.

2 The low priority given to a vocational orientation of studies for fear of creating an academic/vocational divide and of creating a vocational stream for less able pupils with a severely truncated general education. The observation must be made by those promoting technical and vocational education that this divide exists at present, that the purpose of TVEI is to ensure the absorption of technical and vocational studies into the entitlement curriculum, as the *Red Books* define it, for all pupils including the ablest, and that the relationship of all aspects of study (whether traditionally academic, technical or vocational) to life in the community and as an adult should be emphasised. Elsewhere in the report it is stated, 'We are not against vocational

education in school: the curriculum must have a relevance to the world of work and to pupils 'future occupations and occupational aspirations. Some evidently vocational subjects, such as commercial subjects, have a justified place among or across the free options. Pupils have a right to such a vocational element in their studies during the fourth and fifth years. 'It is thus not a question of principle but of priority. It is also worthy of note that the *Research Studies* issued after *Improving secondary schools* concluded that, 'the study has demonstrated the need for subject and courses to be such that their relevance to work, employment, qualifications for employment and generally life outside school, is patently evident to pupils.'

3 The writers' view that 'engaging pupils with the curriculum content, whether it is seen in terms of subject or areas of experience' is a fundamental means of combating under-achievement. The experience of TVEI is that technical and vocational courses have a high success rate in this regard.

4 The notion of additional studies in the options allows continuing support to be given to pupils with special needs, without the stratification which is necessary in less constrained option systems.

Department of Education and Science

The views of the Department of Education and Science, irrespective of changes in political leadership, also point in the same direction. They have been given in: *Education in Schools, a Consultative Document*

A framework for the school curriculum

The School Curriculum

The organisation and content of the 5.16 curriculum

The *Green Book* of 1977 was presented by a Labour Secretary of State. Shirley Williams, who is now President of the Social Democratic Party. It may be taken, therefore, to represent the views of at least two parties. It expressed concern that the curriculum had become overcrowded, the timetable overloaded and the essentials put at risk - a gentler way of referring to 'clutter' in the timetable. It was worried that the curriculum was not matched to life in a modern industrial society. It argued for a bigger core and national guidelines thus, 'it is clear that the time has come to try to establish generally accepted principles for the composition of the secondary curriculum for all pupils. This does not presuppose uniform answers... But there is a need to investigate the part which might be played by a "protected" or "core" element of the curriculum common to all schools'.

The School Curriculum gave guidance to local authorities following consultations based upon the 1980 *Framework* and on an HMI paper. *A view of the Curriculum.* It was issued by Mark Carlisle, a Conservative Secretary of State and came to three major conclusions:

1 'The curriculum offered by a school, and the curriculum received by individual pupils,

should not be simply a collection of separate subjects; nor is it sufficient to transfer, with modifications, the ideas about the curriculum in the separate selective and non-selective schools of an earlier generation into the comprehensive schools attended by most pupils today.'

2 'There is an overwhelming case for providing all pupils between 11-16 with curricula of a broadly common character with substantial common elements.'

3 School education needs to equip young people fully for adult and working life in a world which is changing very rapidly indeed.'

The DES Note of September 1984 continued the theme, but found the task of reaching decisions as difficult as ever and was prepared only to set out 'some tentative and provisional views'. It rejected the notion of short courses, arguing that 'the study of a subject should be sufficient to be of lasting value'. It listed the essential studies, but found that they added up to more than could be crammed into a week. Its main conclusions about the curriculum for 14-16 year olds are:

1 If the curriculum includes as much as 30% of free of unconstrained options, 'some serious sacrifice in curriculum breadth results'; a maximum of 15% is mooted.

2 'It is government policy that there should be option choice for the 4th and 5th years.'

3 These subjects or elements should be compulsory, either as core or as constrained options:

(a) Composite course to include careers, health and social education;

(b) Religious education (either separately or in the composite course);

(c) English (including literature);

(d) Mathematics;

(e) Science—'Government policy is that all pupils should be introduced, *under whatever guise* to all three. Pupils suffer a particular loss of subsequent opportunity if at the end of year 3 they cease to study *any important element of a broad science curriculum'*. One example mentions a school where the pupils gained entrance to Oxbridge to read science, having taken the Schools Council Integrated Science Project's O level syllabus as part of the core.

(f) Modern Languages - a tentative proposition that the least able pupils should not start a foreign language, that a large majority should study one language for 3 years (11-14) and that 'some' should study one language for 5 years and a second language for 2 or 3 years.

(g) Humanities - a proposition for years 1-3, that every pupil should study 'on a worthwhile scale' history and geography and in addition 'under whatever guise' the principles underlying a free society and some basic economic awareness, is followed by a question for years 4 and 5, 'Is it acceptable that any of these three (sic) elements can be dropped in these two years? The question seems to point towards integrated humanities or a seven-day week.

(h) Aesthetic subjects - either art, music or drama, with the unargued and tentative suggestion that 'art now figures more predominantly in the timetable than music or drama, and that should probably continue to be the case.

(i) Application of knowledge and skills, especially in mathematics and science.

(j) Craft, design and technology-it is only a 'possible objective' that this should be compulsory as there are not enough teachers.

4 'Pre-vocational studies are defined as 'technical' or 'commercial' or as a combination of both. TVEL is mentioned; it is 'hoped' that it will show ways in which technical and vocational elements can enrich the curriculum. Co-ordinated course and work experience, of the sort offered in the past to post-16 young people, are also considered capable of making 'a valuable contribution' to the curriculum of 14-16 year olds. A cautionary word about the danger of fostering narrow vocational skills is given.

Two suggestions are offered about how this quart is to be fitted into the pint pot. The main subjects can be taught in less time by 'removing clutter', and time can be found by giving pupils 'more, and better directed, homework'. These thoughts perhaps illustrate the magnitude of the problem rather than solve it.

A further reference to the Note will illustrate how, in present conditions, we have to settle for less than satisfactory solutions. Her Majesty's Inspectors have provided, with comments, examples of existing school curricula. The following three comments all apply to the same school:

1 relatively few pupils take a modern language in years 4-5;

2 the science which all pupils must take is not a balanced science course;

3 the curricular pattern has breadth and balance for all pupils.

The parameters for integrating technical and vocational elements into the curriculum

It will be helpful to draw common threads from these three major searches for curriculum reform.

1 All favour a large common element, consisting of core subjects and constrained potions:

Red Books 70-80%

Hargreaves 50% in his book, 62 1/2% in the ILEA report

DES 70-85%

2 All promote the value of practical work and the application of knowledge to problem-solving.

3 All favour or accept a measure of cross-curricular or unit studies.

4 All retain some options and see merit in limited student choice.

5 They differ fundamentally on their approach to the traditional single-subject based curriculum: *Red Books* see essential elements as experience separate from subjects or disciplines. *Hargreaves* in his book largely favours the end of subject disciplines as we currently understand them, but as a contributor to the

ILEA report he accepts a subject based curriculum with the examinable elements limited to five or six subjects at any one sitting.

DES thinks almost entirely in terms of subjects, except when it is considering topics such as health and careers, or vocational studies.

We also need to acknowledge that none devotes much time to a consideration of how technical and vocational elements may be included. This may be because they were written before the need for such elements was clearly identified. In the case of the ILEA report it may be because of fears about an academic/vocational division. In the case of the DES it may be that, having argued for the inclusion of almost all traditional subject disciplines, the task of embracing additional elements was too daunting. In considering how to include these elements, we have little guidance from the main curricular studies reviewed, although we may take their frameworks as the most likely ones within which we shall have to work.

Before we address ourselves to that problem however, we have to decide what will be the examination or assessment framework which needs to go hand in hand with the curricular framework, for there is no evidence to suggest that Britain, unlike some other countries which are at least its equal in both industrial and cultural achievement, is willing to forego the public and national certification of its youth at the age of 16.

The examination background: a further problem

Britain is currently grappling with the problem of

two new and largely unrelated public assessment systems to be taken by most pupils at the age of 16.

1 General Certificate of Secondary Education (GCSE)

The key decision which sets the parameters of 14-16 curriculum reform was taken by the Secretary of State, Sir Keith Joseph, in June 1984 when he announced a single system of 16+ examining to replace the existing separate GCE O levels and CSE examinations. The etching profession was generally in favour of the merger, as a ratioalisation of 16+ examining to replace the existing separate GCE O levels and CSE examinations. The teaching profession was generally in favour of the merger, as a rationalisation of 16+ examining, but there was a feeling that the long-awaited reform was not only overdue but out-dated. The case against any public examination, taken by the majority of young people at the end of compulsory schooling, is strong. Tim Brig-house, Chief Education Officer for Oxfordshire, was one of those who made an eleventh hour bid to stop Sir Keith Joseph's decision to merge the two systems and thus consolidate 16+ examining, arguing that, 'hitherto the taking of examinations at the end of the fifth year has been a powerful and malign influence on secondary schools'. Brig-house preferred the abolition of 16+ examinations, but knew it was not a possibility and was prepared to settle for the *status quo*. Representatives of head teachers and college principal organisations argued that the 'concept of a curriculum of preparation for adult life... might reduce the dependence placed at the moment on a formal single subject examination at 16+. 'The opposite view was put by members of the Standing Conference on University Entrance whose chief concern was that any changes in 16+ examining should retain syllabuses which provide a sound foundation for GCE Advanced Level and University entrance. The argument is between those who believe that the secondary school curriculum is best designed bottom-up and that this is incompatible with the need to prepare students for single-subject public examinations at 16, and those who see public examinations at 16 and 18, controlled by universities, as the best means of maintaining standards in secondary schools.

The views of employers may have been decisive. In March 1984 Sir Keith wrote to eighteen business organisations asking for their views but first queries the use by employers of examinations as a 'first sift', stating that the knowledge of parents and teachers that this was so,distorted 'the significance which should be attached to examinations' and led to the neglect of 'important skills and personal qualities'. The replies of employer were unambiguous. A Schools Council survey of opinions, which included those of almost 500 employers, showed their overwhelming support for 16+examinations. The Engineering Employers' Federation and the Confederation of British Industry both confirmed their support for a common examining system at 16+.

With secondary school spokespersons preferring the merging of two examinations into one, with some seeing the possibility of ending such examining altogether, and the users of examination results (universities and employers) wanting the retention of public examinations, Sir Keith's decision was in fact widely applauded. 16+ single subject examinations will continue to affect curriculum planning. That fact, welcome or unwelcome, cannot be ignored. The General Certificate of Secondary Education, as the new combined system is called, is here to stay.

Certificate of Pre-Vocational Education (CPVE)

This new education certificate was proposed in a *Consultative Document* prepared for the Secretary of State for Education and presented to him in April 1984. Pilot schemes started in September 1984, with full implementation from September 1985.

It comes from an entirely different horse-box from GCSE, although from the same stable. Much of the thinking has been done at the DES by the Further Education Unit which is co-ordinating a programme of support for the new certificate. Both horses -GCSE and CPVE-have the same owner. They are running in the same race. It is not yet clear which horse the owner is backing.

CPVE is the result of a partnership between the Business and Technician Education Council (B/TEC) and the City and Guilds of London Institute (CGLI), both of which have a vast experience of modular and non-subject-based courses for post-16 students in further education colleges. They have some experience of extending these courses down into the 14-16 curriculum.

The certificate is a whole curriculum based upon an integrated programme covering six elements:

(a) Core, made up of ten components intended to

provide aims and typical learning activities:

personal and career development;

communication;

numeracy;

Science and technology;

industrial, social and environmental studies;

information technology;

problem-solving;

practical skills;

social skills;

creative development

(b) Vocational studies, based upon clusters of studies, e.g. manufacturing through craft and mass production techniques; or narrower activities, e.g. information processing; standards will relate to criteria for entry to employment.

(c) Additional studies, compulsory for centres to provide, but not obligatory for students; includes extensions to (a) and (b), aesthetic subjects, sport, remedial work (these equate roughly to Hargreaves remedial and interest options).

(d) Learning through practical experience, including work experience.

(e) Careers guidance.

(f) Student involvement in all aspects of learning, including assessment, which will include a record of achievement and a profile of performance.

The approach is fundamentally different from the single-subject based GCSE and the assumptions about the 14-16 curriculum in the three routes charted by HMI, Hargreaves and the DES reviewed above. There is, however, a desire to relate the two, in order to establish a progression and a system of credits. The possibility of a part-time CPVE is mooted.

Although planned initially as a one-year course for the 16-17 year olds, the first year of post-compulsory schooling, it has been the intention from the outset to cover the 14-18 age range and thus embrace the same years covered by GCSE. It was stated in January 1984 that the aim was 'to create a new curriculum pathway for that majority of those between the ages of 14 and 18 for whom the traditional academic curriculum is unsuitable'. It is asserted in the *Consulative Document* that GCSE and CPVE can be complementary for 14-16 year olds and that a coherent framework can be worked out.

A way forward

What are we to make of this dichotomy? On the one hand we have a recently confirmed subject-based examining system, designed to cater for the majority and certainly the top 60% of the ability range and well-suited to the type of curriculum emerging from long discussions within the secondary school sphere in which both the DES and HMI have taken a lead. On the other hand we have a model which solves all of the curricular problems arising from the single-subject base, but which seems incapable of covering the main elements to which every pupil is entitled within the years of compulsory schooling. What follows is an attempt to embrace most of the objectives agreed to be desirable within a comprehensive school, with some differentiation by ability but without banding across year groups, using the GCSE single-subject mode, but including some cross-curricular elements. It is not, of course, a model. Even if accepted as a solution to the major curricular problems which we have been considering, it is not capable of being adopted in any particular school. It is obviously not a putative timetable, but a diagrammatic method of presenting curricular elements. It needs to be read with the notes which follow it. The bottom lines relate the subjects or elements of study to the three major curriculum development reviews which have been analysed earlier.

Notes on the curricular framework

(a) The allocation of time for English and Mathematics is a little less than the present average as revealed by the *Red Book* survey, but is the same as recommended in *Improving Secondary Schools.*

(b) Possibilities of additional time for literature and remedial English exist under Options.

(c) Mathematics is seen as a course which embraces not only the knowledge deemed desirable by the subject specialists, but as a genuinely core subject, related to and supportive of science, technical, vocational and economic studies.

(d) It is assumed that an integrated science course will be adopted, embracing the three main elements of says should be studied until the age of 16. This then becomes compulscry for all pupils and gives a broad and coherent science course which is adequate for the needs of all pupils except those who are likely to take separate GCE Advanced Levels post-16.

(e) Humanities remain a problem, as was noted earlier. Unsatisfactory as it is, there seems little alternative but to offer pupils a straight choice of good history and geography courses, unless schools are satisfied that integrated humanities courses do include sufficient of the essential elements of these studies and sufficient content to justify change.

(f) The time allocation allows scope for any of the approaches described in chapter 2 to be adopted:

(i) single-subject 2-year options, similar to existing GCE-CSE courses;

(ii) modular courses;

(iii) two year subject-based courses, but divided into half-term (6-8 week) unit with clear objectives which are known to the pupils at the outset, and with assessment of progress in discussion with each pupil at the end of every unit, as proposed in *Improving Secondary Schools* as a general change for all subjects;

(iv) the non-subject based approach.

(g) Constrained options are offered in the aesthetic, humanities and ethnical and vocational elements. This allocation for Options is the only time when free options are offered. Remedial options are intended to be in the sense used by Hargreaves, i.e. both remedial in the traditional sense of additional help to students have difficulty with basic skills and concepts, and additional studies needed by pupils, irrespective of their general level of work, because they and their teachers see a major gap or gaps in their experience to date.

(h) *Modern language remain a difficulty*. It is proposed that the free option slot be the place where a foreign language may be studied. No allocation is made for a second foreign language may be studied. No allocation is made for a second foreign language below the age of 16. Hargreaves, in *The challenge for the comprehensive school* argues for the abandonment of foreign language studying until students see a possible use for one, when they will acquire at least as satisfactory a standard in a short time by an intensive course at an older age as they do now by the long haul and short doses from 11-16. His argument will persuade many. Certainly the notion of all children spending more than 500 hours studying French from 11-16, in order to achieve the level of proficiency in French-speaking and writing which we know as a nation we have acquired, is hard to justify. However enjoyable for some pupils, and a allocation of time for one is made. The alternatives for a second foreign language would then be as part of a business-orientated vocational course in the technical and vocational slot or as an intensive post-16 course in the technical and vocational slot or as an intensive post-16 course. The former needs to be undertaken with care. One has heard of course, intended to be vocational, which look similar to traditional courses and which have changed their names only to attract resources.

(i) The core is not intended to be modular, which would allow choice. Nor is it intended to be based on a carousel of courses, although there are organisational arguments in favour of this approach and the accommodation of physical education may require it. It is thought of as courses, quite short but of variable length, to be taken by a team of teachers, including some senior teachers such as heads and deputies. The size of teaching group would vary, as would the learning methods. The planning would take account of the fact that careers guidance, for example, needs a big time allocation sometimes and then nothing at all for a period. The proposed arrangement allows considerable blocks of time when it is needed, or for two or three courses to be taught in parallel. Its flexibility is a principal virtue.

Observations on the framework

The success of a framework of the kind proposed depends on the whole staff of the school accepting painful change. Scientists, especially physicists and chemists, who see general science courses as but the necessary preliminary to the narrower study which has been the focus of their own studies and of their professional training since the age of 14, may need some persuasion to look at the problem as an educational one. On the other hand, teachers of aesthetic and creative subjects, and to some extent of technology, will recognise that the frame work gives them reserved allocations. They are no longer competing with science, modern language and other subjects, which in the eyes of parents have primarily a vocational justification, but are in competition only with each other. It would be a welcome paradox if a curricular frame work which is designed to accommodate both current thinking about the curriculum as a whole and the specific needs of technical and vocational studies, were to free music, dance and drama from their greatest handicap—their lack of a raison *d'etre*.

Experience from many of the pilot TVEI project suggests that longer periods of time than we normally allocate are more effective for lessons where process is important as well as content. Half days have commonly been found to be useful. This experience might also be applicable to other subjects or elements, for example science, aesthetic and creative subjects, perhaps even humanities. One of the problems which we currently face with options is the conflicting time requirements of subjects in the same option block. If French and Art are in the same block, the teachers of the first usually like to have four periods on different days, whilst teachers of the latter want at least double periods. The curriculum framework suggested eliminates this disparity of requirements except for the one strand where free options remain.

We have to face the problem analysed earlier - the difficulty of finding compatibility between the GCSE principle of single-subject based examinations and the CPVE principle of a whole curriculum. GCSE will provide an assessment for at least the top 60% of the ability range and will certainly continue to be the examination for all those who would have taken GCEO levels, that is, the ablest. It is not, however, a mere extension of O level, as Sir Wilfrid Cockcroft of the Secondary Examinations Council has emphasized; there is encouragement that more marks be awarded for teacher-assessed course work, for example. Alongside GCSE the DES has been promoting pilot developments of curricula and methods of assessment and validation for the 40% least able pupils under its Low Achievers Project. The two developments could be taken to cover the full ability range, and some of the pilots are designed with this mind. CPVE, on the other hand, could be available in theory to the whole ability range from 14-16, although it does promote itself as 'an alternative route' and it is difficult to imagine that a youngster who could obtain eight GCSEs and regard them as the same as eight GCE O levels will readily forego the opportunity. The choice facing schools therefore seems to be stark. They either use GCSE and the Low Achievers Project as the basis for the curriculum and its validation of all their pupils, ignoring CPVE, or they divide the year group at 14, probably into three groups: GCSE for the ablest and parallel GCSF and CPVE curricula for the average and below. The only other compromise would be a combination of GCSE subjects and a part-time CPVE. This would not avoid the need for a fundamental choice to be made by schools. It would only blur the edges. It is unfortunate that schools should have to face such a choice.

This lack of coherence in planning, which has produced a multiplicity of education and training schemes, many of recent origin, attracted the attention of government in the autumn of 1984. Spurred by a report entitled *Competence and competition*, prepared by the Institute of Manpower Studies at Sussex University at the request of the National Economic Development Office and the Manpower Services Commission, the government began to grasp the nettle which it had itself planted and nurtured. Geoffrey Holland, Director of MSC, complained that existing vocationally-related programmes were not producing the flow of technically competent young people which three major competitors—the USA, Japan and West Germany—were producing. The most important conclusion of the studies made of these three countries is that they give all youngsters a longer period of education and training than Britain does. We can be sure that Britain will move to a *de facto* education/training leaving age of 18 before long, if only as a contribution to the shorter working life which must follow technological advance and unemployment. There is no answer to our dilemma in this report and the discussions which it has promoted. Indeed, the recommendation that 80% of young people should enter the labour market with a qualification relevant to their employment, if coupled to the German example of a selective secondary system to 15 or 16 followed by the equivalent of an A level/vocational education divide, is worrying. If 20% of British students were to take GCSE followed by A levels and 80% were to take CPVE as the basis of a 14-18 curriculum, we should be perpetuating a divide in education, training and society which may be a major cause of our industrial decline as well as being educationally archaic. Perhaps the most important observation in this report is that, 'It is rarely possible to transfer parts of the system of one country into another and achieve similar results'.

Similarly the Secretary of State for education was concerned about the lack of coherence. Referring to proposed GCE A/S level, TVEI, CPVE and YTS, Sir Keith said that. 'The Government aims to define standards of performance and to develop a system of certification which can be applied to both YTS and to pre-vocational courses in schools and further education it would be helpful to schools if the government were to succeed. The schools will not that all four phenomena started or were planned in the same academic year of 1983-84 and may wonder whether it is sensible to design different routes and then try to make them coherent as a secondary activity. We may also note the absence of GCSE and GCE A/S level from Sir Keith's aim to achieve coherence, and may be anxious about the possible reemergence of a duality of routes which we have been trying to discard. Is it too much to hope that we might have in England and Waes what has been proposed by the Secretary of State for Scotland, that is, one examination board for all sub-degree level of education awards?

There are aspects of the framework which are essential and should not be overlooked just because they cannot be represented in the diagram.The first is the need for coherence in each individual *Red Books*. The framework is intended to achieve that coherence, but will not do so if English and mathematics, for example are seen as discrete studies.We know that, in the wake of Bullock and Cockcroft if not before, this should not be the case. However, it often is.

The second is the need to abandon the whole timetable for the whole year group for days, sometimes for a week at a time, in order to send pupils out on work experience or to have some combined activities such as educational industrial visits. Critics will say that this is a further erosion of learning time. It is not. It is a loss of subject teaching time. It will only be a loss of pupil learning time if it is badly done. The week cannot be lengthened. The new cannot come in without concessions from the old. The point is fundamental.

This chapter and the book as a whole are concerned with the 14-16 curriculum, because this is the period of education where young people are approaching the end of compulsory school. Consequently, it is bound to have a different emphasis from what has gone before and what is to follow. There is no need for significantly different curricula for pupils in the first three years of secondary school (ages 11-14) and little variation occurs.After 16 there is a great variety of provision both full-time and part-time in schools, further education and tertiary colleges, company training schools YTS, information technology centres, etc. This is likely to continue. The changes in the 14-16 curriculum are part of general change, however, and they promote it. Changes at 14 which are occurring now, the development of information technology courses for example, may change learning methods in the whole of the secondary school across the curriculum once the principles are understood, the equipment provided and the staff trained. Curriculum planning for the whole school should have regard to the need for a continuum of education and training. Humility and the need to address ourselves to manageable tasks require us to concentrate on parts of the whole. We should not forget the whole.

Curriculum development requires that all teachers who contribute to it in a school have time. We cannot continue to regard classroom work, and its consequences such as marking, as the only activity admissible in the day-time responsibilities of most teachers. The consequence of that is that course planning, the development of learning materials and counselling students are seen as extra curricular activities. This is well understood in schools. It is understood by the DES. Having observed the range of between 72% and 84% for the average teachers' contact time with pupils in different schools (a big variation) the DES Note of September 1984 states that 'schools need to set aside enough non-teaching time for preparation, marking and in-service training and other professional development.' Schools can do a certain amount by increasing class size at the secondary level to achieve this, which is what some schools at the lower level of the contact range are doing. Significant improvement is impossible until the

Secretary of State convinces the Chancellor of the Exchequer.

All curriculum development should consider the appropriateness of teaching styles, the re-training needs of teachers, the monitoring of change to asses whether objective are being achieved, and the additional guidance to the pupils which is required.

10 Monitoring

Why monitor?

The work of schools should be constantly monitored and success in achieving specific objectives should be evaluated. This is done all the time by Her Majesty's Inspectors local authority advisers inspectors projects covering particular aspects of school work such as those conducted in the past by the Schools Council and by individual schools. Monitoring is an aspect of both accountability (letting the community which pays for education know what is being achieved) and development. It has both a passive and an active function. The current reform of the curriculum, to change the content of courses and approaches to learning, is intended to have profound and permanent consequences. It is clearly important that we should know what is happening as it happens, measure progress towards agreed objectives, recognise problems and suggest solutions identify and publicise good practice and expose bad practice.

National monitoring

The Technical and Vocational Education Initiative is being monitored nationally in several ways:

(a) A database containing unidentifiable information on all students and teachers is being compiled.

(b) The curricula followed by TVEI-funded students are being investigated by Professor Harrison of Trent Polytechnic.

(c) A financial database will attempt to provide government with information on the costs of particular courses and on alternative methods of providing them.

(d) HMI are conducting their own survey.

(e) Research institutions have been invited to investigate particular aspects of the initiative. It is important that there should be monitoring of major themes across the initiative as a whole. Questions relating to strategies for avoiding sex-stereotyping, whether the full ability range of students is represented and employer perceptions of the scheme are examples of important issues for which answers still have to be provided. As information is drawn together across the scheme local authorities learn from each other. Later evaluation will need to consider the relative success of different approaches to the basic objectives of TVEI.

(f) There are some university-led research projects which monitor several of the pilot projects for example that being conducted by Lancaster University. The first phase of this research compared the schemes from Barnsley, Wigan and Wirral. An analysis was made of student and teacher attitudes towards TVEI. The expectations of students their career aspirations and their comprehension of the aims of TVEI were explored by the administration of questionnaires. It is intended that this research programme can expand as other projects join the Lancaster monitoring. Their emphasis over the life of the project will be to follow a sample of the first intake of students through the four years and to gather information about subsequent annual intakes, recording any change from previous years and seeking reasons why changes have occurred.

(g) Independent national evaluations, concerned mainly with aspects of curriculum, change are currently being developed by the National Foundation for Education Research and the Education Department of Leeds University.

Local monitoring

It is essential that each individual project is carefully monitored. An example of local monitoring is the Devon project at Exeter where the Education department at Exeter University has appointed a research assistant to follow a monitoring programme through two or three years; other individuals with interests in particular aspects of the scheme will provide research information on a part-time basis. A detailed case-study of the first two months' planning of the project has been compiled by a teacher, seconded to the university for one year; this document provides an important contribution to the Exeter monitoring programme.

A local authority approach

Hertfordshire is one of the first fourteen TVEI projects and is being monitored in three ways:

Monitoring and Assessment Group

This has been established by the County's Chief Adviser and works with the project. It is small group made up mostly of local authority personnel who are not directly involved in the project. Aspects of the project which it is examing are balance between core and technical and vocational elements, work experience and liaison with industry, involvement of further education, counseling and guidance and resource implications for dissemination to the rest of the county.

Independent research into particular/ aspects

The first example of this is the part-time secondment of a deputy headteacher to investigate strategies for ending sex-stereotyping and promoting equality of opportunity for girls and boys as a university supervised research project.

Independent research into the fundamental curriculum change which is being promoted

I have been seconded for four years having been a Senior Teacher and Head of Science in one of the pilot schools to work on monitoring the curriculum in the ten pilot schools. My work is being supervised by an institution of higher education and is a piece of independent research which must meet the academic demands characteristic of such work. As I am locally based I am able to participate in planning meetings, thus gaining insights into thing about future developments and being able to contribute data from my investigations so far.

A framework

A framework for monitoring in Hertfordshire arose from a realisation that the promotion of technical and vocational elements would produce fundamental changes in the curriculum and that the implications for schools were far-reaching. The consolidation of new courses into existing programmes for fourteen to eighteen year olds exerted pressure on an already-overcrowded option system. TVEI was expanding the curriculum in technical and vocational content; it was for the schools to maintain balance and breadth in educational experience whilst responding to the pressures of a changing industrial society.

It was clear at this very early stage that there was a need for schools to assess for themselves what effects were being produced. A major attempt at curriculum reform requires enquiry into the nature of that change; teachers has need to examine the change, considering the implications from all educational perspectives. The uniqueness of the initiative in its impact on curriculum innovation was sufficient stimulus for me to construct a programme of enquiry. It was important that the investigation was rigorous and that any judgments made would be impartial and based only on accumulated evidence deduced from objective information.

The relationship of monitoring and evaluation

It is helpful to distinguish between monitoring and evaluation. Monitoring is a continuous process of gathering information relevant to change. It is a characteristic of monitoring that events are recorded as they happen, that important evidence is not lot. Once data is available, it is possible to appraise what significant changes have taken place and what new directions might be the result of the implementation of the initiative.

Evaluation is the summation of the events which have occurred. It is a statement of the success or failure of the curricular change. Without the solid information provided by monitoring, reliable retrospective judgments cannot be made; monitoring is the essential ingredient of a proper evaluation.

Essential elements of monitoring

How, then does one approach the monitoring of a particular project? There are four important elements:

1 The project has clearly-defined objectives which provide the basis for the enquiry; it is necessary to find accurate ways of measuring success in achieving these objectives.

2 There is need to examine two main aspects of change:

(a) The examination of curriculum patterns within the schools and the shift in emphasis throughout the scheme.

(b) the educational programme for individual students; ways need to be found of measuring change in their total educational experience.

3 It is important to identify unintended adverse consequences and to advise on corrective measures within the life-time of the scheme.

4 Close analysis of what is happening within the schools and careful appraisal of changes that are made provide an objective basis for making a contribution to the development of curriculum reform.

The Hertfordshire project has the distinctive

feature of being carried out in all ten schools in one division of the local authority. To assess the initial impact of TVEI on the curriculum, it was first necessary to explore the option schemes for fourth and fifth year students which already existed in the schools. It was important to identify time spent on core subjects in relation to option time. Criteria has to be devised for assessing the degree of general and vocational elements in the curriculum. It was possible to examine how the vocational courses had been assimilated into the option schemes of each school.

The speed with which change was introduced meant that in the first year schools could do little more than adapt existing curricular patterns to admit new courses. A re-thinking of the curriculum needed more time, and this was given to planning for the second year. Senior staff in the schools have been able to consider more slowly where technical and vocational courses are most appropriately placed within the option schemes and to provide students with the best combinations of subjects for a balanced educational programme. It is crucial that this kind of information is collected for the duration of the scheme, in order to assess the degree of change over a five year period.

The drawing together of this background information took longer than expected. It was important to visit headteachers and senior staff from all schools and one was always conscious of the continual pressures upon them; time for discussion has to be brief. Detailed information was readily available from the schools but its presentation varied from school to school.

Standardistaion of data

The standardisation of curriculum information was the first problem to be tackled. This was facilitated by the fact that curriculum analysis forms are returned by all Hertforshire schools but it was important to represent in a standard form the effect on the curriculum of admitting new courses. Following discussions with members of the team for national monitoring of TVEI curriculum from Trent Polytechnic, an acceptable procedure for representing shift in curriculum patterns was devised. It is possible to show, in standard diagrammatic form central curriculum issues for each educational institution such as:

(a) the original curriculum prior to TVEI;

(b) subjects enhanced by the funding of TVEI;

(c) new subjects in the curriculum as a result of TVEI.

The first year of TVEI is unique in offering measurable information of the specific change in curriculum offered to individual students. Some schools were at an advanced stage of subject choices when the scheme was announced. The students from these schools who joined the scheme had two observable curriculum designs, pre-TVEI and post-TVEI. It has been possible to examine the effects of introducing greater emphasis on technical and vocational elements for particular children.

In order that the objectives of TVEI should be achieved, the Manpower Services Commission laid down certain criteria which had to be met by the local education authorities. A maximum of thirty students from each institution could participate with equal numbers of boys and girls representing the full ability range. It was the staff in the schools who assessed which youngsters were most suited to the course.

The senior careers officers for TVEI and I conducted interviews with staff in five schools to discover how each of the schools set about the process of guidance. These sessions have provided important information and ideas. We have a pool of valuable thoughts and experiences which if shared, offer possibilities for all schools to make improvements in the procedure of option guidance. Staff from the schools have felt able to make suggestions about how they thought the project might make adjustments, which provide important dialogue for planning future directions.

Monitoring the ability range

One of my chief concerns was to monitor the ability range of students. If the full ability range is represented then the scheme is truly comprehensive. If technical and vocational subjects gain equality of status with traditional subjects, if able students are encouraged to include technological and vocational areas in their educational programme without fear of damaging their route to higher education, then the scheme will have brought about significant change. If the full ability range is not represented then the scheme will fall short of its intentions. Technical and vocational education with planned work experience, is for all students.

Monitoring the ability range of TVEI students meant identifying the range of their measurable abilities in relation to other members of their year group. The first task was to investigate the types of 'ability' tests available it was important to examine one's reasons for embarking upon the exercise. It was easy to decide that an objective measure of student abilities was necessary. It was not quite so easy to find a test which met all our requirements and the sensitivities of students being asked to participate in the process. I was certain that several criteria had to be met if testing were to answer our needs.

1 The presentation of the test had to stimulate students to respond, positively, to reveal their true abilities if the test results were to be reliable.

2 The standard of response required by the test had to be appropriate to the age-range of students we were considering.

3 The testing should offer teachers, parents and students positive feed-back of student achievements: it seemed a poor educational reason for testing simply to place students on a standardised scale, without the possibility of real dialogue concerning the outcome of results.

4 The test needed to suit a wide ability range of youngsters, as we were involved in testing approximately 600 students from four schools with an all-ability intake.

5 The test should acknowledge a range of differing abilities which were to be assessed separately.

6 The test needed to allow the possibility of re-testing at different points in the scheme if information were to be accumulated over a period of time.

Advice was sought from several people experienced in the field of psychological testing. We were slow to decide which test should be used. Finally we were satisfied with the process of testing. Students responded well; even those who resisted initially became absorbed by the demands of the test. The test gave the measurements we needed. We recognise the limits of this kind of testing and are conscious of the need to provide a range of evidence in the assessment of cognitive abilities when coming to conclusions regarding individual students.

The criterion relating to equal opportunities for boys and girls that there should be an equal number of each cn the scheme and that courses should be designed to avoid sex-stereotyping, was considered to be of such major concern that it is being monitored separately as already indicated.

Post 16 monitoring

The monitoring of changes in educational provision beyond the age of sixteen promises to be more demanding than the monitoring exercise thus far. The schools are grouped into consortia for 16-18 courses. The complexity of planning increases as the arrangements between the schools develop further, as further education becomes integrated into the process, and as the diversity of courses becomes much greater.

There is a wide range of information about individual students which needs to be monitored as they enter the scheme. Their reasons for participating, their abilities and aspirations are matters of prime importance throughout the scheme.

What happens to students as they leave the scheme, which skills and qualifications they have acquired and where their vocational orientations finally lead will need careful monitoring.

The growth of links between industrialists and educationists is central to the reform. There is important information concerning employer perceptions of TVEI to be gained from the monitoring of works experience programmes. TVEI has generated employer involvement in curriculum planning and in the writing of examination syllabuses. As employers and teachers work together towards documentation for the school-leaver which is more detailed and useful than past records, so mutual understanding increase.

These issues, which in Hertfordshire are considered to be central to the monitoring of curriculum change, can be summarised in the diagram though it must be said that if monitoring is fulfilling its function, the programme will be flexible and adjustments will be made as need dictates.

The education of teachers

Proposal for curriculum change based on pre-vocational and vocational initiatives present teaching staffs in secondary schools with a formidable challenge. They are no less demanding of those who provide programmes of teacher training to those entering the profession or to practising teachers. All such proposals require a major shift in attitudes and approaches. Essentially what they challenge is the exercise of benevolent authority upon which so much of the tradition of schooling rests. They question whether in a learning environment in which the teacher wields authority partly by disciplining behaviour from a position of guardianship, in *loco parentis*, and partly by disciplining learning from a position of authority in knowledge, are helpful or inhibiting to students who are about to enter in adult world in progressing towards independence, autonomy, assurance and self-sufficiency. Furthermore, they invoke teachers to revise their practice in quite specific ways:

— to change the basis of staff/student relationships

— to design programmes of active, participative, experiential learning, applying the principle of cooperative rather than competitive learning, instead of programmes based on the transmission of knowledge.

— to establish learning objectives to include skills and competencies and the practice and reinforcement of those skills.

— to offer flexible, modular courses within which young people may negotiate what and how they will learn

— to relate learning objectives to include skills and competencies and the practice and reinforcement of those skills.

— to offer flexible, modular courses within which young people may negotiate what and how they will learn.

— to relate learning directly to applications in the changing world of adult life and employment

— to embrace new forms of assessment, seeing assessment as an integral and continuous part of the educative process, rather than as serving the functions of screening, selecting and certificating

— to offer constructive guidance and counselling towards better educational and vocational achievement

— to work with others in team coördination, including those outside the school who can contribute substantially to the total learning experience.

This is not an exhaustive list, but enough to make clear the magnitude of the task and the fundamental nature of the change. If the challenge is to be met, teachers will need to work together to establish these new interpretations within their institutions. They will need the support of staff development programmes which provide the necessary experience and time for reflection upon it, so that they can work with confidence based on understanding and conviction, not merely upon exhortation or encouragement.

This perception of the wider objectives pursued through a new curriculum may best be achieved by immersion in courses of training which provide the same relationships, the same forms of experiential and reflective learning, the same mode of assessment and self-appraisal which are consonant with the curricular development which the training is designed to support. Too often the training courses exemplify a tradition they are pledged to reform.

There is little reason to suppose that any significant onslaught on the problem can be mounted through initial training in the immediate future. The system which now operates offers courses of two kinds: three or four year concurrent courses which combine undergraduate higher education, including education studies, with training leading to a teaching qualification (BEd courses): and one-year courses for graduates in subject disciplines, which combine education studies and professional training (PGCE courses). Both types of courses are available for those training to teach in primary or secondary schools, but the BEd route is becoming increasingly restricted for secondary training to subjects in which there is shortage of qualified teachers in schools or in which there is only limited opportunity for study in higher education in institutions other than those training teachers. Religious Education, Mathematics and Physics fall into the first category, Business Studies, Home Economics and Craft, Design and Technology into the second. The numbers of teachers training to teach these subjects in secondary schools through the BEd, relative to the total number in training, is very small.

It is easier to influence attitudes and to immerse students in new approaches and methodologies in concurrent courses of some years duration, such as the BEd courses. However, postgraduate courses which concentrate upon preparing new teachers for new interpretations of their subjects, combined with new approaches to teaching and learning, might effectively meet these ends, at least as 'awareness arousing' introductions to be consolidated later through experience. The proposed lengtheing of the PGCE courses to thirty-six weeks may serve to strengthen this possibility.

Even supposing that both types of courses could be so designed and organised as to bring students to understand and practise in the recommended fashion, the impact on the system as a whole should be marginal, since the total numbers of new entrants required in the secondary sector in the next decade is so small. The projections made by the Department of Education and Science (DES) in a report published in March 1984 include annual average number of new entrants to secondary schools as 5100 to 1990 and 9200 from 1990-95, joining a total teaching force of secondary teachers falling from 240000 to 200000 in the same period. Projections of the future age distribution of the teaching force in these same ten years show that the over 40s will form almost two thirds of the total with teachers aged 40-49, the new entrants during the expansion of the late 1960s and 1970s, as the largest single age-group. This is the same group of teachers covered in the report by Her Majesty's Inspectors (HMI) *Aspects of Secondary Education in England* published in December 1979, who at that time 'had less than ten years experience' and who had their professional initiation in the period when secondary education moved from a largely selective to a largely comprehensive system, with all the disruption which that entailed, at a time of greatly expanding pupil numbers. The report commented that 'institutional change in these circumstances can lead to a basic lack of confidence and this in turn to a tendency to play safe, to fall back on the familiar and the known. It can thus strengthen the tendency to conservatism which is a built-in feature of the teaching profession'. Institutional change was not all that was required of teachers in this period: the

Certificate of Secondary Education (CSE) was established as an alternative to the earlier GCE O level examination at 16+: there were numerous curriculum development projects emanating from the Schools Council affecting most areas of the curriculum and new assessment procedures to support the new examinations; then in 1973 the school leaving age was raised to 16 years. Much of this change was seriously underfunded but, in particular and most significantly, it was achieved on totally inadequate staff development programmes.

A further difficulty in the present situation is that surveys of the work of schools in recent years have expressed a particular concern about the low level of qualification of many teachers in the subjects they are teaching. As examples, in the schools surveyed in *Aspects*. HMI reported that 14% of those teaching French recorded no qualification in the subject; the report of the Cockroft committee *Mathematics Counts* 1981 estimated that 38% of all mathematics teaching in maintained secondary schools was being undertaken by teachers whose qualifications were 'were' (17%) or 'nil' (21%); in other words almost two-fifths of all mathematics teaching was in 'unstable' hands. This situation has led to the promulgation of criteria recommended to parliament by the Secretaries of State in a White Paper Teaching Quality in March 1983, by which courses of initial teacher training will in future be judged before approval is granted.

The broad requirements set out in the White Paper lay first emphasis on 'at least two full years' of course time devoted to subject studies at a level appropriate to higher education'. This requirement would recognise teachers' need for subject expertise, if they are to have the confidence and ability to enthuse pupils and respond to their curiosity in their chosen subject fields. Furthermore, all training courses should include adequate attention to teaching method in the chosen main subjects, differentiated by age of intended pupils.

These requirements, indisputably worthy in themselves, may do much to limit the attention given to the fundamental difference of offering an education 'through' curriculum subjects rather than 'in' the individual subjects of study. They seem likely to continue, if not to increase, the emphasis on the notion of 'pure' subject studies; there is no mention here of 'application' or 'connection' or 'relevance'. At best this may be an example of an opportunity missed, at worst it might be seen as a continuation of the confusion illustrated in paragraph 10.9 of the Green Paper *Education in Schools* which stated : 'in addition to their responsibility for the academic curriculum schools must prepare their pupils for the transition to adult working life'; as if the academic, subject-based curriculum was in some special way separated from these other considerations.

More recent authoritative statements concerning initial training are scarcely reassuring; the dichotomies are less obvious, the separations no less pervasive. In a paper *Teacher Training and Preparation of Working Life* HMI, after enunciating as a first priority (students) need to teach their subjects well and effectively went on to say, 'initial training institutions should also make positive efforts to ensure that future teachers understand the part that their subject plays in the economic and cultural life of their society. Similarly a statement by HMI on the *Content of Initial Training Courses for Teachers* attempts to resolve the difficulty in this way: 'Methodology of the main subject should include consideration of the contribution which the subject may make to the personal, social and academic development of pupils: the contribution which the subject well enough to understand how it can be made accessible to pupils of different ages and abilities; links between the subject and other subjects and a very close knowledge of inter-related subjects.

The two-fold failure of the present subject curriculum is its lack of relevance to that big majority of pupils who will not proceed to advanced study in any of the disciplines and inappropriateness of presents knowledge in the form of conceptual abstractions and organising principles to pupils whose level of intellectual development and experience do not match the demands of the material offered.

The central issue for subject curriculum designers, in response to the widespread concern that pupils in schools should gain experience more directly related to life, is the selection of subject contents and learning activities which will give meaning to pupils experiences as they move about the world and will enable them to engage confidently with the range of personal and social challenges with which they are faced in making the transition from youth to adulthood.

The dangers inherent in laying undue emphasis on pure subject studies in initial training deserve mention, because of the considerable effect they have in shaping the attitudes and ultimately, the professional identity of the student becoming a teacher. Perceptions built within the present subject-ridden curriculum are supported by early specilistion and so-called 'single-subject' examination qualifications. Students entering training may well have chosen their teaching subject specialism at the age of thirteen or fourteen and it may be as narrow as a single science, physics, for example, so that they may argue, with HMI, that they are ill-equipped, 'unsuitable' to teach biology in a combined science course with eleven and twelve year-olds. In evidence to the Parliamentary Committee on *Education, Science and Arts*. Mr Arnold Jennings of the Schools Council, a headmaster of many year' experience summarised the situation like this: 'A head who has notions of what is called "general science" has to do battle with graduate staff who say, "But I'm a physics graduate, Mr Jennings, I can't teach biology. "I say, "I take it you know some biology. Possibly you could cope with the academic demands of the second form. 'And they are really sniffy at this suggestion.'

Too often the commitment to subject provides the central reason why students choose a career in secondary teaching. It is a common experience in interviewing candidates for training to have them say that they wish to share their love of the subject with pupils, so that the system becomes self-regenerating. Vocational considerations can then be interpreted and satisfied through the examination system, where study of subjects given instrumental purpose in providing qualifications based on judgments unrelated to their use in screening or selecting candidates for a wide range of industrial or commercial careers. If subject certification has any vocational validity it may be in identifying those who might proceed to teaching.It is perverse feature of the system that for teachers all subjects are vocational, if learned or taught with entry to the teaching profession as the end goal. The problem here is that subject teaching thus becomes introverted and never looks belong the world of scholarship for kits justification. To continue with a system of initial training which embodies this priority may be self-defeating, if there is any expectation that newly-trained teachers may be enlisted as agents of change.

The case for extensive provision of in-service education and training of teachers (INSET) has been well made over many years. The James Report, *Teachers Education and Training* proposed the systematic induction of probationary teachers as the second phase of initial teacher training and in-service training as a continuing process throughout the whole of a teacher's career. Following the report, INSET committees have been established on a local and regional basis to monitor the programmes of courses provided in any area, with a view to ensuring that the provision meets the expressed needs of the service. Although the effectiveness of these committees is often called in question, their presence marks a significant move towards the establishment of a systems of in-service education and training designed to service perceived needs.

May local education authorities have, at the same time, developed policies for course provision and the secondment of teachers in line with explicit priorities. These developments are in line with recent proposals made in a European Community (EC) report, Policies of Transition which summarises the work of thiry-eight projects undertaken throughout the member states to examine approaches to the problem facing young people in the transition to adulthood. The report suggests the development of local or regional networks in order, among other objectives, to establish co-operation between schools, colleges and training institutions, as well as industrial and commercial training agencies, and to ensure the support of the 'administrative authorities', whether central or regional.

Change on the scale envisaged in proposals made for new vocational and prevocational programmes cannot be achieved in the absence of clear, coherent and co-ordinated policies of in-service training developed at every level; national, regional, local and institutional. Critical to the ultimate success of INSET provision however, is the acceptance by staff of the need for training to meet the challenge of change. The Standing Committee for the Education and Training of Teachers (SCETT) in a document *Inservice Education and Training of Teachers* argues for 'promoting a sense of personal, professional training obligation' to be closely related to the defined needs of the school which the teacher serves'. In this respect 'involvement in the processes for identifying needs, establishing procedures,k recommending priorities where interests compete, reviewing provision, modifying policy as changing circumstances require and evaluating the effectiveness of the in-service undertaken' might serve as the basic in-service right, responsibility and training experience for every teacher. The EC report provides a critical insight. Its projects demonstrated 'that it is often the lack of clear and consistent policies on the part of administrators and the heads of institutions which prevents staff development, rather than the resistance of staff themselves' and 'trhat many staff are willing, given support, to develop new skills, new approaches to their work and more flexible, non-traditional attitudes. Many are increasingly open to the idea that their role should be that of facilitator, rather than the giver and controller of knowledge, which has been the more commonly accepted role of the teacher.'

The Inner London Education Authority (ILEA) in its report *Improving Secondary Schools* proposes that the process of staff development should start with the appointment of a senior officer with the responsibility for staff development committee to establish and service the school's priorities for INSET in relation to the authority's central responsibility for employing authorities and the heads of institutions in which teachers, who are increasingly expected to have regard for the vocational aspirations of their students, pursue their own careers, are not yet realised in practice. A report by the ILEA research and Statistical Branch, *Management Training for Senior Staff* showed that only ten per cent of headteachers rated INSET the career development of teachers and probatiuoners as a major managerial task, and only two percent of heads and deputies had taken courses on staff development INSET.

At he national level the chorus of demand for improved INSET provision is growing and the case for better planning and major funding is being won. The Advisory Committee on Supply and Education of Teachers (ACSET) has recommended major changes.

A press notice summarises its report to the Secretaries of State including these among its recommendations:

— a general to LEAs for INSET should be introduced, to provide some safeguard that resources intended for INSET are devoted to that purpose and to reduce the disparity that exists in opportunities for INSET between different part of the country.

— each LEA should develop clear and coherent policies towards INSET

— LEAs should set budgets for INSET based on a target equivalent to about 5% of their expenditure on teachers salaries: this target should be taken into account in the determination of the overall level of the general grant to LEAs

— a review of each school's INSET needs should be carried out annually

— each school should satisfy itself that there are adequate staffing resources for each school to enable school-based INSET to take place

— the Secretaries of State should invite proposals for area INSET committees to act as 'broker' between LEAs and higher education institutions in promoting a match between INSET needs and provision.

— including award-bearing courses

The Advisory Committee suggests that taken as a whole its recommendations. imply the need for something like a doubling current LEA expenditure on INSET. It does not suppose that such an increase would be possible without the provision f additional resources for INSET.

The setting up of proper frameworks within which systematic programmes of training and retraining may be mounted would not of itself ensure either trhat sufficient priority would be given to work in this area, nor that such work would achieve the desired effect, but it is an essential prerequisite to the successful implementation of the policy.

Undertaking curriculum change makes heavy demands upon teacher time, and time in schools is a scarce resource. In *Aspects of Secondary Education* (HMI), a significant section examines reasons why teachers find it difficult to thing and plan collectively:

'The planning of coherent policies and their effective implementation require the collective involvement of the whole staff. They also require clear and effective leadership, by heads and by heads of departments and senior staff. The indications are that collective thinking and planning are difficult to achieve, even where there is appreciation of the need. The reasons will not be the same for all schools. Onwe which can be confidently adduced in many cases has already been touched on - lack of time. The discussion of policies, their translation into the planning of speciric programmes of work in the classroom, their regular reassesssment and evaluation take more time than many teachers have available to them if they are also to keep up with daily preparation and routine marking. The time available is further reduced if, for entirely valid reasons, teachers are also asked to make more contacts with parents and the outside world, both to enrich their own teaching programmes and to interpret the work of the school to others who have interest in and responsibility towards it.'

Policy proposals need the support of adequate resourcing if trhey are to succeed.

Among the first'pump priming' initiatives to provide teachers with the opportunity for extended study in the pre-vocational field were course of six weeks' duration at designated institutions under a scheme of direct funding by the DES. This section gives a brief acount of one such course as an exemplar of such provision together with a participant's descriptive evaluation of the course and its outcomes.

On 1 September 1982 the Secretary of State annoounced his intention to introduce a scheme of direct grants for in-service teacher training in 1983-4. The main purpose of the scheme was to give direct finnancial assistance through the neww Teacher Training Grants Scheme (Department of Education and Science to local authorities when serving teachers were released for training on designated courses. Within DES Circular 3/83 one of the four specified priority areas for retraining was pre-vocational education in schools. This was included again in Circular 4/84 with the following statement of intent :

Schools have a key role to play in preparing older secondary pupils for vocational education and training, notably but not exclusively in the Youth Training Scheme (YTS); they are also involved to an increasing extent, in the Technical and Vocational Education Initiative (TVEI) for 14-18 year olds, and in courses leading to the Certificate of Pre-Vocational Education (CPVE) for 16 year olds. Teachers may require assistance in preparing suitable pre-vocational programmes for their students. The courses may require assistance in preparing suitable pre-vocational programmes for their students. The courses currently eligible under the scheme, of six weeks' duration, are based on establishments which offer significant programmes of teacher trainining, and draw on the experience of those secondary schools and FE institutions which are already working in the field. There is a strong emphasis on the nees of the world or work, especially in the areas of language, technology and mathematicvs, and on identifying appropriate skills, teaching styles and materials, and forms of social and personal education. In particular

Teachers are encouraged to consider how links between pre-vocational programmes and industry and commerce might be developed. In addition to these opportunities, the Further Education Unit's programme of staff development opportunities, targeted on the needs of CPVE techers, may be appropriate to school as well as FE teachers, and the Department will give favourable consideration for grant purposes to arrangements for school teachers to attend such opportunities jointly with FE teachers.

The number of instituions offering six-weeek in service courses is incresed from thirteen in 1983-4 to eighteen in 1984-5 when local authorities were allocated increased financial assistance to release teachers for this area of retraining. In the Eastern Division, Homerton College was designated as a providing institution. Teachers are recruited from the six counties; Bedfordshire, Cambridgeshire, Essex, Hertfordshire, Norfolk and Suffolk, as well as from the North London boroughts of Barking and dagenham, Enfield, Haringay, Havering, Newham and Redbridge. After liaison with local authority representatives a decision was made to split the thirty-day course into two parts.

The first part of fifteen days, the Orientation Phase, aims to provide the teachers with a good background of the current state of pre-vocational education. This phase offers:

— clarification and identification of the rationales, aims and principal components of pre-vocational education.

— a broad base on which more informed development of pre-vocational courses can be made

— an opportunity to extend industrial, commercial and community contacts and to examine ways of promoting liaison

— an opportunity to study new approaches to teaching and learning and to study techniques and purposes for assessment

— development of some new area of activity for the teachers to exemplify these new approaches to learning and assessment

— exploration of personal and supportive curriculum
— an increased awareness of the network of support services, nationally and locally, for pre-vocational work. Time is given to maintain contact with the local authority co-ordinator

Between the two phases of the course participants return to their posts in schools for the Interim Phase. This kin-school period provides the opportunity to test ideas developed during the Orientation Phase, to examine and consider curricular and institutional implications and to establish local links.

The second part of fifteen days, the Exploration Phase, is structured in modules so that the teachers can extend their studies from phase 1 to develop and intensify areas which best suit their needs and the needs of their schools. Modules are :

— communication skills
— numeracy
— science and technology
— information technology
— community education
— economic literacy
— health education
— recreational and leisure pursuits
— visual arts
— computer literacy
— education for enterprise

During this phase participants consider the design and implementation of learning programmes for their schools including programmes for their school including programmes of staff appraisal and development and implications of the new programmes.

Evaluation

The course adopts an active mode as the dominant mode of engagement for all course members, both tutors and teachers alike. Members, both tutors and teachers alike. Members are involved in alternative approaches to study for example investigations, problem solving, simulations and game situations and in alternative methods of assessment such as profiling and records of achievement.

Visits are made to industry, commerce and the whole range of supporting services and alternative provisions; those who are active and experienced in these fields are invited to contribute to the course.

There is direct contact with young people in contexts in which they feel some confidence and with people who work successfully with them outside school; youth leaders, social workers, sport club leaders, for example.

All the work is supported with resources such as films, audio programmes, video materials, simulations, business games and computer programmes as well as with a collection of course and programme outlines and the accumulated literature in this field.

Contributors to the course are drawn from the college and outside bodies such as the Careers

Research and Advisory Centre the National Institute for Careers Education and Counselling, the Joint Board for Pre Vocational Education, the Economics 14-16 Project, the Central; Council for Physical Recreation, the Secondary Science Curriculum Review, Project Trident and Young Enterprise. Other contributors are a Technical and Vocational Education Initiative project director, an Understanding British Industry regional director, HMI, local authority inspectors and advisers, managers of education liaison from industry and local teachers.

Course members are expected to develop materials and programmes for their own schools. Simultaneously the group looks at common problems and possibilities between schools across the region. At appropriate times course membership is extended to include senior management from members' own schools to examine and advise on the institutional implications of applying the emerging approaches and course arrangements.

Pre-vocational education implies a departure from traditional syllabus-bound 'chalk and talk' approaches and the introduction of more student-centered and participatory forms of learning. The in-service courses should reflect this methodology. When traditional lecture format is used in the course, course members appreciate authoritative and flexible speakers but they are intolerant and critical when speakers appear unable to depart from formal presentation. Active, experiential learning has been entered into enthusiastically especially where the approach is then discussed in terms of its application to school work. Participants are anxious to develop materials suited to their own areas rather than fall back on commercially-produced materials. Avoidance of re-inventing the wheel, though, is a common concern.

HMI invited all courses co-ordinators from the thirteen 3/83 providers to a conference in Oxford in June 1984. Although many courses, like the one at Homerton College, had involved senior management from participants' schools at some stage during the course, and close liaison with local authority representatives had been established, it was felt that participants of the courses would feel frustrated and despondent on their return to school and authority if no follow-up support was offered. It has been encouraging in the Eastern Region to know that teachers who have attended a 3/83 course are being called together by their local authority co-ordinators with a view to establishing their role as pre-vocational tutors within the authorities. Certainly this is already happening in some authorities where the teacher-tutor is acting as co-ordinator for activities within that authority alongside the Homerton College tutor for subsequent 4/84 courses.

Continuing liaison between course providers and local authorities can only help to maximise the experience gained by everyone involved in these new course. Local authorities, and the schools and further education colleges within them, will develop a policy for prevocational education which must include a coherent policy for in-service provision.

11 Learning to Solve Problems and Learning as Problem Solving

It was noted that modern industry requires workers who are capable of applying their knowledge in a flexible, adaptable way and that there is a need to embed the teaching of thinking skills in vocational education and training, it is through thinking more efficiently that we become better problem solvers at work and in our own personalities lives.

For nearly a century psychologists have been working at understanding thinking. The intention in this chapter is to present only those aspects of psychological theorising which are necessary to crease sufficient understanding for you to incorporate the teaching of thinking into your vocational programmes.

Obviously thinking happens inside people's heads. Techniques for direct observation of what is happening inside people's heads when they are thinking havenot yet been developed, nor are they likely to be in the foreseeable future. Descriptions of thinking are based on indirect evidence. Various techniques are used which permit inferences to be made about the thinking process underlying task performance. One technique is the verbal protocol.

This is obtained by asking people to describe their thinking by talking aloud as they are completing a problem. Psychologists are particularly interested in charting the thinking of experts in different occupational areas on the assumption that their thinking processes are the most efficient ones for the tasks which they tackle in their working lives.

This chapter begins with a brief consideration of whether it is possible to teach people to think more efficiently. If thinking is manifested in solving problems, it is necessary to have a working definition of 'problem'. Therefore, the chapter goes onto introduce a definition used by psychologists for the purpose of developing descriptions of thinking which can inform the teaching of thinking and problem solving. This definition and a simple but valid description of thinking are explained and illustrated by examples which highlight the main points in a reader-friendly fashion. In the last part of the chapter there is a discussion of the adequacy of the definition offered of a 'problem'. Finally, the notion that efficient learning is an instance of problem solving is discussed.

What about intelligence?

It might be argued that the many entrants to vocational programmes who have poor school achievements are simply not bright enough to learn how to cope with tasks other than the more routine ones. Poor achievement is often interpreted as a reflection of low 'intelligence, in the sense of having poor 'hard wiring', which sets a ceiling on achievement. However, this view of intelligence and the evidence which supported it have been seriously undermined in the last twenty years. There is now good evidence that intelligence in the sense of efficient thinking can be taught. In Japan, for example, the average teenage IQ, which is a frequently sited measure of thinking ability, has been raised to 117 compared with 100 in Britain. 'Although it is not doubted that under some vastly improved system of instruction mental ability may set an upper limit to individuai learning attainment, the view that present levels are so constrained is largely discredited'.

If you cannot complete this task within four minutes you may wish to look at a list of mental operations at the end of this chapter which are sufficient to achieve a solution. When you have learned these operations and produced a solution, are you more 'intelligent'? The approach in this book is based on the view now shared by many researchers, that 'intelligence' is learnable, in the sense that 'intelligence' consists of a repertoire of concepts and mental operations. Sequences of operations build up into procedures. A Scottish further education lecturer often uses the problem in Figure to introduce the idea that mental procedures to deal with problems in an electrical engineering module can be learned. The procedure for the MENSA task is mastered fairly easily even by students who have poor O-level qualifications, and students can learn to transfer it to other relevant tasks.

MENSA task two

If you would like to test your grasp of the procedure for dealing with the MENSA question, you might like to try a second version of the original problem, which has appeared in MENSA advertisements.

The solution is at the end of this chapter. You might like to try these two problems on friends. Find a friend who needs to be shown the procedure for the first problem, and present the second version without mentioning that the problems require similar mental operations. Research suggests that most people do not transfer a procedure to another relevant problem unless it is pointed out very explicitly that the problems are similar. Try the two problems again with another friend who needs to be shown the procedure for the first problem, but this time tell the friend that the procedure for solving the second problem is similar.

One of the reasons why the teaching thinking movement has not developed as rapidly in this country as in the United States is that certain traditional views of intelligence have been so widely disseminated through the media and in other ways that they are often not questioned by education and training practitioners. This book offers a description, based on current research on learning and thinking, which enables you to understand shortcomings in thinking and problem solving as a temporary stage on a route to further development, and to understand why that development is highly susceptible to instruction. Without such a description it is difficult for you to understand shortcomings other than in terms of irreversible limitations of learners' cognitive equipment. Unless you are provided with a reasonably detailed and accurate description of the mental processes which underlie the problem-solving processes which you are being exhorted to promote, you can hardly be expected to achieve much success in helping learners to think efficiently.

What is a problem

The introduction of 'core skills' into NVQs reflects employers' demands for efficient occupational problem solving and the growing evidence that this competence can be taught. One of these core skills is problem solving, which is thinking in relation to some task whose solution is not immediately obvious to the task performer. Psychologists have been investigating 'problem solving' for most of this century. The essence of definitions in cognitive research is that a problem exists when:

> you want something and do not know immediately what series of mental operations you can use to get it.

In modern societies, problems, as defined above, arise frequently not only in high-level jobs but at all occupational levels. The above description allows a task to be a problem for one person but not for another who has previously encountered that task. The following description is taken from a novel where a professor is trying to use a typewriter. This is again consistent with our everyday experience that even people who are regarded as 'intelligent' often have trouble with simple but new tasks.

> I'd no idea a typewriter was such a complicated beast. It took a good ten minutes to find the little catch that lets the thing loose. And even when the roller was moving freely, I had enormous difficulty feeding the paper in and winding it up straight.

There is extensive evidence that most people are not good at dealing with tasks they have not previously encountered. For example, try the following tasks.

The none-dot problem
Draw four straight lines (without raising your pencil from the paper) which will pass through all nine dots.

The selection task
You are shown a panel four cards (a), (b), (c) and (d) together with the following instructions:

Which of the hidden parts of these cards do you need to see in order to answer the following question decisively?

For these cards is it true that if there is a circle on the left there is a circle on the right? If you cannot produce the answer within ten minutes you should turn to the solution at the end of the chapter.

Problems with problems solving at work
In the following examples the problems were minor ones, in that the tasks deviated only slightly from their routine versions, but failure to deal with them has significant effects on the organisation's goals. They are presented to illustrate further the definition of 'problem' on page 15 and to introduce a way of describing what is involved in solving problems. They are all reports of real situations reported by vocational trainers and help to explain the current concern with core skills in the NVQ system. The examples are intended to emphasise that problem solving is required at all levels of work and that it has to be learned. There is extensive evidence that the gap between understanding what has to be done in relation to a task and actually doing it is often seriously underestimated. The need for practice in learning practical skills seems to be

almost universally recognised, whereas it is often almost overlooked in the case of intellectual skill.

Some illustrations of the definition of 'problem'

A new eighteen-year-old typist who had good academic achievements as well as a secretarial qualification was given a hand-written letter to type which was to include the works 'European Social Fund'. As this was referred to frequently in the organisation's correspondence, the writer had abbreviated it to E...S...F... The letter was presented for signature with European Social Fund typed as it had been written - E...S...F... The writer of the letter explained that while abbreviations were used to save time they were usually typed in full, and she wrote at the bottom of the letter 'European Social Fund'. The letter was altered and presented again for signature. This time 'European Social Fund' was indeed typed in full - but at the bottom of the letter with the abbreviated E...S...F... still appearing in the body of the letter.

In this example the typist, who was very eager to do well, clearly wanted to produce a mailable letter. Her failure to produce one suggests that she did not know that certain elementary mental operations were necessary, such as generating appropriate questions to herself; for example, during my training, what kind of changes did I have to make? How can I find out what these abbreviations stand for? And later when making the alteration: does this fit in with my previous experience of typing letters?

The task faced by the typist also illustrates the point that the description given of the term 'problem' allows a task to be a problem for one person, but not for another who has previously encountered it. Experienced typists are assumed by the error reported above in carrying out what seems to them a trivial task.

The next example emphasises this point, that whether a task can be classified as a problem or a routine task depends on the state of knowledge of the problem solver.

Your current wage is 121 a week, which includes a 10 per cent pay rise you have just received. What was your wage before you received this 10 per cent pay rise?

If you were unable to produce the correct answer you will be better able to appreciate why the employees in the remaining examples made errors. You are likely to find the correct answer if you ask yourself the questions, 'Have I come across a similar problem - if so, what procedure did I use? If not, was the previous wage more or less? What percentage of the previous wage is 121? (121 is 110 per cent of the previous wage.) Can I write out this information in the form of an equation?

You may now have converted the problem into a task for which there is a routine procedure. If you do not know this procedure you can look it up in a basic mathematics book.

In a coffee bar a customer asked the waitress for black coffee with cold milk. In this coffee bar it was usual to serve coffee which had been made up with hot milk. The waitress served black coffee with two ice cubes in it but no milk. As in the first example, this waitress seems to have had no awareness that she should have been generating appropriate questions to herself, such as:

Is this request different from the standard order?

What feature is different? (temperature of milk)

What effect on the coffee is the customer trying to achieve? (flavour)

Is cold milk available? (If not) are there alternative ways of achieving the effect wanted by the customer?

By means of questions like these learners manipulate and transform their existing knowledge in order to solve problems. Such questions are described as mental operations. A sequence of mental operations is described as a mental procedure. What has to be learned can therefore be described in terms of mental operations and procedures.

You might be unconvinced that it is necessary to learn to generate questions in order to deal with a task such as the above. Whether you describe a task as routine or as a problem depends on the gap between the mental procedures - namely, sequences of mental operations known by the task performer - and the procedures required for the successful solution of the task. A person can be a good problem solver by learning a large repertoire of mental operations organised into procedures, and by learning to manipulate these when new tasks are encountered. Manipulation involves, for example, combining parts from different sequences of mental operations to generate the new sequences required for a particular task. In the MENSA task, you are combining questions which seek out the parts of the problem which have most information with questions which eliminate one of two pieces of information when a decision has to be made about which bit should fill a particular slot. Most adults would immediately produce the answer for the following arithmetic task, whereas many six-year-old would need to be taught the mental operations listed below:

Jason has 9 sweets and he gives 3 of these sweets away to Andrew. How many sweet does Jason now have? In order to produce the correct answer, young children have to engage in the mental operation of asking themselves whether this is an 'adding' or 'taking away' task and, having classified it as 'taking away', to engage in the mental operations of asking questions such as the following:

Is one number larger than the other? (Yes)

Do I start with the larger or smaller number? (The larger one:9)

Do I go backwards or forwards from 9? (Backwards)

How many times do I go backwards? (3 times)

What number am I at now? (6)

The manipulation of knowledge to solve this problem is simple, but it is not in its essentials different from many problems tackled in occupational life. Consciousness that mental operations are used in problem solving seems to be one of the necessary conditions for transfer

Interrogation of your own knowledge is a significant component of problem-solving skill, but learning to ask others the right questions is also important. In the following activity, asking questions which yield the maximum relevant information is of great practical significance.

A bomb threat

Imagine that you are working in a large organisation and that one day the telephone rings and a voice tells you that a bomb has been placed in your organisation's premises.

List about six questions which would extract the maximum useful information from the caller. Pay particular attention to prioritising the questions with those at the end of the chapter.

The following are just a few of the mental operations which have been identified by many psychologists as contributing to efficient thinking:

— generate alternative courses of action;

— identify future consequences of proposed courses of action;

— describe advantages and disadvantages of courses of action;

— recall similar problems and actions taken and generalise these to the current problem;

— find a starting point in a problem which allows you to move forward;

— check solutions against facts;

— look for features of a problem which reminded you of a problem previously tackled successfully.

As noted earlier, these operations often take the form of questions to yourself; for example, what are the advantages or disadvantages? Can you recall similar problems?

The following activity is intended to raise your awareness of the mental operations you use every day.

Questions to solve a work problem

Think of a problem you have encountered at work recently. Which of the above mental operations did you use, if any, in tackling the problem?

Decision making, organising, prioritising and planning are familiar examples of mental procedures which they can select and recall and adapt with little or no conscious effort, building new procedures by putting together parts of existing ones. Consciousness of the need to search for a procedure is an early signal that a task to be carried out is not routine one but a problem.

It should be emphasised at this point that there are usually several mental procedures which would produce a solution to any particular problem. It is not implied at any point in this book that there is only one correct procedure. What is being argued is that, if learners do not know any procedures or cannot put together a procedure for a problem, it is in their interest that they should be taught a procedure. This is intended to be a starting point for learners, a first introduction to the possibility that they can learn to construct such procedures for themselves and that, as their repertoire of procedures grows, they will be able to take parts from various procedures and combine them to create new procedures of their own.

It is also important for you to remember that, in teaching problem solving, the emphasis is on teaching mental operations and procedures as well as teaching behaviours. The following example helps to clarify distinction.

A neighbour has the problem that she has difficulty in starting her elderly car, even although the car has been recently serviced and is in good running order.

You have found that you can start the car first time by adopting the following behaviours which could be taught to your neighbour:

apply maximum choke;
depress clutch fully;
depress accelerator fully and release slowly;
depress accelerator gently and turn ignition key.

Learning these behaviours would not equip the driver with any competence which is transferable to other problems with cars. A problem-solving approach would involve you in thinking about the information this driver needs to understand the problem, teaching the information and then asking her to suggest some useful questions which would point the way to a solution. If this fails, in your role as tutor you could say, 'I would ask myself what could be done to take some of the load off the engine parts' and then ask the driver to suggest how this could be done.

A word about automatisation of mental procedures

Once people become efficient at using mental operations which are sufficient to deal with various types of task, these sequences of operations fade from their consciousness until they are no longer aware of using them. Psychologists would describe these mental operations as 'automised' or 'enfolded'.

'Experts' are people who have automised or enfolded certain mental operations. Automatisation is necessary if you are to deal efficiently with all the tasks which confront you at work and in everyday life. If you had to be conscious of all the sequences of mental operations you use, you could not perform tasks at the speed expected by employers, or at a speed which would enable you to fit in the huge number of things that you expect to be able to do in the course of pursing a happy and interesting life. In the other hand, this efficiency has a cost - it makes it difficult for you to make your mental operations visible to learners when you are coaching them. If you do not reveal to learners the most efficient, operations for a task, they are left to try and discover them for themselves. Learners vary in their ability to discover the most rational sequence of mental operations for a task which is new to them (that is, a problem). A few learners discover most of the appropriate operations while others discover some of the operations, but many discover very few of them. A much larger percentage of school leavers might achieve the entrance qualifications for higher education if thinking processes were taught effectively.

Thus teaching problem solving involves an instructional approach which targets both the learning of information and its application in solving problems.

If you produced a correct solution on the first trial of the nine-dot problem you have probably automatised or enforced the appropriate mental operations. By generating this question the solution becomes fairly clear.

Interactions between information and mental operations

Although the emphasis so far has been on mental operations that efficient problem solving; requires both mental operations/procedures and task-relevant information. problem solving involves an interrogation of the information which you hold in memory or which can be found by using reference books and other resources. At this point it is useful to think of knowledge as having two aspects.

Information: all the ideas which you are conscious of knowing. These ideas are often referred to as concepts, which are connected to form propositions; e.g., traffic lights give instructions to motorists. These instructions are backed by legal sanctions.

Mental operations which are built up into *mental procedures*. A question to oneself is an example of a mental operation, and the sequences of questions used would be an example of the operations being built into procedures.

For example, are the traffic lights at green?
If yes: proceed with caution.
If no: are they at red?
If yes: then stop.

You solve problems when you have or can construct adequate information and mental procedures. There is a constant interaction between these two aspects of memory which have been described above as information and procedures.

Suppose you wanted to buy a used diesel car. You want to avoid one which has been used as a taxi but are not confident about eliciting an honest answer as to the car's origins. You need a mental procedure which would begin with a self-question such as, what features does a taxi have which are not features of a car in normal use? This question would direct a memory search which might result in retrieval of information such as plates showing taxi licence information. The procedure might continue with, where are they usually fixed? In response to which you might retrieve 'bumpers'. This might lead to your concluding that small holes in the bumper would raise suspicion that the car had been used as a taxi. The interplay between mental procedures and information can be traced in more complex tasks.

Suppose you have a double garage with two doors but no internal partition and you have the problem that you find difficulty in driving the car into the garage without scraping it against the door post. You might start to tackle this problem using the mental operation of generating alternative solutions. Having asked yourself this question about alternatives, you might go into your long-term memory store and come up with:

1 practice driving into tight spaces;

2 remove the two doors and replace with one door.

Another mental operation would be evaluating these solutions by asking yourself about the advantages or disadvantages of each. In order to do this you need to use the mental operation of generating relevant factors. In evaluating the solution of changing the doors you might retrieve from your long-term memory store that cost is a factor. In order to use the mental operation of evaluating the cost, you need to generate components of cost. Until you can produce the information to answer this question, you cannot proceed further in solving the problem.

You might retrieve from memory the information that components of cost would include removal of the two single doors and the cost of a new double door. However, if you did not also retrieve or find out information about other components of cost such as insertion of a supporting beam, your answer to the 'evaluating the cost' question and he eventual solution would be flawed.

Try the following activity. Its purpose is to illustrate further the relationship discussed above between mental operations and task relevant information.

The thinking DIY

Suppose you want to put up book shelves, approximately 6 feet tall by 8 feet wide, in your lounge.

— Write questions which you might ask yourself as part of the planning for this task.

— Find someone who is a trained carpenter or an experienced DIY enthusiast and ask him or her to generate appropriate questions for this task.

— Compare your list of questions with those of the more expert person in (2) above.

(If you do not have a DIY friend, you will find an 'expert' list at the end of this chapter.)

You will have noticed that the questions you ask yourself are dependent to some extent on the information you have stored in memory, while, as already noted, some questions are useful in almost every situation. For example, 'Have I come across a problem life this before? How does this problem differ from previous similar ones? Are those differences significant?' Others are quite specific to the task and depend on subject knowledge. The joiner's questions will be based on information about woods, fixing materials and so on. If you do not know that different types of wood are more likely to bend or less likely to bend under the weight of books, you cannot generate the likely to bend under the weight of books, you cannot generate the questions 'What type of wood will hold up under the weight of the books?' Without expert information you cannot generate some questions, let alone answer them. In order to be effective, your knowledge of a subject must be linked to your knowledge of how to apply the subject.

Clearly, this view of the content of human memory has some resemblance to descriptions of how computers work. Artificial Intelligence has had a very strong influence on theorising about thinking and its manifestation in problem solving. One useful way of describing the relationship between Artificial Intelligence and theories of problem solving is to say that Artificial Intelligence is a metaphor for thinking about thinking.

Index